How to use this book!

Latin Grammar offers you all the **important points of gram.**

Grammar → starting on page 4

If you want a simple, easy-to-understand review of Latin grammar or would like to look up specific items, you're definitely in the right place here.

The detailed index will help you get answers to your questions quickly, because this grammar book offers you a **neatly arranged breakdown** of the Latin language, and the **clearly formulated rules** are illustrated with meaningful examples.

In the **Glossary** (starting on page 172), you'll find key terms explained again.

Verb Tables → starting on page 181

In the **verb tables**, you'll find neatly arranged paradigms with inflected forms of regular and irregular verbs of all conjugations. Each individual form is translated into English. The table of **principal parts of important verbs** (starting on page 236) is arranged by conjugation and by method of forming the perfect tense. It is followed by an **alphabetical list of verbs** with an indication of the number assigned to each in the table of principal parts and a code indicating the appropriate conjugation paradigm (starting on page 255).

Index → starting on page 262

If you want to look up something specific, the extensive **index** in the back of the book will quickly lead you to the right page of the grammar section or to the verb form you're seeking.

Have fun, and we wish you great success in your study of Latin!

Grammar

BARRON'S

FOREIGN LANGUAGE GUIDES

LATIN

Grammar

Edited by Raffaela Maidhoff

BARRON'S

First edition for the United States and Canada published in 2011 by
Barron's Educational Series, Inc., Hauppauge, NY, USA.

Editor: Raffaela Maidhoff

All inquiries should be addressed to:
Barron's Educational Series, Inc.
250 Wireless Boulevard
Hauppauge, NY 11788
www.barronseduc.com

ISBN-13: 978-0-7641-4721-0
Library of Congress Control Number: 2010939096

Printed in China
9 8 7 6 5 4 3 2 1

How to use this grammar book

In working with this grammar, you will find the following symbols helpful:

 The exclamation point makes you aware of aspects of grammar that often are overlooked or misunderstood, unfortunately, and that can lead to silly mistakes in understanding a text or making a translation.

 The two facing arrows make you aware of places where Latin and English exhibit serious differences. If these differences are not properly grasped, messy errors on tests, class work, and exams that lead to deduction of points can be the result here as well.

Grammar is a complex structure in which everything is interrelated. A small arrow ▶ is used here to designate references to related areas in other sections or chapters, so that you can keep the complete picture in sight at all times.

A tip for those of you who are animal lovers: We would never do anything to hurt a rabbit (or any other animal), either. But sometimes drastic examples are a good way to commit something to memory! Does that statement seem cryptic to you right now? Once you start working with this grammar, you'll see right away what we're talking about.

Contents

Contents

Contents

Contents

PART I: MORPHOLOGY

1 Parts of Speech

Latin is a highly **inflected** language; that is, the grammatical function of a word within a sentence is made clear in part by altering the word, by **inflecting** (**flectere** *to bend inward*) it. Latin is more overtly inflected than English, which is described as a "weakly inflected" language.

Ferdinand reads the book.
Caroline is the book**'s** owner/the owner of the book.

In the first example, "the book" performs the grammatical function of **direct object**; in the second sentence, it has a **modifying** or **limiting** role, conveying here the idea of **possession**. In the second sentence, an apostrophe plus the ending **-s** is attached to the noun "book" to signal its role in the sentence. In English, possession also can be indicated by using the preposition "of."

   (But that brings us to the topic of syntax. You'll find more on that in the section **Objects in Various Cases** in Chapter 17.)

   Latin has both variant (**inflected**) and invariant (**uninflected**) word classes.

Words that are inflected include
- Nominals (**nōmen, -inis** n. *name, appellation*), which are **declined** (**dēclīnāre** *to bend, deflect, turn aside*): nouns, adjectives, pronouns, and numerals. Nominals are parts of speech that share some characteristics of nouns; they are nouns or word groups that can function as nouns.
- Verbs, which are **conjugated** (**coniungere** *to join together*).

An uninflected word is called a particle (**particula, -ae** f. *particle*). This category includes adverbs, prepositions, conjunctions and subjunctions, interjections, modal particles (filler words such as "like," "okay," "so"), and negative particles (such as "not").

 Latin, unlike English, has neither a direct article ("the") nor an indirect article ("a," "an").

2 Word Formation

Inflected words in Latin can be broken down into specific components. They consist of the **stem** and an **ending**. The stem is the **carrier of meaning**. Therefore, words (vocables) in a semantic field (lexical field, word-field) that are similar in meaning often have the same stem.

   A recurring stem in the semantic field of "king," which includes "ruler" and "regal," is, for example, **reg-**.

The ending, in turn, shows the **grammatical form** of the word and gives information about the grammatical function of that word within the sentence (**syntactic function**).

The stem, in turn, usually consists of a one-syllable word root and a simple sound, a **thematic vowel**. The words in the semantic field of "king" are formed as follows, according to these rules:

REG-	E-	RE	TO RULE
Stem	Vowel	Infinitive Ending	
rēg-	**ĭ-**	**na**	*queen*
rēx		(from **rēg-s**)	*king*
rēg-		**-num**	*kingdom*

3 Inflected Parts of Speech: The Noun

The inflection of various grammatical forms of a noun is known as **declension** (**dēclīnāre** *to bend*). From the declined form, you can identify the **number** (**numerus, -i** m. *number*) and **case** (**cāsus, -ūs** m. *case*) of a noun. Only in some cases can the **gender** (**genus, generis** n. *gender*) be reliably identified as well.

 The endings do identify case and number, but sometimes the same endings are used in Latin for different cases and numbers. When you want to find out which case or number is intended, you also have to take the context into account.

Gender

Latin has three genders: **feminine**, **masculine**, and **neuter**. In dictionaries and vocabulary lists, nouns are always given along with their gender. The genders are abbreviated as follows: **m.**, **f.**, and **n.**

For many nouns, the gender can be deduced from the ending that is attached or from affiliation with a declension group. This does not apply to all nouns, however. Only with some nouns does the grammatical gender coincide with the gender based on the sex of the noun, as with personal names, such as **Cornelia** and **Marcus**, or with gender-specific terms, such as **māter** f. *mother* or **filius** m. *son*. When this is the case, we speak of **natural gender**. All other nouns are declined on the basis of their **grammatical gender**. In English, nouns usually have no gender. An exception is the word "ship," which can be referred to as "she."

 The gender of a Latin noun has to be memorized. There is no reliable way to predict which gender category a noun is assigned to.

In accordance with their natural gender, all male persons are **masculine**. Names of **peoples**, **rivers**, and **winds** are also viewed as masculine.

In accordance with their natural gender, female persons are **feminine**. In addition, **names of trees**, **streets**, **islands**, and **countries** usually are feminine in gender.

With collective nouns for persons or animals where the natural gender is clearly known, feminine and masculine forms often exist side by side in Latin. There are three ways to tell the feminine and the masculine forms apart: specific **derivational suffixes**, separate **words**, or **accompanying words and antecedents**.

Sometimes the feminine form is derived from the masculine one and characterized by a specific **derivational suffix**:

filius m.	*son*	**filia** f.	*daughter*
puer m.	*boy*	**puella** f.	*girl*
rēx m.	*king*	**rēgina** f.	*queen*
lupus m.	*wolf*	**lupa** f.	*she-wolf*

Sometimes the feminine form also has a word of its own.

pater m.	*father*	**māter** f.	*mother*
frāter m.	*brother*	**soror** f.	*daughter*
vir m.	*man*	**mulier** f.	*woman*
taurus m.	*bull*	**vacca** f.	*cow*

With some words, only accompanying words or antecedents make it clear that it is explicitly the feminine, not the masculine, form that is meant:

hic/haec cīvis	*this (male/female) citizen*
coniunx meus/mea	*my (male/female) spouse*
sacerdōs pius/pia	*the pious (male/female) priest*
dux optimus/optima	*the best (male/female) leader*

 When collective nouns denote a group of persons, they follow the grammatical gender:
magnae cōpiae *large forces* or **vigiliae armātae** *armed watchmen*

With animals, in contrast to designations of persons, attention is paid to clearly labeling the intended gender only if it is essential to the context. Otherwise, these nouns have **one** grammatical gender:
passer m. *sparrow*   **aquila** f. *eagle*   **tigris** f. *tiger*

Exceptions:
* **mancipium** *slave*, as a "salable good," is neuter.
* All words that cannot be declined are treated as neuters, for example:
    maximum nefās *a serious crime*
    suprēmum valē *the last farewell*

Case

The case tells what role a word plays within a sentence. It defines its **syntactic function**.

In addition, the case can indicate that several words in the sentence belong together. When adjectives, participles, or pronouns complement another nominal and thus have an attributive function, they are **congruent**, or in **agreement**, with it; that is, they agree with it in **case**, **number**, and **gender**. English, by comparison, does not have much agreement.

Despite the agreement in case, number, and gender, the endings of words that go together may be different because they belong to different declensions and have other forms.
▶ You will learn more about agreement in the following chapters on **declensions**, **adjectives**, and **pronouns**.

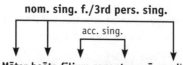

Māter beāta filium rogantem nōn audit.
The happy mother does not hear her pleading son.

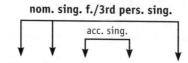

Fēlis nigra cunīculum album persequitur.
The black cat pursues the white rabbit.

 Latin, unlike English, has **no articles**. In Latin, **word order** has little influence on the role of a word in the sentence; English word order is far less flexible. Therefore, because the **syntactic function** of a word is determined solely by its ending and the context, it is especially important to recognize the corresponding Latin cases by their endings.

Latin has **five distinct cases**. In addition, it also has a **vocative**, a way of expressing **direct address** (**vocāre** *to call*), which can be seen as a separate case. It is not given in the declension tables because it uses the same forms as the nominative, except for singular nouns of the second declension ending in **-us** and **-ius**.

	QUESTION	ABBREVIATION
Nominative	who or what?	nom.
Genitive	whose?	gen.
Dative	to or for whom?	dat.
Accusative	whom or what?	acc.
Ablative	by/with whom/what? when? where?	abl.
Vocative	—	voc.

Only the **nominative** and the **vocative** are independent, uninflected cases (**casūs rectī**); the other cases cannot appear without a constituent in the nominative. They depend on another constituent and therefore are inflected and known as **oblique cases** (**casūs obliquī**).

In Latin, two cases of the Proto-Indo-European language, the **locative** (where?) and the **instrumental** (by/with what?), merged with the **ablative**. The ablative generally is rendered in English with a preposition in a prepositional phrase: *in the yard, with the car, at that time*, etc.

Number

Latin, like English, has two grammatical numbers: singular and plural. Some nouns, because of their meaning, occur only in the singular (**singulāria tantum**), others only in the plural (**plūrālia tantum**).

These are **singulāria tantum**:
- **Proper names**, such as **Cicerō, Caesar**, or **Rōma**
- Designations of **materials**, such as **aurum, -ī** n. *gold* or **aes, aeris** n. *bronze* (The word **aera** appears in rare instances in the plural, but then it means *bronze statues* or *bronze tablets!*)
- **Abstract terms**, such as **scientia, -ae** f. *knowledge, science, skill* or **supellex, -ectilis** f. *household utensils*

These are **plūrālia tantum**:
- Designations for a related group of **living things**, such as **liberī, -ōrum** m. *children,* **penātēs, -ium** m. *household deities,* **maiōrēs, -um** m. *ancestors,* or **posterī, -ōrum** m. *descendants*
- **Body parts** that occur only in pairs or are thought of as having several parts, such as **nārēs, -ium** m. *nose* (*nostrils*) or **viscera, -um** n. *intestines*
- Periods of time and festivals that usually last several hours or days, such as **Kalendae, -ārum** f. *the first day of the month,* **Sāturnālia, -ium** n. *the Saturnalia festival,* **Olympia, -ōrum** n. *the festival of the Olympic games,* or **nuptiae, -ārum** f. *wedding*
- **Things** made up of **several parts**, such as **reliquiae, -ārum** f. *remains,* **scālae, -ārum** f. *stairs,* **arma, -ōrum** n. *weapons, arms,* or **insidiae, -ārum** f. *treachery, ambushes*
- **Geographical designations**, such as **Athēnae, -ārum** f. or **Alpēs, -ium** f.

Especially in poetry, unusual forms sometimes occur, so that one or two singulāria tantum in rare instances can appear in the plural, and vice versa (for example, nāris, -is f. sing. *nostril* or vīscus, -eris n. sing. *flesh, internal organ*). Nevertheless, it is a good idea to memorize the nominative and genitive forms of the noun as given in the vocabulary lists, so that you can tell whether the word in question is singular or plural.

Because vocabulary lists usually give the nominative and genitive of the noun, it always is obvious whether a word is singular or plural.

Actually, there are also nouns that have **different meanings** in the singular and in the plural, and for this reason they must be learned separately. For example:

cōpia, -ae f.	plenty, abundance	cōpiae, -ārum f.	troops
littera, -ae f.	letter (of the alphabet)	litterae, -ārum f.	letter (note, missive), literature
auxilium, -ī n.	help, aid	auxilia, -ōrum n.	auxiliaries
finis, -is m.	end, limit, boundary	finēs, -ium m.	territory

Latin still contains vestiges of a third grammatical number, the **dual**, the Indo-European form referring to precisely two. It is very rare, however. Examples: **duo** *two* or **ambo** *both*.

4 Declensions

Each noun can be unequivocally assigned to a **declension** (**dēclīnāre** *to bend*) and declined accordingly. That is, it receives a special ending for each case and number. With adjectives, gender also is taken into account.

Latin has seven different declensions, which can be condensed into **five major declensional groups**. The affiliation is based on the final letter of the stem, which can be either a vowel or a consonant. The stem ending is usually easiest to recognize from the genitive plural form. The declensions are as follows:

GEN. PL.	STEM	DECLENSION
amicā-rum	amica-	first declension (a)
dominō-rum	domino-	second declension (o)
rēg-um	rēg-	third declension (consonant stems)
mari-um	mari-	third declension (i-stems)
urbi-um	urb(i)-	third declension (mixed i-stems)
domu-um	domu-	fourth declension (u)
rē-rum	re-	fifth declension (e)

The consonant stems, i-stems, and mixed i-stems are condensed into a single declension (third declension) because they share common characteristics.

Some case rules apply to all declensions equally:

- The **neuters** have **three identical cases** in the singular and plural: nominative, accusative, and vocative.

ingenium n.	*innate or natural quality, intelligence (nom. sing or acc. sing.)/ (What) intelligence! (vocative)*
verba n.	*words (nom. pl. or acc. pl.)/Words! (vocative)*

- The **vocative** generally is the same as the **nominative.** (Only in the second declension, for words ending in -us and -ius, are there exceptions!)
- The **ablative plural** is identical in form to the **dative plural.**

First Declension (a)

All words ending in **-a** in the nominative singular and **-ae** in the genitive singular use the forms for the first declension. Their earmark is the stem ending **-a-**, which appears in all cases except the dative and ablative plural.

In terms of grammatical gender, they all are **feminine**, with the exception of those that have a natural gender, such as **poēta** m. *poet* or **nauta** m. *sailor.*

The word **anima, -ae** f. *soul, spirit, life, breath* is used to illustrate the declension of first-declension nouns:

	SINGULAR		PLURAL	
Nom.	**anima**	the soul	**animae**	the souls
Gen.	**animae**	of the soul	**animārum**	of the souls
Dat.	**animae**	to/for the soul	**animīs**	to/for the souls
Acc.	**animam**	the soul	**animās**	the souls
Abl.	**animā**	by/with/from the soul	**animīs**	by/with/from the souls

Adjectives ending in **-us**, **-a**, **-um**, and in **-er**, the perfect passive participle, and the future active participle also base their feminine forms on the first declension.

Exceptions:

- Because of their natural gender, the following nouns are masculine:

poēta, -ae m. *poet*	**agricola, -ae** m. *farmer*
nauta, -ae m. *sailor*	**incola, -ae** m. *inhabitant*

 In fact, Latin has no feminine forms for these terms, whereas English has at least the antiquated *poetess*. Even when speaking of *a learned woman poet,* Latin uses **poēta doctus.**

- These occur only in the plural:

dīvitiae, -ārum f. *wealth*	**īnsidiae, -arum** f. *treachery*

- These exist only as singular nouns:

iūstitia, -ae f. *justice*	**scientia, -ae** f. *knowledge, science, skill*

- Some nouns have different meanings in the singular and plural:

cōpia, -ae f. *abundance, plenty*	**cōpiae, -ārum** f. *troops*
littera, -ae f. *letter (alphabet)*	**litterae, -ārum** f. *letter (note), literature*

- In addition, a few older forms that have been preserved can appear in place of the usual ones.
  In the **genitive singular**, these forms occur:
  pater familiās (plural **patrēs familiās**) *father of a family, family man*
  māter familias (plural **mātrēs familiās**) *housewife*
  In the **dative/ablative**, **dea** *goddess* and **filia** *daughter* use the older ending **-bus** when combined with the masculine, for clarity:

deīs et deābus	**cum filiīs filiābusque**
gods and goddesses	*with the sons and daughters*

- The locative (ablative) **Rōmae** *in Rome* is formed from **Rōma, -ae**. It answers the question "where?"
  Marcus et parentēs Rōmae **habitant.**   *Marcus and his parents live in Rome.*

Second Declension (o)

All words ending in **-us**, **-er**, or **-um** in the nominative singular and **-i** in the genitive singular belong to the second declension (o). Its distinguishing feature is the stem ending **-o-**, which is seen in the genitive plural.

All second-declension nouns that end in **-er** are **masculine** in gender; all words that end in **-um** are **neuter**. Most words ending in **-us** are **masculine**.

Memorize the following:
A few nouns of the second declension (names of trees, towns, countries, islands) that end in **-us** are **feminine**.
Example: **mālus frūctuōsa** *the fruitful apple tree*

Nouns Ending in -us

The word **amicus, -i** m. *friend* is used to illustrate the declension of second-declension nouns ending in **-us**.

	SINGULAR		PLURAL	
Nom.	amīcus	the friend	amīcī	the friends
Gen.	amīcī	of the friend	amīcōrum	of the friends
Dat.	amīcō	to/for the friend	amīcīs	to/for the friends
Acc.	amīcum	the friend	amīcōs	the friends
Abl.	amīcō	by/with/from the friend	amīcīs	by/with/from the friends

The singular vocative of second-declension nouns is the only place where the vocative and nominative forms are not identical. Nouns ending in -us use the vocative ending -e: domine! *(my) lord!* or amice! *(my) friend!* Nouns ending in -ius use the vocative ending **-ī**: filī! *(my) son!*

Not all nouns ending in **-us** belong to the second declension! They can also belong to the fourth declension (u). Always learn the genitive singular along with the meaning of the word, so that you know which declension the word belongs to.

Nouns Ending in -er

Nouns ending in **-er** fall into two groups: With some words, such as **puer, -ī** m. *boy*, the **-e-** is retained in all cases, while for most nouns of this declension, such as **liber, librī** m. *book*, the **-e-** is present only in the nominative singular.

The noun **puer, -ī** m. *boy* is used to illustrate the declension of second-declension nouns ending in **-er**:

	SINGULAR		PLURAL	
Nom.	**puer**	the boy	**puerī**	the boys
Gen.	**puerī**	of the boy	**puerōrum**	of the boys
Dat.	**puerō**	to/for the boy	**puerīs**	to/for the boys
Acc.	**puerum**	the boy	**puerōs**	the boys
Abl.	**puerō**	by/with/from the boy	**puerīs**	by/with/from the boys

Nouns Ending in -um

Many neuter second-declension nouns end in **-um**. The word **templum, -ī** n. *temple* is used to illustrate the declension of these nouns:

	SINGULAR		PLURAL	
Nom.	**templum**	the temple	**templa**	the temples
Gen.	**templī**	of the temple	**templōrum**	of the temples
Dat.	**templō**	to/for the temple	**templīs**	to/for the temples
Acc.	**templum**	the temple	**templa**	the temples
Abl.	**templō**	by/with/from the temple	**templīs**	by/with/from the temples

 Adjectives ending in **-us, -a, -um** and in **-er**, the perfect passive participle, and the future active participle form their masculine forms in the same way as second-declension nouns.

Exceptions:

- The following nouns are exceptions; they are **not masculine:**

humus, -ī f. *earth, soil*	**virus, -ī** n. *poison*
vulgus, -ī n. *people*	**Corinthus, -ī** f. *Corinth*

Third Declension

This declension group includes three different sets of nouns: nouns with **consonant stems**, **pure i-stem** nouns, and **mixed i-stem** nouns, which "mix" characteristics of the other two sets and differ from the nouns with consonant stems only in the genitive plural, where they employ the ending **-ium**.

The third declension contains a great many nouns that show very different stems: All words whose **genitive singular** ends in **-is** belong to the third declension. The nominative singular endings vary widely, and frequently give no indication of the stem, as in the case of **senex**, **senis** m. *old man* or **opus, -eris** n. *work*. This shows that the genitive singular absolutely must be memorized along with the nominative: for example, **virtūs, -ūtis** f. *valor, prowess*.

 The third declension contains nouns of all three **genders**. Generally two-syllable words ending in **-or** are **masculine**. All words ending in **-io** are **feminine**. Beyond that, it is not possible to establish a uniform rule, and thus the gender must be memorized along with the noun!

Nouns with Consonant Stems

Nouns whose stem ends in a consonant, such as **lēx, lēgis** f. *law*, belong to this subcategory. It consists of masculine, feminine, and neuter nouns. (So you absolutely must memorize the genitive along with the nominative!) Masculine and feminine nouns follow the paradigm below:

	SINGULAR		PLURAL	
Nom.	**lēx**	the law	**lēgēs**	the laws
Gen.	**lēgis**	of the law	**lēgum**	of the laws
Dat.	**lēgī**	to/for the law	**lēgibus**	to/for the laws
Acc.	**lēgem**	the law	**lēgēs**	the laws
Abl.	**lēge**	by/with/from the law	**lēgibus**	by/with/from the laws

The example **opus, -eris** n. *work* illustrates the declension of neuter nouns with consonant stems:

	SINGULAR		PLURAL	
Nom.	opus	the work	opera	the works
Gen.	operis	of the work	operum	of the works
Dat.	operi	to/for the work	operibus	to/for the works
Acc.	opus	the work	opera	the works
Abl.	opere	by/with/from the work	operibus	by/with/from the works

Peculiarities:

* With some words, the nominative has a very different stem, as in

  Iuppiter, Iovis m. *Jupiter*   **iter, itineris** n. *way*

* In the third declension, there are a few irregular nouns, such as **bōs, bovis** m./f. *ox, cow* and **vās, vāsis** n. *vessel*, and they must be memorized in addition:

	SINGULAR	PLURAL	SINGULAR	PLURAL
Nom.	bōs	bovēs	vās	vāsa
Gen.	bovis	boum	vāsis	vāsōrum
Dat.	bovī	būbus/bōbus	vāsī	vāsis
Acc.	bovem	bovēs	vās	vāsa
Abl.	bove	būbus/bōbus	vāse	vāsis

> **!** Only eight adjectives are declined like third-declension nouns: **vetus**, **veteris** *old*, **dīves**, **dīvitis** *rich*, **pauper**, **pauperis** *poor*, **prīnceps**, **prīncipis** *the first*, **compos**, **compotis** *having mastery of*, **superstes**, **superstitis** *surviving*, **sōspes**, **sospitis** *unharmed, safe and sound*, and **particeps**, **participis** *participating, participant*.

Pure i-stem Nouns

Some names of rivers and places, such as **Tiberis, -is** m. and **Neāpolis, -is** f., the seven nouns (all feminine) **sitis, -is** f. *thirst,* **puppis, -is** f. *stern of a ship,* **turris, -is** f. *tower,* **tussis, -is** f. *cough,* **febris, -is** f. *fever,* **secūris, -is** f. *axe, hatchet,* **vīs** f. *strength, force,* and the neuters **mare, -ris** n. *sea,* **animal, -ālis** n. *animal, living being,* **vectīgal, -ālis** n. *tax, revenue* belong to the i-stem subcategory. All these nouns are characterized by **-i** in certain places.

 For **febris, puppis, secūris, turris, tussis, sitis, vīs, Tiberis, Neāpolis,** don't forget the i-stem.

The declension of **turris, -is** f. *tower* illustrates the pattern of endings for feminine i-stem nouns:

	SINGULAR		PLURAL	
Nom.	**turris**	the tower	**turrēs**	the towers
Gen.	**turris**	of the tower	**turrium**	of the towers
Dat.	**turrī**	to/for the tower	**turribus**	to/for the towers
Acc.	**turrim**	the tower	**turrēs/-īs**	the towers
Abl.	**turrī**	by/with/from the tower	**turribus**	by/with/from the towers

Neuter nouns such as **animal, -is** n. *animal, living being* are declined as follows:

	SINGULAR		PLURAL	
Nom.	**animal**	the animal	**animālia**	the animals
Gen.	**animālis**	of the animal	**animālium**	of the animals
Dat.	**animālī**	to/for the animal	**animālibus**	to/for the animals
Acc.	**animal**	the animal	**animālia**	the animals
Abl.	**animālī**	by/with/from the animal	**animālibus**	by/with/from the animals

 Adjectives ending in **-is,** such as **brevis, -is** *short,* in **-ns,** such as **cōnstāns, -antis** *constant,* and **-x,** such as **audāx, -ācis** *bold,* take the same endings as i-stem nouns. The masculine and feminine accusative singular, however, ends not in **-im,** but in **-em.**

Peculiarities:

- The noun **vis** f. *strength, force* has special forms. It has neither a genitive nor a dative singular. The accusative singular is **vim**, the ablative **vī**. The plural, however, is declined in the regular way, from the stem **vīr-** (**vīrēs, vīrium, vīribus, vīrēs, vīribus**). The singular and the plural differ in meaning: **vis** f. *strength, force*, but **vīrēs, -ium** f. *armed forces*.

Mixed i-stem Nouns

This class includes:

- all nouns that end in **-es** or **-is** in the nominative singular, have the same number of syllables in the nominative and the genitive singular, and are not pure i-stem nouns, such as **hostis, -is** m. *enemy* or **navis, -is** f. *ship*.
- and all nouns whose stem ends in two consonants, such as **urbs, urbis** f. *city* or **ars, artis** f. *art*.

The only difference from consonant-stem nouns is the ending **-ium** for the **genitive plural**.

 Exceptions are **pater, patris** m. *father*, **māter, mātris** f. *mother*, **frāter, frātris** m. *brother*, **iuvenis, -is** m. *young man*, and **canis, -is** m./f. *dog*. They are declined as consonant-stem nouns.

Some words have two genitive plurals, both of which are in common use: **parentēs, -(i)um** m. *parents*, **mēnsis, -is** m. *month*, **vātēs, -is** m. *prophet*, **mūs, mūris** m. *mouse,* and **fraus, fraudis** f. *fraud*.

The example of **hostis, -is** m. *enemy* illustrates the declension of mixed i-stem nouns:

	SINGULAR		PLURAL	
Nom.	**hostis**	the enemy	**hostēs**	the enemies
Gen.	**hostis**	of the enemy	**hostium**	of the enemies
Dat.	**hostī**	to/for the enemy	**hostibus**	to/for the enemies
Acc.	**hostem**	the enemy	**hostēs**	the enemies
Abl.	**hoste**	by/with/from the enemy	**hostibus**	by/with/from the enemies

 There are no adjectives that use the mixed i-stem declensional endings, but they are used to decline the present active participle.

Fourth Declension (u)

Only a small group of nouns ending in **-us** or **-ū** in the nominative singular and **-ūs** in the genitive singular belong to the fourth declension, or u-declension. Examples are **passus, -ūs** m. *step* and **cornū, -ūs** n. *horn*. Their distinguishing feature is the stem ending **-u-**.

All words ending in **-us** are masculine, with these exceptions: **domus, -ūs** f. *house,* **manus, -ūs** f. *hand,* **tribus, -ūs** f. *division of the Roman people, tribe,* **porticus, -ūs** f. *arcade, gallery,* and **īdus, -uum** f. *Ides (13th or 15th day of the month);* they are feminine. Only a few nouns ending in -u, such as **cornū, -ūs** n. *horn,* are neuter.

The example of **passus, -ūs** m. *step* illustrates the declension of masculine and feminine u-declension nouns.

	SINGULAR		PLURAL	
Nom.	**passus**	the step	**passūs**	the steps
Gen.	**passūs**	of the step	**passuum**	of the steps
Dat.	**passuī**	to/for the step	**passibus**	to/for the steps
Acc.	**passum**	the step	**passūs**	the steps
Abl.	**passū**	by/with/from the step	**passibus**	by/with/from the steps

Neuters are declined like **cornū, -ūs** n. *horn:*

	SINGULAR		PLURAL	
Nom.	**cornū**	the horn	**cornua**	the horns
Gen.	**cornūs**	of the horn	**cornuum**	of the horns
Dat.	**cornū(ī)**	to/for the horn	**cornibus**	to/for the horns
Acc.	**cornū**	the horn	**cornua**	the horns
Abl.	**cornū**	by/with/from the horn	**cornibus**	by/with/from the horns

Peculiarities:
- Some nouns have the ending -ubus rather than -ibus in the dative and ablative plural. This applies to **arcus, -ūs** m. *bow, arc,* **artus, -ūs** m. *joint,* and **tribus, -ūs** f. *division of the Roman people, tribe,* which use the forms **arcubus, artubus,** and **tribubus.**
- Dative forms ending in **-ū** can, as an exception, also occur in the case of words ending in -us, such as **exercitū** *to/for the army.*

- **domus, ūs** f. *house* is declined in part as a second-declension noun and has special forms:

	SINGULAR	PLURAL
Nom.	domus	domūs
Gen.	domūs	domōrum/domuum
Dat.	domuī	domibus
Acc.	domum	domōs (rarely domūs)
Abl.	domō	domibus

Memorize the following forms of **domus**, which appear with frequency:

domī *at home*   **domum** *home* (acc. of place)   **domō** *from home*

 There are no adjectives that use the fourth-declension endings.

Fifth Declension (e)

The fifth declension includes only a few words, which end in **-es** in the nominative singular and in **-(ē)i** in the genitive singular. Frequently used nouns in the group include **rēs, -eī** f. *thing* and **diēs, -ēī** m./f. *day/specific day, date.* Their distinguishing feature is the stem ending **-e-**.

All these words are **feminine** in gender, with the exceptions of **diēs, -ēī** m. *day* and **merīdiēs, -ēī** m. *midday*, which are masculine.

The example **rēs, -eī** f. *thing* is used to illustrate the declension of fifth-declension nouns:

	SINGULAR		PLURAL	
Nom.	rēs	the thing	rēs	the things
Gen.	reī	of the thing	rērum	of the things
Dat.	reī	to/for the thing	rēbus	to/for the things
Acc.	rem	the thing	rēs	the things
Abl.	rē	by/with/from the thing	rēbus	by/with/from the things

Peculiarities:

- The noun **rēs, -eī** f. *thing* frequently appears in connection with other nouns or adjectives and can have a great variety of meanings, such as:

rēs militāris	*military matters*	**rēs futūrae (pl.)**	*future*
rēs secundae (pl.)	*prosperity, success*	**rēs adversae (pl.)**	*misfortune*
rēs familiāris	*property*	**rēs gestae (pl.)**	*deed*
rēs Rōmānae (pl.)	*Roman history*	**rēs pūblica**	*state*

 There are no Latin adjectives that use the fifth-declension endings.

5 Adjectives

Adjectives are modifiers, words that describe or identify or quantify a person, thing, or condition. They can modify a noun, as here: **atropa venēnāta** *poisonous nightshade*, **discipulus protervus** *the impertinent pupil*, or **otium diūtinum** *boring leisure time*.

So that readers can associate adjectives with the nouns they modify, adjectives in Latin **agree with** their **antecedent**; that is, they use the same **case**, **number**, and **gender**. Then they perform the syntactic function of an **attribute**.

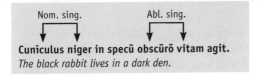

Nom. sing.   Abl. sing.

Cuniculus niger in specū obscūrō vitam agit.
The black rabbit lives in a dark den.

 In Latin, unlike English, attributive adjectives do not necessarily precede the word they modify. Agreement in terms of case, number, and gender provides the first clue to understanding the meaning of a sentence by indicating which words belong together. As there sometimes are several possibilities, at times you have to base your understanding on the **context**. The stylistic device known as **hyperbaton**, a deliberate separation of words that belong together, is a way of emphasizing individual words.

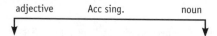

adjective   Acc sing.   noun

Aequam mementō rēbus in arduīs servāre mentem!
Remember to keep a calm mind in difficult times!

Adjectives, like nouns, are declined. Unlike nouns, they have forms for all cases, numbers, and genders, to agree with the word they modify:

cunīculo nigrō *to/for the black rabbit; by/with/from the black rabbit (dat. sing.; abl. sing.)*, **cāseum dēlicātum** *the delicious cheese (acc. sing.)*, **feminae laetae** *the glad women (nom. pl.); of/to/for the glad woman (gen. sing./dat. sing.)*.

Adjectives and nouns can belong to different declensions; that is, when they are in agreement with each other, they can use different endings. That is why a good knowledge of forms and an alert eye are essential when translating a sentence!

Fēlis nigra cunīculum felicem strepitū ferōci terret.
The black cat frightens the happy rabbit with a fierce noise.

The syntactic function of an adjective can vary. In addition to the attributive function, adjectives can be used in two other ways: as **predicate nominals** or as **predicatives**.

The Adjective as Predicate Nominal

When an adjective takes on the role of a predicate nominal, it usually occurs as the complement of the auxiliary verb **esse** *to be*, which cannot function as a predicate on its own. Here too, the adjective agrees with its antecedent, which is the subject of the sentence:

Cunīculus niger est.	*The rabbit is black.*
Fēlis alba pulchra est.	*The white cat is pretty.*
Feminae laetae sunt.	*The women are glad.*

Nouns, too, can take on the syntactic function of a predicate nominal, which in turn can be more precisely defined by an adjectival attribute.

Cuniculus albus animal pulchrum est.	*The white rabbit is a beautiful animal.*
Marcus homo magnus est.	*Marcus is a great man.*

The Adjective as Predicative

A predicative is often confused with an attribute, in part because the Latin sentence does not differentiate between attributive usage and predicative usage. Whether one or another possible translation is more appropriate is something that must be decided on the basis of the context.

There is an important **difference in meaning** between an attribute and a predicative, however: an attribute expresses a property that generally lasts for a long period of time, while a predicative describes a property that is significant only at the moment of the verbal action, as in this example:

Cuniculus salvus viam trānsiit.

Attributive usage	*The unharmed rabbit crossed the street.*
Predicative usage	*The rabbit crossed the street unharmed.* At the time the rabbit is crossing the street, it is (still) unharmed.

▶ For more on **predicatives**, see Chapter 17.

Adjectives of the First (a) and Second (o) Declensions

Adjectives of the first (a) and second (o) declensions are divided into two groups, which differ only in the nominative singular: The larger group has the following endings in the nominative singular: masculine, **-us**, feminine, **-a**, and neuter, **-um**.

A smaller number of adjectives end as follows in the nominative singular: masculine, **-er**, feminine, **-(e)ra**, and neuter, **-(e)rum**.

The latter group, in turn, distinguishes between adjectives that retain the **-e-** in all cases, and adjectives that exhibit the **-e-** only in the nominative (and vocative) singular masculine. Here, therefore, adjectives behave exactly like the nouns of the corresponding group.

Morphology

In the following adjectives, the **-e-** is present in all cases:

asper, aspera, asperum	*rough, harsh*
lacer, lacera, lacerum	*torn*
tener, tenera, tenerum	*tender*
liber, libera, liberum	*free*
miser, misera, miserum	*wretched, miserable*

In addition, the **-e-** is retained in adjectives with the component **-fer** or **-ger**, such as **frūgifer, -era, -erum** *fruitful* and **armiger, -era, -erum** *armed, arms-bearing*. **Dexter, -era, -erum** *right, right-hand* can be declined in both ways and also has the forms **dexter, dextra, dextrum.**

The declension of an adjective of the a-/o- declension depends on the word it modifies. If its antecedent is a masculine noun (regardless of the declension to which the noun belongs), it is declined like an o- declension noun. If the word it modifies is feminine, it is declined like a noun of the a- declension; if it refers to a neuter noun, the forms are based on the neuter o- declension endings.

This is illustrated by the example of **albus, -a, -um** *white:*

SINGULAR	M.		F.		N.	
Nom.	cunīculus	albus	fēlis	alba	animal	album
Gen.	cunīculī	albī	fēlis	albae	animālis	albī
Dat.	cunīculō	albō	fēlī	albae	animālī	albō
Acc.	cunīculum	album	fēlem	albam	animal	album
Abl.	cunīculō	albō	fēle	albā	animālī	albō
PLURAL	M.		F.		N.	
Nom.	cunīculī	albī	fēlēs	albae	animālia	alba
Gen.	cunīculōrum	albōrum	fēlum	albārum	animālium	albōrum
Dat.	cunīculīs	albīs	fēlibus	albīs	animālibus	albīs
Acc.	cunīculōs	albōs	fēlēs	albās	animālia	alba
Abl.	cunīculīs	albīs	fēlibus	albīs	animālibus	albīs

Note the following peculiarity:
- The vocative singular masculine, like the nouns of the second (o) declension, has a special form: **albe.**

Participles, too, are declined like adjectives. The perfect passive participle (PPP), the future active participle (FAP), the gerund, and the gerundive are declined like the adjectives of the first and second declensions ending in **-us, -a, -um.**

Example: **agere, agō, ēgī, āctum** *act, do, conduct, make*

PPP:	āctus, ācta, āctum	PFA:	āctūrus, āctūra, āctūrum
Gen. sing.	āctī, āctae, āctī		āctūrī, āctūrae, āctūrī
Gerund:	gen.: agendī	gerundive:	agendus, -a, -um
Dat. sing.	agendō	gen. sing.	agendī, -ae, -ī, etc.

For more on participles, gerunds, etc., see the corresponding sections in Chapter 17.

Adjectives of the Third Declension

Besides the adjectives of the first and second declensions, there are also adjectives that are inflected like third-declension nouns. As with the nouns, a distinction is made between those that are declined like **consonant-stem** nouns and those that are declined like pure i-stem nouns.

 There are no adjectives that are declined like mixed i-stem nouns.

Adjectives with Consonant Stems

Only eight adjectives follow this pattern. All are **one**-ending adjectives; that is, they have the same form for all three genders in the nominative singular. The second form typically given in vocabulary lists is the genitive.

vetus, veteris	*old*	**compos, compotis**	*having mastery of*
dīves, dīvitis	*rich*	**superstes, superstitis**	*surviving*
pauper, pauperis	*poor*	**sōspes, sospitis**	*unharmed, safe and sound*
prīnceps, prīncipis	*the first*	**particeps, participis**	*participating, participant*

The example of **pauper, pauperis** *poor* illustrates the declension of these adjectives:

SINGULAR	M.	F.	N.
Nom.	pauper	pauper	pauper
Gen.	pauperis	pauper	pauperis
Dat.	pauperī	pauperī	pauperī
Acc.	pauperem	pauperem	pauper
Abl.	paupere	paupere	paupere
PLURAL	M.	F.	N.
Nom.	pauperēs	pauperēs	paupera
Gen.	pauperum	pauperum	pauperum
Dat.	pauperibus	pauperibus	pauperibus
Acc.	pauperēs	pauperēs	paupera
Abl.	pauperibus	pauperibus	pauperibus

Characteristic of such adjectives are the endings **-e** in the ablative singular, **-a** in the neuter plural, and **-um** in the genitive plural.

Adjectives with Consonant Stems (i-stems)

The adjectives that are declined like i-stem nouns are divided into **three groups**, according to the number of forms they have in the **nominative singular**:

- **three**-ending adjectives, which have a separate form for each gender in the nominative singular, such as **ācer** m., **ācris** f., **ācre** n. *sharp*
- **two**-ending adjectives, which have only two forms in the nominative singular, such as **gravis** m. and f., **grave** n. *heavy*
- **one**-ending adjectives, which have the same form for all three genders in the nominative singular, such as **ingēns** m., f., n. *huge, enormous*

The examples **celer, celeries, celere** *fast,* **fortis, fortis, forte** *brave,* and **felix, felix, felix** *happy* illustrate the declension of i-stem adjectives:

SINGULAR	M.	F.	N.
Nom.	celer	celeris	celere
Gen.	celeris	celeris	celeris
Dat.	celerī	celerī	celerī
Acc.	celerem	celerem	celere
Abl.	celerī	celerī	celerī
PLURAL	M.	F.	N.
Nom.	celerēs	celerēs	celeria
Gen.	celerium	celerium	celerium
Dat.	celeribus	celeribus	celeribus
Acc.	celerēs	celerēs	celeria
Abl.	celeribus	celeribus	celeribus

SINGULAR	M.	F.	N.
Nom.	fortis	fortis	forte
Gen.	fortis	fortis	fortis
Dat.	fortī	fortī	fortī
Acc.	fortem	forte	forte
Abl.	fortī	fortī	fortī
PLURAL	M.	F.	N.
Nom.	fortēs	fortēs	fortia
Gen.	fortium	fortium	fortium
Dat.	fortibus	fortibus	fortibus
Acc.	fortēs	fortēs	fortia
Abl.	fortibus	fortibus	fortibus

SINGULAR	M.	F.	N.
Nom.	fēlix	fēlix	fēlix
Gen.	fēlicis	fēlicis	fēlicis
Dat.	fēlici	fēlici	fēlici
Acc.	fēlicem	fēlicem	fēlix
Abl.	fēlici	fēlici	fēlici
PLURAL	M.	F.	N.
Nom.	fēlicēs	fēlicēs	fēlicia
Gen.	fēlicium	fēlicium	fēlicium
Dat.	fēlicibus	fēlicibus	fēlicibus
Acc.	fēlicēs	fēlicēs	fēlicia
Abl.	fēlicibus	fēlicibus	fēlicibus

! The adjectives that are inflected like i-stem nouns differ from the nouns of this declension class in that their accusative singular masculine and feminine ends in **-em** rather than **-im**.

Occasionally adjectives occur without an antecedent. Frequently they refer to a noun in the immediately preceding sentence, and in this instance they can be treated like nouns and also translated as such. Then they are called **substantivized adjectives.**

Fēlis mūrem ēdit. Rūrsus fortis parvum vīcit.
The cat ate the mouse. Once again the strong conquered the weak.

Latin adjectives, like English ones, have degrees of comparison.
▶ You'll learn more about that in the chapter on **comparison of adjectives and adverbs.**

6 Adverbs

Latin, like English, has a great many adverbs, which can perform different functions in a sentence. Adverbs, like adjectives, are modifiers, but they apply to **verbs** rather than to nouns: *translate* **carefully,** *work* **judiciously** = **ad verbum** *(added) to a verb*. More rarely, an adverb also can more precisely define the meaning of an adjective ("**very** restful weeks"), a **participle** ("**deeply** affected"), or another **adverb** ("**very** quickly"). Adverbs are classified as **particles**, and they cannot be declined or conjugated.

Noctū fēlis nigra cito **appropinquāvit.** Subito **cuniculum** tantopere **parvum terruit. Sed cuniculus ā**criter **territus** sērō **fūgit.**
At night the black cat approached quickly. *Suddenly the* very *small rabbit was frightened. But the rabbit, which had been* badly *scared, fled* too late.

	ANSWER THE QUESTION
Adverbs of time:	when? how long? how often?
Adverbs of place:	where? to where? from where?
Adverbs of manner:	how/in what way is the action occurring?
Adverbs of cause:	why? for what reason?

Adverbs Formed from Adjectives

In Latin, there are two ways to derive an adverb from the corresponding adjective:

- For adjectives of the first and second declensions, the ending is usually replaced by **-ē**: **pulchrē** *beautifully,* **magnē** *significantly,* **liberē** *freely*
- For adjectives of the third declension, the ending **-iter** is usually added, with stems ending in **-nt-** adding only **-er,** as in **fēliciter** *happily,* **sapienter** *wisely*

> **!** There are a few exceptions to the rules on adverb formation, however, and these words must be memorized.

ADVERBS ENDING IN -Ō FROM SECOND-DECLENSION ADJECTIVES

citō	quickly	**tūtō**	safely
crēbrō	frequently	**perpetuō**	constantly
falsō	falsely	**sērō**	late, tardily
meritō	deservedly	**sēcrētō**	secretly
necessāriō	necessarily	**subitō**	suddenly
prīmō	in the first place	**rārō**	rarely
postrēmō	finally		

DIFFERENTIATE BETWEEN:

vērō	truly, but	**vērē**	truthfully
certō	dependably, unfailingly	**certē**	surely, assuredly

ACC. SING. NEUTER OF THE ADJECTIVE AS ADVERB

multum	much	**parum**	very little, insufficient
plūrimum	very much	**cēterum**	moreover
plērumque	usually	**potissimum**	chiefly, principally
nimium	too much	**prīmum**	first
paulum	a little	**dēmum**	only now, just now
facile	easily	**impūne**	with impunity
nōn facile	with difficulty	**saepe**	often

"FROZEN" CASE FORMS OF NOUNS AS ADVERBS

ABLATIVES

vesperī	in the evening	**magnopere**	greatly
noctū	at night	**tantopere**	so much
diū	for a long time	**quantopere**	how much
hodiē	today	**modo**	only
cottīdiē	daily	**quōmodo**	how, in what way
prīdiē	the day before	**forte**	by chance
postrīdiē	the day after	**grātīs**	without charge
ūnā	together	**frūstrā**	in vain
omnīnō	completely		

"FROZEN" CASE FORMS OF NOUNS AS ADVERBS

ACCUSATIVES

partim	in part	sēnsim	gradually
statim	at once	nōminātim	by name
passim	everywhere	paulātim	gradually
praesertim	especially	prīvātim	privately
palam	openly, plainly	clam	secretly

NOMINATIVE

satis	enough	rūrsus	again

"FROZEN" COMPOUNDS WITH A PREPOSITION AS ADVERBS

anteā	before, previously	dēnuō	anew, once again
posteā	later	imprīmīs	in the first place
intereā	meanwhile	īlicō	on the spot
praetereā	besides	extemplō	immediately
proptereā	on that account	sēdulō	diligently
invicem	mutually, by turns	obviam	toward

ADVERBS FORMED WITH THE SUFFIX -TUS, DENOTING POINT OF ORIGIN

antīquitus	in ancient times	penitus	wholly, entirely
funditus	totally	rādīcitus	utterly, by the roots

COMPOUNDS WITH -PER

semper	always	nūper	recently
paulīsper	a little		

OTHER EXCEPTIONS:

nunc	now	vix	hardly, scarcely
crās	tomorrow	sīc	thus, so
mox	soon	simul	at the same time

Some adjectives that occur with great frequency form their adverbs irregularly. These must be memorized:

bonus	*good*	▶	**bene**	*well*
audāx	*bold*	▶	**audācter**	*boldly*
alius	*another*	▶	**aliter**	*otherwise*

In the chapters on pronouns and numerals, you will learn more about adverbs that are derived from pronominal stems or numerals. Adverbs, like adjectives, have forms that indicate degrees of comparison.

7 Comparative Adjectives and Adverbs

Latin, like English, uses different forms of adjectives and adverbs to make comparisons between two or more living beings or things.

*There are strong and weak animals. No matter what, a cat is **stronger** than a rabbit. The **strongest**, however, is the lion, the king of beasts.*

These forms indicate various degrees of comparison (**comparāre** to compare).

Both adjectives and adverbs have three degrees of comparison:

the strong animal	*the stronger animal*	*the strongest animal*
positive	**comparative**	**superlative**

Forming the Comparative and Superlative Degrees of Adjectives

The Latin comparative generally is formed by adding the ending **-ior** to the stem of masculine and feminine adjectives and the ending **-ius** to the stem of neuter adjectives.

POSITIVE	COMPARATIVE (nom. sing. m./f.)	SUPERLATIVE (nom. sing. n.)
prūdēns, -tis *wise*	**prūdent-ior** *wiser (m./f.)*	**prūdent-ius** *wisest (n.)*
fortis, -e *strong*	**fort-ior** *stronger (m./f.)*	**fort-ius** *strongest (n.)*
altus, -a, -um *high*	**alt-ior** *higher (m./f.)*	**alt-ius** *highest (n.)*

The comparative forms are declined like consonant-stem adjectives ending in **-r**. Only the neuter singular in the nominative/accusative case is an exception: The comparatives in this case have a special ending, **-ius**.

SINGULAR	M.	F.	N.
Nom.	prūdentior	prūdentior	prūdentius
Gen.		prūdentiōris	
Dat.		prūdentiōrī	
Acc.	prūdentiōrem	prūdentiōrem	prūdentius
Abl.		prūdentiōre	

PLURAL	M.	F.	N.
Nom.	prūdentiōrēs	prūdentiōrēs	prūdentiōra
Gen.		prūdentiōrum	
Dat.		prūdentiōribus	
Acc.	prūdentiōrēs	prūdentiōrēs	prūdentiōra
Abl.		prūdentiōribus	

To form the Latin superlative degree, most adjectives add the ending **-issimus, -a**, or **-um** to the stem. Some adjectives ending in **-tis** add **-limus, -a**, or **-um** to the stem, while adjectives ending in **-er** add **-rimus, -a**, or **-um** to the **nominative singular masculine**. The superlative forms are declined like adjectives of the first and second declensions ending in **-us**.

Morphology

POSITIVE	SUPERLATIVE
longus, -a, -um *long*	**long-issimus, -a, -um** *longest*
facilis, -e *easy*	**facil-limus, -a, -um** *easiest*
pulcher, -a, -um *pretty*	**pulcher-rimus, -a, -um** *prettiest*

Forming the Comparative and Superlative Degrees of Adverbs

The **accusative singular neuter form of the comparative degree of the adjective** serves as the comparative degree of all adverbs. For example: **facilius** *more easily,* **altius** *higher,* **prūdentius** *more wisely.*

The superlative forms are generally formed like the adverbs derived from the adjectives of the first and second declensions, by adding the ending **-e** to the stem, as follows: **facillimē** *most easily,* **altissimē** *highest,* **prūdentissimē** *most wisely.*

 Occasionally, both the comparative and superlative degrees of adjectives and adverbs do not express comparison. Instead, like adjectives and adverbs, they refer to a property. Then they are translated into English by adding words such as *too, quite,* or *very* for the **comparative**, and *extremely* for the **superlative**.

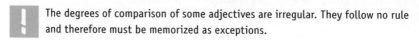

Cunīculus minor **est.**	*The rabbit is quite small.*
Fēlis māior **est.**	*The cat is very big.*
Leō est fortissimus **et** prūdentissimus.	*The lion is extremely brave and wise.*

 The degrees of comparison of some adjectives are irregular. They follow no rule and therefore must be memorized as exceptions.

Comparative Adjectives and Adverbs

Adjectives that use a different stem for the comparative and superlative:

bonus, -a, -um *good*	**melior, -ius** *better*	**optimus, -a, -um** *best*
malus, -a, -um *bad*	**peior, peius** *worse*	**pessimus, -a, -um** *worse*
magnus, -a, -um *big*	**maior, -ius** *bigger*	**māximus, -a, -um** *biggest*
parvus, -a, -um *small*	**minor, -us** *smaller*	**minimus, -a, -um** *smallest*
multum *much*	**plūs** *more*	**plūrimum** *most*
multī *many*	**plūrēs, -a** *more*	**plūrimī** *most*

Adjectives that use magis *more* and māximē *most* to form the comparative and superlative degrees (especially adjectives ending in -eus and -ius):

idōneus, -a, -um *suitable*	**magis idōneus** *more suitable*	**māximē idōneus** *most suitable*
necessārius *necessary*	**magis necessārius** *more necessary*	**māximē necessārius** *most necessary*

Prepositions that can have adjectival forms of comparison:

intrā *inside*	**interior** *inner*	**intimus** *inmost*
extrā *outside*	**exterior** *outer*	**extrēmus** *outermost*
infrā *under*	**inferior** *lower*	**infimus/īmus** *lowest*
suprā *above*	**superior** *upper*	**suprēmus/summus** *uppermost*
prāe *before*	**prior** *former*	**prīmus** *first*
post *behind*	**posterior** *latter*	**postrēmus/postumus** *last*
dē *down from*	**dēterior** *worst*	**dēterrimus** *worst*
prope *near to*	**propior** *nearer*	**proximus** *nearest, last*

8 Pronouns

Pronouns are classified as follows, according to meaning:

Personal pronouns	**egō** *I,* **tū** *you* (sing.), **nōs** *we,* **vōs** *you* (pl.), etc.
Reflexive pronouns	**sē** *-self/selves* (third-pers. sing. and pl.), **suī** *his,* etc.
Possessive pronouns	**meus** *my,* **tuus** *your,* **suus** *his,* etc.
Demonstrative pronouns	**hic/is** *this,* **iste** *this,* **ille** *that,* **īdem** *the same,* **ipse** *he himself*
Relative pronouns	**quī** *who, which,* etc.
Interrogative pronouns	**quis?** *who?* **quid?** *what?* etc.
Indefinite pronouns	**aliquis** *someone,* **quīdam** *a certain,* etc.
Correlative pronouns	**tālis** *such,* **tantus** *so great,* etc.

As their name indicates, pronouns (**prō nōmine** *in place of a noun*) can take the place of a noun by standing in for a **noun** from the preceding sentence (or one that is already known from the context). Pronouns, however, are not treated only **as nouns**; they can also be used **adjectivally**.

If a pronoun is used **as a noun (substantively)**, the pronoun and the antecedent must agree in gender and number, so that the reader can tell that they belong together. When used **adjectivally**, the pronoun, like other attributes, agrees with the noun in **case**, **number**, and **gender**.

Fēlis nigra cunīculum album fugat. Haec semper illud animal terret.
The black cat puts the white rabbit to flight. It always terrifies that animal.

In the preceding sentence, the demonstrative pronoun **haec** *this* replaces the noun **fēlis** *cat* (and all amplifications, such as **nigra** *black*). To make it clear that they go together, the two words agree in **number** and **gender**. Their case, however, does not necessarily have to agree.

▶ For more on demonstrative pronouns, see that section later in this chapter.

Fēlis nigra cunīculum album fugat. Hoc animal ab illā semper terrētur.
The black cat puts the white rabbit to flight. This animal is always frightened by that one.

If the neuter pronoun is used, it occasionally can also refer to the entire content of the preceding sentence or clause.

Fēlis nigra cunīculum album fugat. Hoc initium fābulae tristis est.
The black cat puts the white rabbit to flight. This is the beginning of a sad story.

 The declension of pronouns, in many respects, follows the pattern of the first and second (a and o) declensions, but there are a few points of **divergence**. A common feature of many pronouns is that all genders end in **-ius** in the genitive singular and in **-i** in the dative singular.

Personal Pronouns

The personal pronoun differs from the other pronouns in that it has no forms for the various genders, but instead has only a **single form** for all. It refers to the first- or second-person singular (**egō** and **tū**) and plural (**nōs** and **vōs**). The personal pronouns can be inflected. The genitive forms are derived from the possessive pronouns.

SINGULAR	1ST PERSON		2ND PERSON	
Nom.	**egō**	*I*	**tū**	*you*
Gen.	**meī**	*my*	**tuī**	*your*
Dat.	**mihī**	*to/for me*	**tibī**	*to/for you*
Acc.	**mē**	*me*	**tē**	*you*
Abl.	**ā mē (mēcum)**	*by/from me (with me)*	**ā tē (tēcum)**	*by/from you (with you)*

PLURAL	1ST PERSON		2ND PERSON	
Nom.	**nōs**	*we*	**vōs**	*you*
Gen.	**nostrī/nostrum**	*our*	**vestrī/vestrum**	*your*
Dat.	**nōbīs**	*to/for us*	**vōbīs**	*to/for you*
Acc.	**nōs**	*us*	**vōs**	*you*
Abl.	**ā nōbīs** **(nōbīscum)**	*by/from us* *(with us)*	**ā vōbīs** **(vōbīscum)**	*by/from you* *(with you)*

In the genitive case of **nōs** and **vōs**, these functions exist:

genitīvus obiectīvus (genitive of the object):	**fidēs vestrī**	trust **in** you
	fidēs nostrī	faith **in** us
genitīvus partitīvus (partitive genitive):	**ūnus vestrum**	one **of** you
	duo nostrum	two **of** us

To indicate the third person (*he, she, it* sing. and *they* pl.), Latin also uses a personal pronoun. Unlike the personal pronouns for the first and second persons, the third-person pronoun has both **reflexive** forms (of **sē**, *-self*) referring to the subject and **nonreflexive** forms: **is**, **ea**, **id** *this (one)*.

SINGULAR/PLURAL	3RD PERSON REFLEXIVE FORM	
Nom.	–	–
Gen.	**suī**	*his/her/its/their*
Dat.	**sibī**	*to/for himself,* etc.
Acc.	**sē**	*himself,* etc.
Abl.	**ā sē (sēcum)**	*by/from himself,* etc. *(with himself,* etc.*)*

The **reflexive** forms are used only when the personal pronoun refers to the subject.

Marcus eum laudat.
Marcus praises him.

Marcus sē laudat.
Marcus praises himself.

In the first sentence, it is not Marcus himself who is praised, but another person (nonreflexive), while in the second sentence Marcus is praising himself, not someone else (reflexive). The demonstrative pronouns **is**, **ea**, **id** *this (one)* function as personal pronouns to substitute for nouns. For their declension, see the section on **demonstrative pronouns**.

Unlike English, Latin does not require the use of a personal pronoun; in Latin, the personal pronoun is used only to place special emphasis on the person. Otherwise, the predicate itself, through the ending, indicates the person. Occasionally the personal pronoun is given particular emphasis by attaching **-met** (**egomet** *I*), by attaching **-te** (**tūte**, *you* nom., **tēte** *you* acc.), or by doubling the reflexive (**sēsē**, *-self*).

Egō linguam Latīnam valdē utilem exīstimō.
I think Latin is a very useful language (though you may disagree).

Possessive Pronouns

Possessive pronouns (**possidēre** *to possess*) indicate possession or "ownership." They are used as adjectives, occasionally as nouns (**substantivized**), and thus agree in case, number, and gender with the word to which they refer. They are declined like adjectives of the first and second (a and o) declensions.

SINGULAR			PLURAL	
1st Pers.	**meus, -a, -um**	*my*	**noster, -tra, -trum**	*our*
2nd Pers.	**tuus, -a, -um**	*your*	**vester, -tra, -trum**	*your*
3rd Pers.	**suus, -a, -um** (reflexive)	*his, her, its*	**suus, -a, -um** (reflexive)	*their*
	eius (nonreflexive)	*his, her, its*	**eōrum bzw. eārum** (nonreflexive)	*their*

Just as with the personal pronouns, the third-person forms of **suus** are only used reflexively, and in nonreflexive usage they are replaced by the genitive forms of **is, ea, id**.
Note the difference between:

Rūfus avum eius (Gāi) vīsitat.   **Rūfus avum suum vīsitat.**
Rufus visits his (Gaius's) grandfather.   *Rufus visits his (own) grandfather.*

 The vocative singular masculine of **meus** is **mī**:
Mī pater! *My father!* but **Mea puella** *My girl!*

In addition, memorize the following expressions:

meā, tuā, suā sponte	*of my, your, his/one's (etc.) own will*
meā, tuā, suā sententiā	*in my (etc.) opinion*
meō, tuō, suō iūre	*in my (etc.) own right*
suō tempore	*in its time, at the right time*

 Unlike English, Latin states the possessive pronoun explicitly only if the context makes it absolutely necessary to emphasize the possessor.

amīcus fīlium servāvit	**amīcus fīlium meum servāvit**
my friend rescued his son	*my friend rescued my son*

Demonstrative Pronouns

Demonstrative pronouns (**dēmōnstrāre** *to demonstrate, show*) are words with which the speaker identifies or specifies an object (persons or things). Both English and Latin have several demonstrative pronouns, which in some instances differ only in shades of meaning but are deliberately chosen by the speaker.

PRONOUN	FIELD OF APPLICATION	EXAMPLE
hic, haec, hoc *this*	indicates things or persons that usually are close to the speaker in terms of space or time	**Hic liber Cornēliae est.** *This book is Cornelia's.*
ille, illa, illud *that*	the things or persons indicated usually are farther from the speaker in terms of space or time or are generally known to the listeners	**Ille liber Claudiō est.** *That book is Claudius's.* **Illa sententia Sōcratis nobis nota est.** *That saying of Socrates's is known to us.*
iste, ista, istud *this (here)*	indicates things or persons that are near the speaker in terms of space; frequently with a disparaging undertone	**iste vir** *this (bad) man here* **istae litterae** *this letter here*
is, ea, id *this*	1. indicates something already named or following 2. replaces the nonreflexive personal pronoun for the third person and 3. in the genitive replaces the nonreflexive possessive pronoun 4. indicates a following relative clause	1. **is vir** *this man* **ea fāma** *this news* 2. **Eōs invitāvī.** *I invited them.* 3. **cunīculus eius** *his rabbit* 4. **is amīcus, quī** *this friend, who*
ipse, ipsa, ipsum *-self*	adds special emphasis or delimits, but can also have other shades of meaning; usually agrees with the subject and often must be translated loosely	**Ipse hoc dīxit.** *He himself said it.* **ipsam virtūtem contemnere** *to despise even virtue* **trigintā diēs ipsī** *exactly 30 days*
idem, eadem, idem *the same*	refers to a previously named person or thing	**Idem faciō, quod tū.** *I'm doing the same thing as you.*

The demonstrative pronoun **hic, haec, hoc** *this* has the following forms:

	SINGULAR			PLURAL		
	M.	F.	N.	M.	F.	N.
Nom.	hic	haec	hoc	hī	hae	haec
Gen.	huius	huius	huius	hōrum	hārum	hōrum
Dat.	huic	huic	huic	hīs	hīs	hīs
Acc.	hunc	hanc	hoc	hōs	hās	haec
Abl.	hōc	hāc	hōc	hīs	hīs	hīs

The demonstrative pronoun **ille, illa, illud** *that* has the following forms:

	SINGULAR			PLURAL		
	M.	F.	N.	M.	F.	N.
Nom.	ille	illa	illud	illī	illae	illa
Gen.	illīus	illīus	illīus	illōrum	illārum	illōrum
Dat.	illī	illī	illī	illīs	illīs	illīs
Acc.	illum	illam	illud	illōs	illās	illa
Abl.	illō	illā	illō	illīs	illīs	illīs

The demonstrative pronouns **iste, ista, istud** *that, that ... of yours* (sometimes used contemptuously) and **ipse, ipsa, ipsum** *himself, herself, itself* (intensifier) are declined according to this pattern.

> **!** In contrast to all other demonstrative pronouns, **ipse** ends in **-um**, rather than **-ud**, in the nominative and accusative singular neuter.

Is, ea, id *this, that* is declined as follows:

	SINGULAR			PLURAL		
	M.	F.	N.	M.	F.	N.
Nom.	is	ea	id	iī/eī	eae	ea
Gen.	eius	eius	eius	eōrum	eārum	eōrum
Dat.	eī	eī	eī	eīs/iīs	eīs/iīs	eīs/iīs
Acc.	eum	eam	id	eōs	eās	ea
Abl.	eō	eā	eō	eīs/iīs	eīs/iīs	eīs/iīs

The personal pronoun **idem, eadem, idem** *the same* is derived from the forms **is, ea, id** and is declined correspondingly. The genitive singular is **eiusdem**, the dative singular **eīdem**, etc. However, **idem, eadem, idem** also has variant forms, which you need to memorize: In the accusative singular masculine and feminine, the **-m-** changes to **-n-** and the forms are **eundem** and **eandem**. The same thing occurs in the genitive plural of all genders: **eōrundem, eārundem, eōrundem**.

Relative Pronouns

Relative pronouns introduce a subordinate clause. They relate to a noun (more rarely, a pronoun) that has already been mentioned (in a main clause or a dependent clause), and give more information about it. Thus they perform the function of an **attribute**.

The relative pronoun agrees in **number and gender** with its antecedent, but the **case** varies, depending on the pronoun's relationship to the verb in the relative clause.

Fēlis, quae semper cuniculum parvum terret, nigra est.
The cat that always frightens the little rabbit is black.

Fēlis cuniculum nigrum terret, quōcum cuniculus albus semper lūdit.
The cat frightens the black rabbit, with which the white rabbit always plays.

If the relative pronoun is used in the neuter, it can refer to the content of the entire main clause.

Cuniculus sēcrētō mactātus est, quod sine dubiō pūniendum est.
The rabbit was secretly slaughtered, which without doubt must be punished.

The Latin relative pronoun **quī, quae, quod** *who, which, what, that* is declined as follows:

SINGULAR	M.		F.		N.	
Nom.	**quī**	*who*	**quae**	*who*	**quod**	*which*
Gen.	**cuius**	*whose*	**cuius**	*whose*	**cuius**	*of which*
Dat.	**cui**	*to/for whom*	**cui**	*to/for whom*	**cui**	*to/for which*
Acc.	**quem**	*whom*	**quam**	*whom*	**quod**	*which*
Abl.	**quō**	*by/with/from whom*	**quā**	*by/with/from whom*	**quō**	*by/with/from which*

PLURAL	M.		F.		N.	
Nom.	**qui**	who	**quae**	who	**quae**	which
Gen.	**quōrum**	whose	**quārum**	whose	**quōrum**	of which
Dat.	**quibus**	to/for whom	**quibus**	to/for whom	**quibus**	to/for which
Acc.	**quōs**	whom	**quās**	whom	**quae**	which
Abl.	**quibus**	by/with/ from whom	**quibus**	by/with/ from whom	**quibus**	by/with/ from which

Relative clauses also can be introduced by the indefinite relative pronoun **quicumque, quaecumque, quodcumque** *whoever, whatever*. Its forms are produced by adding the suffix **-cumque** to the declined relative pronoun **qui, quae, quod**. In the singular, it is used as an adjective; in the plural it can also be used substantively.

Quisquis, quidquid *whoever, whatever* is used as a substantive. This pronoun has only three forms: **quisquis** (nom. sing. masc.) and **quidquid** (nom. sing. neut. and acc. sing. neut.).

A special feature of Latin is the **conjunctive use of the relative pronoun**. Here the relative pronoun refers to a preceding noun, but introduces a **main clause** rather than a dependent clause. Then it is translated with a **demonstrative or personal pronoun**.

Fēlis nigra cunīculum cepit; quem irrītāre vōluit.
The black cat caught the rabbit; it (the cat) wanted to tease it (the rabbit).

The following expressions often introduce a relative conjunctive pronoun:

quō factō	*upon this*	**quārē**	*wherefore*
quod sī	*but if*	**quibus rēbus gestīs**	*after which*
quā dē causā	*for which reason*	**quō**	*thereby*
quam ob rem	*for which reason*		

These conjunctives should be memorized as vocabulary words.

In English, a relative clause follows the noun it modifies. Only when the antecedent is not a single word but a group (for example, *the rabbits from the city park, which*) is the pronoun separated from the noun it modifies. In Latin, that is not always so. A relative clause can also be at some distance from its antecedent. Pay close attention to the **agreement of case and number**, and always check to see which nouns are possible antecedents!

▶ For more on relative pronouns, see the section on **Relative Clauses.**

Interrogative Pronouns

Interrogative pronouns (**interrogāre** *to ask*) introduce interrogative clauses. With regard to their inflection, they have certain things in common with the relative pronouns.

The substantivally used **quis**, **quid** *who, what?* are declined like the relative pronoun, except for the forms **quis** and **quid**:

PLURAL	M./F.		N.	
Nom.	**quis?**	*who?*	**quid?**	*what?*
Gen.	**cuius?**	*whose?*	**cuius?**	*of what?*
Dat.	**cui?**	*to/for who?*	**cui?**	*to/for what?*
Acc.	**quem?**	*whom?*	**quid?**	*what?*
Abl.	**quō?**	*by/with/from whom?*	**quō?**	*by/with/from what?*

The forms of the relative pronoun **quī**, **quae**, **quod** *what, which, what kind of?* serve as adjectival interrogative pronouns.

The following are used as substantives and as adjectives when it is a question of one of two alternatives: **uter, utra, utrum** (**utrīus, utrī**, etc.) *which (of two)?*

Uter cunīculus sēcrētō mactātus est?
Which rabbit was secretly slaughtered? (There are only two, a black one and a white one.)

▶ For more on interrogative clauses, see the section on **Types of Sentences.**

51

Indefinite Pronouns

Indefinite pronouns are used when a thing or person is not or cannot be specified. Many of them are based on the **interrogative pronoun/relative pronoun** and a **suffix**. In each instance, only the interrogative/relative component is declined.

 There are different Latin forms, depending on whether the pronoun is used as a **substantive** or as an **adjective**. Generally, the **interrogative pronoun** is used to form the former, while the **relative pronoun** is used for the latter.

The indefinite pronoun **aliquis, aliquid** *someone, somebody, something* is used **substantivally**. In the neuter, some forms are supplemented with the word **rēs** *thing, matter*.

	M./F.	N.
Nom.	**aliquis**	**aliquid**
Gen.	**alicuius**	**alicuius** reī
Dat.	**alicui**	**alicui** reī
Acc.	**aliquem**	**aliquid**
Abl.	**aliquō**	**aliquā** rē

The particle **ali-** is added to the relative pronoun **qui** for use as an adjective. An exception is the form **aliqua** in the nominative singular feminine and nominative and accusative plural neuter.

 After some words, the **ali-** preceding the pronoun is dropped. Such words include **sī, nisī, nē** and **num, quō, quantō**, and **cum**.

Sī quis venit, portam nōn aperiō.
If someone comes, I'm not opening the door.

In sentences that contain a negation, **quisquam, quicquam** (**cuiusquam, cuiquam**, etc.) and **ūllus, -a, -um** are used in the same meaning.

Cuniculus sine cuiusquam misericordiā mactātus est.
The rabbit was slaughtered without mercy from anyone.

Rarely, **aliquis** is replaced by **quisquam, quidquam** (for nouns) or **quispiam, quaepiam, quodpiam** (for adjectives) *someone, somebody, something.*

Latin also has the following indefinite pronouns:

Substantival	Adjectival	Meaning	Examples
quīdam, quaedam, quiddam*	quīdam, quaedam, quoddam*	*a certain (one or thing)*	**Quīdam senātōrum ōrātiōnem habuit.** *One of the senators gave a speech.* **Philosophus** quīdam **hoc dīxit.** *A certain philosopher said that.*
quisque, quidque	quisque, quaeque, quodque	*each (one, person)*	**Quisque vestrum Rōmānus est.** *Each of you is a Roman.* **Cuique puerō dōnum dō.** *I give each boy a present.*
quīvīs, quaevīs, quidvīs	quīvīs, quaevīs, quodvīs	*any (one, thing)*	**Quīvīs nostrum cantāre potest.** *Any of us can sing.* **Marcus** quodvīs **animal capit.** *Marcus catches each (any) animal.*
quīlibet, quaelibet, quidlibet	quīlibet, quaelibet, quodlibet	*whatever, whichever; any (one, thing)*	**Quaelibet illārum uxor est.** *Any (and every) one of them is a married woman.* **Quamlibet fēminam adiuvāmus.** *We help any woman.*

* Note: In the accusative singular masculine and feminine, **-m-** becomes **-n-**: **quendam, quandam.** The same thing is true in the genitive plural of all genders: **quōrundam, quārundam, quōrundam.**

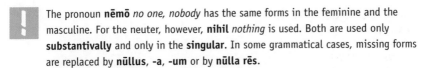

The pronoun **nēmō** *no one, nobody* has the same forms in the feminine and the masculine. For the neuter, however, **nihil** *nothing* is used. Both are used only **substantivally** and only in the **singular**. In some grammatical cases, missing forms are replaced by **nūllus, -a, -um** or by **nūlla rēs.**

Nom.	nēmō	nihil (nīl)
Gen.	nūllīus	nūllīus reī
Dat.	nēminī	nūllī reī
Acc.	nēminem	nihil (nīl)
Abl.	ā nūllō	nūllā rē

Cunīculus ā nūllō servātus est. Quid fēcistī? Nihil.
The rabbit was saved by no one. What did you do? Nothing.

Pronominal Adjectives

The following adjectives are known as **pronominal adjectives** because in their case endings in the genitive singular (**-ius**) and dative singular (**-ī**) and in their meaning, they resemble pronouns.

The pronominal adjectives include the following:

ūnus, -a, -um	one, single, alone
sōlus, -a, -um	alone, only, the only
tōtus, -a, -um	entire, whole
ūllus, -a, -um	any
nūllus, -a, -um	not any, no, none
uter, -tra, -trum	which (of two)
neuter, -tra, -trum	neither (of two)
alter, -era, -erum	the other (of two), second
alius, -a, -ud (alterīus in the genitive!)	other, another
aliī ... aliī	some ... others

 Alius, -a, -ud has special forms in the nominative/accusative singular neuter and in the genitive singular (**alterīus**) of all genders.

The pronominal adjectives with special genitive and dative endings must be memorized:

> **ūnus, sōlus, tōtus, ūllus,**
> **uter, alter, neuter, nūllus,**
> and **alius** all require
> **-ius** in the genitive.
> In the dative, they always
> end in a long **-ī**.

The remaining forms, such as **nūllus, -a, -um**, follow the pattern of the o- and a-declensions:

	SINGULAR			PLURAL		
	M.	F.	N.	M.	F.	N.
Nom.	nūllus	nūlla	nūllum	nūllī	nūllae	nūlla
Gen.	nūllīus	nūllīus	nūllīus	nūllōrum	nūllārum	nūllōrum
Dat.	nūllī	nūllī	nūllī	nūllīs	nūllīs	nūllīs
Acc.	nūllum	nūllam	nūllum	nūllōs	nūllās	nūlla
Abl.	nūllō	nūllā	nūllō	nūllīs	nūllīs	nūllīs

Notes on the use of the pronominal adjectives:

- For adjectival use, **nēmō** replaces **nūllus** with masculine nouns denoting persons: **nēmō civis** *no citizen*
- **alter** and **alii** often are doubled to convey a special meaning:

alter – alter	**alii – alii**
(the) one – the other	*some – others*

- There are slight differences in meaning among the following words:

alii	*others*
cēterī	*the others* (in the sense of *the rest, the remaining ones*)
reliquī	*the rest, the remaining ones*

Morphology

Pronominal Adverbs

The following pronominal adverbs occur in Latin:

INTERROGATIVE	RELATIVE	DEMONSTRATIVE	INDEFINITE
ubī? *where?*	**ubī** *where*	**ibī** *there*	**alicubī** *somewhere*
	ubicumque *wherever*	**hīc** *here*	**usquam** *somewhere*
		istic *there*	**ubīque** *everywhere*
		illic *there*	**alibī** *somewhere else*
		ibīdem *in the same place*	
unde? *from where?*	**unde** *from which*	**inde** *from there*	**alicunde** *from somewhere*
	undecumque *from whatever place*	**hinc** *from here*	**undique** *from all sides*
		istinc *from there*	**aliunde** *from somewhere else*
		illinc *from there*	
quō? *to what place?*	**quō** *whither*	**eō** *thither*	**aliquō** *to some place*
	quōcum-que *wherever*	**hūc** *hither*	**aliō** *to some other place*
		istūc *to that place*	
		illūc *to that place*	
		eō-dem *to that same place*	
quā? *in which way?*	**quā** *where, how*	**eā/hāc** *in this way*	**aliquā** *somewhere, in some way*
	quācumque *whenever, however*	**istāc/illāc** *in that way*	
quando? *when?*	**cum** *when*	**tum** *then*	**aliquan-dō** *at some time*
	quandō-cumque *whenever*	**tunc** *then*	**umquam** *ever*
		ōlim *once; in the future*	**num-quam** *never*
			aliās *at another time*
quōmodo? *how?*	**ut/sīcut/quōmodo/ quemad-modum** *as*	**ita/sīc** *so, thus*	**utique** *in every way*
		item *also, likewise*	
quam? *how?*	**quam** *how (much)*	**tam** *to such a degree*	

Correlative Pronouns

Correlative pronouns give information about quantity or quality and are used when comparing two persons, groups, or things. They cannot stand alone, but must be used in **correlation with another correlative**.

Tantus timor cunīculum invāsit, quantus numquam ante.
The rabbit felt such (great) fear as never before.

The most important correlative pronouns are the following:

tālis, -e	*such, of such a sort*	**quālis, -e**	*of what kind*
tantus, -a, -um	*so great, so large*	**quantus, -a, -um**	*how great, how much*
tot	*so many*	**quot**	*how many*
tantum	*so much*	**quantum**	*how much*

Tālis and **quālis** follow the pattern of the third declension, while **tantus** and **quantus** use the endings for the first and second a- and o-declensions. **Tot** and **quot** are indeclinable.

In addition, there are **correlative adverbs**:

quō	*where, whither*	**eō**	*there, thither*
quō/quantō	*ever, at any time*	**eō/tantō**	*all the (more), so much the (better, etc.)*
quotiēns	*how often*	**totiēns**	*so many times*

Morphology

9 Prepositions

Prepositions (**praepōsitus** *put in front*) are classified as particles and cannot be inflected. They can either serve as prefixes in combination with verbs (**ab-īre** *to go away* from **īre** *to go*, **circum-stāre** *to stand around* from **stāre** *to stand*), or be linked with a noun.

Although prepositions play an important role in the composition of verbs, the types of prepositions dealt with in this chapter are those that are combined with nouns. Prepositions precede their object.

post merīdiem	*in the afternoon (after midday)*
extrā mūrōs	*outside the (city) walls*
sub monte	*at the foot of the mountain (under the mountain)*

 The Latin system of prepositions is very different from the English system. Latin prepositions always require the use of a certain case. You will have to memorize which Latin preposition is used with which case, in order to tell which noun is associated with a preposition. Most prepositions take the **accusative** or the **ablative**. Some, however, can take more than one case, depending on the meaning being conveyed.

Prepositions with the Accusative

ad *to, up to, near to* (used for place, time, and figuratively)	
ad mūrōs proficīscī	*advance to the city walls*
ad id tempus	*up to this time*
ad haec dīxit	*hereupon he replied*
adversus *toward, facing; against*	
adversus hostēs	*against the enemies*
adversus amīcōs	*toward friends*
adversus rem pūblicam facere	*to act against the state*
ante *in front of; before* (time or place)	
ante portās	*before the gates*
ante multōs diēs	*many days ago*

apud *among, at the house of, in the presence of*	
apud Marcum esse	*to be at Marcus's house/in the presence of Marcus*
apud maiōrēs	*among our ancestors*
circā, circum *around* (place and time)	
circum Rōmam	*around Rome*
circā merīdiem	*around noon*
contrā *against, across from, opposed to*	
contrā Galliam	*opposite to Gaul*
contrā lēgem	*against the law*
contrā Germānōs	*against the Germans*
ergā *toward*	
amīcitia ergā cunīculum	*friendship toward the rabbit*
extrā *beyond, outside* (place and in figurative sense)	
extraōrdinem	*out of order, irregularly*
extrā mūrōs	*beyond the city walls*
infrā *below, beneath, inferior to* (place, time, and in figurative sense)	
infrā pontem	*beneath the bridge*
infrā cōnsulem esse	*to be below the consul (in rank)*
inter *between, among* (place, time, and in figurative sense)	
inter montem et flūmen	*between the mountain and the river*
inter decem annōs	*during ten years*
inter cunīculōs	*among rabbits*
intrā *within* (place and time)	
intrā mūrōs	*inside the city walls*
intrā paucās hōrās	*within a few hours*
iuxtā *near, close to, next to*	
iuxtā urbem	*close to the city*
ob *toward; on account of* (place or in figurative sense)	
ob oculōs versārī	*to hover before the eyes*
ob eam causam	*for that reason*
per *through* (place, time, and in figurative sense)	
per prōvinciam īre	*to go through the province*
per vim	*by force*
per decem annōs	*for ten years*
per sē	*by itself, by themselves*

post *after, behind* (place and time)	
post mē	*after/behind me*
post multōs annōs	*after many years/many years later*
praeter *beyond, past; except* (place and in figurative sense)	
praeter castra	*past the camp*
omnēs amīcī praeter ūnum	*all the friends except one*
prope *near, near to* (place)	
prope silvam	*near the forest*
propter *on account of, because of; near* (place and in figurative sense)	
oppidum propter Rōmam	*the town near Rome*
propter inopiam frūmentī	*because of the grain shortage*
secundum *following, in accordance with, along* (place, time, and in figurative sense)	
secundum flūmen	*along the river*
secundum nātūram vīvere	*to live in accordance with nature*
secundum quiētem	*right after going to sleep*
suprā *above* (place and time)	
suprā modum	*beyond measure*
suprā multōs annōs	*over many years*
trāns *across* (place)	
trāns Rhēnum	*across the Rhine*
trāns Alpēs	*across the Alps*
ultrā *on the other side, beyond* (place or in figurative sense)	
ultrā montēs	*on the other side of the mountains*
ultrā vīrēs	*beyond his strength*

Prepositions with the Ablative

ā, ab, *(rarely:* **abs***) from, away from; by* (place, time, and in figurative sense) (**ā** only before consonants)	
ab urbe discēdere	*to go away from the town*
ab urbe conditā	*from the founding of the city (Rome)*
ā castrīs	*away from the camp*
ā Germanīs dēfendere	*to defend from the Germans*
cum *with* (time, or to express a connection)	
cum amīcīs esse	*to be with friends*

cum prīmā lūce	*at daybreak (with the first light)*

dē *from, down from; concerning, about* (place, time, and in figurative sense)

dē montibus	*down from the mountains*
dē tertiā vigiliā	*during the third night watch*
dē pāce agere	*to negotiate about peace*

ē, ex (ē only before consonants) *out of, from within, from; by reason of, on account of* (time, place, and in figurative sense)

ex oppidō	*out of the town*
ex eō tempore	*since that time*
pōculum ex aurō	*a drinking-cup of (made from) gold*

prae *before; in favor of; in front of* (place or to explain an obstacle)

prae sē ferre	*to show, exhibit (carry in front)*
prae tumultū nihil audīre	*to hear nothing because of the noise*
prae lacrimīs	*because of the tears*

prō *in front of, before, on behalf of, in return for, instead of, for* (place or in figurative sense)

prō castrīs	*in front of the camp*
prō lībertāte pugnāre	*to fight for freedom*

sine *without* (figurative)

sine ūllā spē	*without any hope*
sine causā	*without cause*

Prepositions with the Accusative or the Ablative

in

with Acc.: *in, into, to*
(place and in figurative sense; answers the question *where to?*)

in prōvinciam īre	*to go to the province*
in diem vīvere	*to live for the day (the moment)*
in servum	*toward the slave*

with Abl.: *in*
(place and in figurative sense; answers the question *where?*)

in urbe	*in the city*
in rēbus adversīs	*in adversity*
in pāce	*in peace*

with Acc.: *under, toward* (place and time; answers the question *where to?*)	
sub montem venīre	*to come to the foot of the mountain*
sub lūcem, sub vesperem	*toward daybreak, toward evening*
with Abl.: *under* (place, time, and in figurative sense; answers the question *where?*)	
sub monte	*at the foot of the mountain*
sub Tiberiō Caesare	*under (in the reign of) the Emperor Tiberius*
sub imperiō alicuius esse	*to be under someone's control*

The ablatives **causā** (from **causa, -ae** f. *reason, cause*) and **grātiā** (from **grātia, -ae** f. *favor, gratitude*), when used as prepositions, take the genitive and are rendered as *because of, on account of, for the sake of*. They follow, rather than precede, their objects (postpositions).

exemplī grātiā/causā	*for example*
honōris grātiā/causā	*for the sake of honor*

! Prepositions can also occur in an intermediate position. This word order usually is adopted to place greater emphasis on the word in front.

magnā cum laude	*with high honors*
eā dē causā	*for this very reason*

You will learn more about comparison of prepositions in the section on **Comparative Adjectives and Adverbs**.

10 Numbers

The Latin numbers include the following:

cardinal numbers	*one, two, three, ...*
ordinal numbers	*first, second, third, ...*
distributives	*one each, two each, three each, ...*
multiplicatives	*once, twice, three times, ...*

Numbers: An Overview

Number		Cardinal Numbers how many?	Ordinal Numbers how many in order?	Distributives how many each?
1	I	ūnus, -a, -um	prīmus, -a, -um	singulī, -ae, -a
2	II	duo, duae, duo	secundus	bīnī
3	III	trēs, tria	tertius	ternī
4	IV	quattuor	quārtus	quarternī
5	V	quīnque	quīntus	quīnī
6	VI	sex	sextus	sēnī
7	VII	septem	septimus	septēnī
8	VIII	octō	octāvus	octōnī
9	IX	novem	nōnus	novēnī
10	X	decem	decimus	dēnī
11	XI	ūndecim	ūndecimus	ūndēnī
12	XII	duodecim	duodecimus	duodēnī
13	XIII	trēdecim	tertius decimus	ternī dēnī
14	XIV	quattuordecim	quārtus decimus	quarternī dēnī
15	XV	quīndecim	quīntus decimus	quīnī dēnī
16	XVI	sēdecim	sextus decimus	sēnī dēnī
17	XVII	septendecim	septimus decimus	septēnī dēnī
18	XVIII	duodēvīgintī	duodēvīcēsimus	duodēvīcēnī
19	XIX	undēvīgintī	undēvīcēsimus	undēvīcēnī
20	XX	vīgintī	vīcēsimus	vīcēnī
30	XXX	trīgintā	trīcēsimus	trīcēnī
40	XL	quadrāgintā	quadrāgēsimus	quadrāgēnī
50	L	quīnquāgintā	quīnquāgēsimus	quīnquāgēnī
60	LX	sexāgintā	sexāgēsimus	sexāgēnī
70	LXX	septuāgintā	septuāgēsimus	septuāgēnī
80	LXXX	octōgintā	octōgēsimus	octōgēnī
90	XC	nōnāgintā	nōnāgēsimus	nōnāgēnī

Number		Cardinal Numbers how many?	Ordinal Numbers how many in order?	Distributives how many each?
100	C	centum	centēsimus	centēnī
200	CC	ducentī	ducentēsimus	ducēnī
300	CCC	trecentī	trēcentēsimus	trecēnī
400	CD	quadringentī	quadringentēsimus	quadringēnī
500	D	quīngentī	quīngentēsimus	quīngēnī
600	DC	sescentī	sescentēsimus	sescēnī
700	DCC	septingentī	septingentēsimus	septingēnī
800	DCCC	octingentī	octingentēsimus	octingēnī
900	CM	nōngentī	nōngentēsimus	nōngēnī
1000	M	mīlle	mīllēsimus	singula mīlia
2000	MM	duo mīlia	bis mīllēsimus	bīna mīlia

Declension of Numbers

Only a few **cardinal numbers** are declined:

- **Ūnus, duo**, and **trēs** are declined like adjectives. **Trēs** is declined like a two-ending adjective of the i-stem group in the plural, while **ūnus** and **duo**, with the variations noted below, are declined like a- or o-declension adjectives. The numbers from **quattuor** *four* on up are not declined!
- All the hundreds from **ducentī, -ae, -a** *200* on up are regular in their declension, following the pattern of a- or o-declension adjectives.

	M.	F.	N.	M.	F.	N.	M./F.	N.
Nom.	ūnus	ūna	ūnum	duo	duae	duo	trēs	tria
Gen.	ūnīus	ūnīus	ūnīus	duōrum	duārum	duōrum	trium	trium
Dat.	ūnī	ūnī	ūnī	duōbus	duābus	duōbus	tribus	tribus
Acc.	ūnum	ūnam	ūnum	duōs	duās	duo	trēs	tria
Abl.	ūnō	ūnā	ūnō	duōbus	duābus	duōbus	tribus	tribus

The plural **milia** *thousands* of **mille** *1000*, as well as the compound numbers from 2000 up are treated like nouns and declined like the i-stems of the third declension: **milia, milium, milibus, milia, milibus.** A noun that is associated with them is always in the genitive: **duo milia navium** *2000 ships* (but: **mille naves** *1000 ships*).

The **ordinal numbers** are declined like adjectives of the a- or o-declensions. They are used in Latin to state the **year** and the **time of day.** The **time of day** is given as a certain hour from sunrise on (about 6 a.m.).

anno sescentesimo nono (ab urbe condita)	*in the 609th year (since the founding of Rome)*
hora nona	*around the ninth hour (at 3 p.m.)*

The **distributives** (**distribuere** *to distribute*) indicate the "distribution" of a quantity of something. They modify nouns in the plural and follow the a- or o-declensions.

centeni milites	*100 soldiers each*
binae litterae	*two letters each*

In addition, there are numeral adjectives, which are formed by adding **-plex, -plicis.** They are declined like single-ending adjectives (such as **audax, -acis** *bold*) of the i-stem group.

simplex	*simple*	**quadruplex**	*fourfold*
duplex	*twofold*	**quincuplex**	*fivefold*
triplex	*threefold*	**decemplex**	*tenfold*

Adverbs of Number

Adverbs of number specify frequency and answer the question, **how often?** The **singular neuter** form of the ordinal numbers (except for **iterum**) is used as the adverb of number.

prīmum	**iterum**	**tertium**	**quārtum**	etc.
first, in the first place	*a second time, again*	*third, in the third place*	*fourth, in the fourth place*	

In addition, Latin has the following adverbs of number:

Fixed terms:		**Regularly formed by adding -iēs:**	
semel	*once*	**quīnquiēs**	*five times*
bis	*twice*	**sexiēs**	*six times*
ter	*three times*	**septiēs**	*seven times*
quater	*four times*	**octiēs**	*eight times*
		etc.	

11 Verbs

Verbs (action words) rank after nouns as the second-largest group of **inflectable** parts of speech. Unlike nouns, they are not **declined**, but **conjugated** (**coniugāre** *to unite*). Latin organizes verb conjugations, like noun declensions, into different sets known as classes.

The most important syntactic function of the verb is to act as the predicate (**praedicāre** *to state, express, or declare*), a basic component of every sentence. It modifies or provides information about the subject; that is, it tells what **action** is carried out and at what **time**.

1	**Cunīculum irrītat.**	*She annoy the rabbit.*
2	**Fēlēs nigrae cunīculum irrītābant.**	*The black cats annoy the rabbit.*
3	**Fēlis nigra cunīculum irrītābit.**	*The black cat will annoy the rabbit.*

In Latin, unlike English, the subject (person or thing) of the action is clearly readable from the form of the predicate. The **subject** of a Latin sentence, therefore, can be **expressed in the predicate** and needs no additional mention, as in the first example below. In examples 2 and 3, however, a **nominative form** of **fēlis** appears as the subject. If the subject of a Latin sentence is also present in the form of a **nominative**, the **subject** and the **predicate** must **agree** in **number.** In the case of **irritā-ba-nt** in the example above, we are dealing with a plural form, which could either be translated as *they annoyed* or modified by a nominative form in the plural; **irritā-bi-t** is a third person singular verb form. The predicate, unlike attributes, gives no indication of the grammatical gender of the subject.

In addition to the number, the Latin predicate contains **four other pieces of information.** It gives unambiguous information about
* the **person or thing performing the action**, by using **personal markers** to identify one of six possible agents (three in the singular and three in the plural: *I, you* (sing.), *he/she/it, we, you* (pl.), *they*).

 In Latin, unlike English, for the first and second persons, the subject generally is expressed only in the predicate. For the third person, too, the subject does not absolutely have to be mentioned. Thus even a single word can constitute a grammatically complete sentence: **Ambulat.** *He is taking a walk.*

* the **tense** (**tempus, -oris** n. *time*) in which an action is accomplished. Latin has **six tenses**: present, imperfect, future I, future II, perfect, and pluperfect.
* the relationship of the statement to reality, which is expressed in one of three **moods** (**modus, -i** m. *mode, manner*): **indicative** (realistic mood, indicating that something actually is or is not the case), **subjunctive** (irrealistic mood, for discussing hypothetical or unlikely events), and **imperative** (command form).
* the **voice**. It tells whether an action is occurring in the **active** voice or is being accomplished in the **passive** voice.

As all these pieces of information can be **read from a word**, Latin verbs have **numerous, usually unambiguous forms**, so that the reader understands what is meant. As with nouns, these forms are produced almost exclusively by **attaching suffixes** to the **verb stem**, which carries the meaning. Depending on the tense, it appears as the **present, perfect, or participial stem** (also known as the **supine stem**).

VERB STEM	TENSE
present stem	present, future, imperfect
perfect stem	perfect, future II, pluperfect
participial stem (supine stem)	perfect passive, future II passive, pluperfect passive, perfect passive participle, future active participle

To designate tense and mood, **tense and mood markers** are added to the respective verbs; to **designate person** and **voice** (tense too, at times), **endings** are added: **vocā-tis** *you* (pl.) *call,* **vocā-bā-tis** *you* (pl.) *called.*

Verb forms occur not only as predicates, which are **finite** with respect to the criteria listed above, but also as indefinite **infinite** forms. In addition to **infinitives**, these include **participles**, **gerunds**, and **gerundives**. They are used **adjectivally** or **substantivally** and thus are also known as nominal forms.

The Conjugation of Verbs

Every verb, on the basis of the **ending of the present stem**, can be assigned to one of **five conjugations**. The present stem is obtained by removing the infinitive ending **-(e)re.**

laudā-re	a-conjugation (first conjugation)
monē-re	e-conjugation (second conjugation)
audī-re	i-conjugation (fourth conjugation)
aɡ-ere	consonant conjugation
cap-e[1]re	mixed conjugation (also: consonant conjugation with i enhancement)[2]

[1] The stem **-e** of **capere** is weakened from **-i.**

[2] These verbs, with few exceptions, are inflected like verbs of the **i** conjugation: The present infinitives resemble those of the consonant conjugation; in the 2nd person present passive indicative, **-eris** replaces -iris.

Present Stem

The finite indicative and subjective forms of the **present** and **imperfect** tenses and the **future I** forms (active and passive) are derived from the present stem. In addition, the present stem is used to form the **imperative I and II** and the infinite forms of the **present active participle (PAP)**, the **gerund**, and the **gerundive**.

Present Tense Forms (Indicative and Subjunctive) in the Active Voice

For these tenses, the following personal endings are used:

1st pers. sing.	**-o/-m**	1st pers. pl.	**-mus**
2nd pers. sing.	**-s**	2nd pers. pl.	**-tis**
3rd pers. sing.	**-t**	3rd pers. pl.	**-nt**

In the formation of the present active indicative, the endings are attached to the stem; for the sujunctive, the -a- of the present subjunctive is also included. Only in the a-conjugation does the -a- of the stem fuse with the -a- of the present active subjunctive to become -e-.

Tense	Person	a-conjugation	e-conjugation	i-conjugation	Consonant conjugation (consonant stems)	Consonant conjugation (i-stems)
Present indicative	1.	laudō	moneō	audiō	agō	capiō
	2.	laudās	monēs	audis	agis	capis
	3.	laudat	monet	audit	agit	capit
	1.	laudāmus	monēmus	audīmus	agimus	capimus
	2.	laudātis	monētis	audītis	agitis	capitis
	3.	laudant	monent	audiunt	agunt	capiunt
		I praise	I warn	I hear	I act	I seize
Present subjunctive	1.	laudem	moneam	audiam	agam	capiam
	2.	laudēs	moneās	audiās	agās	capiās
	3.	laudet	moneat	audiat	agat	capiat
	1.	laudēmus	moneāmus	audiāmus	agāmus	capiāmus
	2.	laudētis	moneātis	audiātis	agātis	capiātis
	3.	laudent	moneant	audiant	agant	capiant

The present indicative is translated as such into English. To learn more about the various ways of translating the subjunctive, see the chapter on the **subjunctive**!

Morphology

The Imperfect in the Active Voice

The **imperfect indicative** of all conjugations is formed by adding the imperfect tense indicator -**ba**- plus the **personal ending** to the present stem. The **imperfect subjunctive** is formed by combining the **present infinitive stem** and the **personal ending**. With verbs of the consonant conjugation and the i-conjugation, an -**e**- is added between the present stem and the -**ba**-.

Tense	Person	ā- conjugation	ē- conjugation	ī- conjugation	Consonant conjugation (consonant stems)	Consonant conjugation (i-stems)
Imperfect indicative	1.	laudābam	monēbam	audiēbam	agēbam	capiēbam
	2.	laudābās	monēbās	audiēbās	agēbās	capiēbās
	3.	laudābat	monēbat	audiēbat	agēbat	capiēbat
	1.	laudābāmus	monēbāmus	audiēbāmus	agēbāmus	capiēbāmus
	2.	laudābātis	monēbātis	audiēbātis	agēbātis	capiēbātis
	3.	laudābant	monēbant	audiēbant	agēbant	capiēbant
		I was praising, I used to praise	*I was warning, I used to warn*	*I was hearing, I used to hear*	*I was acting, I used to act*	*I was seizing, I used to seize*
Imperfect subjunctive	1.	laudārem	monērem	audīrem	agerem	caperem
	2.	laudārēs	monērēs	audīrēs	agerēs	caperēs
	3.	laudāret	monēret	audīret	ageret	caperet
	1.	laudārēmus	monērēmus	audīrēmus	agerēmus	caperēmus
	2.	laudārētis	monērētis	audīrētis	agerētis	caperētis
	3.	laudārent	monērent	audīrent	agerent	caperent

The imperfect is rendered in English by indicating that the action was going on in the past, or was repeated or habitual. The chapter on the **subjunctive** contains additional information on ways of translating the Latin imperfect subjunctive.

Future I, Active Voice

Unlike the other tenses, the **future** has **no subjunctive forms**. The indicative is formed in various ways, depending on the conjugation:

- **a- and e-conjugations:** The future tense indicator **-bi-** and the **personal endings** are attached to the present stem. In the first person singular, the indicator blends with the personal ending to create the ending **-bo**. In the third person plural, the future tense indicator is irregular: **-bu-**.
- **i- and consonant conjugations:** The future tense indicator is **-e-** (in the first person singular, it is irregular: **-a-**).

First and Second Imperatives

The imperative (**imperāre** *to command*) is, along with the indicative and the subjunctive, one of the three **moods** of the verb.

Latin has two types of imperatives. The more commonly used **first imperative** is used for **requests** and **commands** or **suggestions**. It addresses the second person singular or plural directly, but is not accompanied by a personal pronoun. For example, **venī!** (sing.) or **venīte!** (pl.) *Come!*

For **commands addressed to the first person plural**, the **hortative** is used, while the **jussive** expresses **commands to the third person plural**. Both can be paraphrased in Latin by using forms of the **subjunctive**. For negative commands to the second person, there are two possibilities: **nōlī/nōlite + infinitive** and **nē + second person perfect subjunctive**. For other guidelines, see the section on the **subjunctive** in Chapter 15.

A wish or command that is to be implemented in the near or distant future is expressed by the **second imperative**. It is less common than the first imperative, and it usually is used for **general regulations**, **laws**, and **maxims**. It addresses the second or third person.

Pār-ētō lēgibus! *You shall obey the laws!*

▶ For more information on the use of the Latin imperative, see the section **Independent Commands and Wishes** in Chapter 18.

The **first** and **second imperatives** are formed as follows in the various conjugations:

Tense	Person	a- conjugation	e- conjugation	i- conjugation	Consonant conjugation (consonant stems)	Consonant conjugation (i-stems)
First imperative	2. 2.	laudā! laudāte! *praise!*	monē! monēte! *warn!*	audī! audīte! *hear!*	age! agite! *act!*	cape! capite! *seize!*
Second imperative	2./ 3. 2. 3.	laudātō! laudātōte! laudantō! *you/he shall praise!*	monētō! monētōte! monentō! *you/he shall warn!*	audītō! audītōte! audiuntō! *you/he shall hear!*	agitō! agitōte! aguntō! *you/he shall act!*	capitō! capitōte! capiuntō! *you/he shall seize!*

Passive Tenses of the Present Stem

In changing the active to the passive, only the active **personal ending** is removed and the passive one added. Everything else remains the same.

The personal endings for the passive voice are:

1st pers. sing.	**-or/-r**	1st pers. pl.	**-mur**
2nd pers. sing.	**-ris**	2nd pers. pl.	**-mini**
3rd pers. sing.	**-tur**	3rd pers. pl.	**-ntur**
Infinitive: **-(r)ī** (-rī or a-, e-, and i-conjugation; for all others -ī)			

In the second person singular, future I, passive voice, the forms for the a- and e-conjugations are not, as one would expect, **laudā-bi-ris** or **monē-bi-ris**, but **laudā-be-ris** and **monē-be-ris**. Among the verbs of the consonant conjugation and the mixed conjugation, there is another irregular form: The second person singular present passive indicative is not **ag-i-ris** or **cap-i-ris**, but **ag-e-ris** and **cap-e-ris**.

Tense	Person	a- conjugation	e- conjugation	i- conjugation	Consonant conjugation (consonant stems)	Consonant conjugation (i-stems)
Present indicative	1.	laud**or**	mone**or**	aud**ior**	ag**or**	cap**ior**
	2.	laud**āris**	mon**ēris**	aud**īris**	ag**eris**	cap**eris**
	3.	laud**ātur**	mon**ētur**	aud**ītur**	ag**itur**	cap**itur**
	1.	laud**āmur**	mon**ēmur**	aud**īmur**	ag**imur**	cap**imur**
	2.	laud**āminī**	mon**ēminī**	aud**īminī**	ag**iminī**	cap**iminī**
	3.	laud**antur**	mon**entur**	aud**iuntur**	ag**untur**	cap**iuntur**
		I am praised	*I am warned*	*I am heard*	*I am driven*	*I am seized*
Present subjunctive	1.	laud**er**	mon**ear**	aud**iar**	ag**ar**	cap**iar**
	2.	laud**ēris**	mon**eāris**	aud**iāris**	ag**āris**	cap**iāris**
	3.	laud**ētur**	mon**eātur**	aud**iātur**	ag**ātur**	cap**iātur**
	1.	laud**ēmur**	mon**eāmur**	aud**iāmur**	ag**āmur**	cap**iāmur**
	2.	laud**ēminī**	mon**eāminī**	aud**iāminī**	ag**āminī**	cap**iāminī**
	3.	laud**entur**	mon**eantur**	aud**iantur**	ag**antur**	cap**iantur**

Active Tenses of the Perfect Stem

The perfect stem is used for the finite indicative and subjunctive forms of the **perfect**, **pluperfect**, and **future II**, as well as the **perfect infinitive**.

Latin has **two regular methods of forming the perfect**:
- For almost all verbs of the **a-conjugation** and some others, the perfect is formed with a **-v**. The perfect stem is obtained by adding a **-v** to the present stem. For example, **laudāv-ī** *I praised*.
- Many verbs of the **e-conjugation** form the perfect with a **-u**. The **-e** of the present stem is replaced by a **-u**. For example, **monu-ī** *I warned*.

> All other verbs form the perfect in an **irregular** way. These irregular forms simply must be memorized along with the vocabulary words. For irregular forms, the **principal parts** usually are given along with the vocabulary entry. These parts include the present and perfect active forms, each in the first person singular indicative, and—if one exists—the passive perfect participle of a verb. The principal parts of **agere** *to act, do*, for example, are **agō - ēgī - āctum**.

▶ A selection of the most important **principal parts** is given at the end of the chapter.

There are **four irregular methods of forming the perfect**:
- **Lengthening** (lengthening of the vowel in the first syllable, in some cases modification of -a- to -e-), as here:
  lēg-ī *I read* from **legere**
  fēc-ī *I made* from **facere**
- **Reduplication** (usually, doubling of the first syllable), as in these examples:
  cu-curr-ī *I ran* from **currere**
  pe-perc-ī *I spared* from **parcere**
- **Use of an s**, as below:
  scrīps-ī *I wrote* from **scribere**
  fīx-ī (from **fīg-sī**) *I fastened* from **figere**
- **No change in stem** (no change in present stem), as here:
  dēfend-ī *I defended* from **dēfendere**
  vert-ī *I turned* from **vertere**

To form the perfect, the appropriate **personal ending** is attached to the **perfect stem**. The **perfect** has its own **personal endings**, which occur only in the perfect indicative, active voice.

1st pers. sing.	**-ī**	1st pers. pl.	**-imus**
2nd pers. sing.	**-istī**	2nd pers. pl.	**-istis**
3rd pers. sing.	**-it**	3rd pers. pl.	**-ērunt**
Infinitive: **-isse**			

Accordingly, the forms of **laudāre** in the **perfect active indicative** are:

laudāv-ī	*I praised*
laudāv-istī	*you praised*
laudāv-it	etc.
laudāv-imus	
laudāv-istis	
laudāv-ērunt	

The **perfect of all other verbs** is formed according to this pattern. The Latin perfect can be rendered in English as a simple past or present perfect.

▶ On the use of the perfect (relative to the imperfect, for example), see the chapters on **Tenses** and **Temporal Relationships**.

All other forms of the perfect stem are formed with the same endings as the following examples:

Perfect active subjunctive:

monu-erim	*For possible translations, see chapter on subjunctive.*
monu-eris	
monu-erit	
monu-erimus	
monu-eritis	
monu-erint	

Pluperfect active indicative (perfect stem + imperative indicative of **esse** *to be*):

monu-eram	*I had warned*
monu-erās	*you had warned*
monu-erat	*etc.*
monu-erāmus	
monu-erātis	
monu-erant	

Pluperfect active subjunctive (perfect infinitive + personal ending):

monu-isse-m	*For translation, see chapter*
monu-issē-s	*on subjunctive*
monu-isse-t	
monu-issē-mus	
monu-issē-tis	
monu-isse-nt	

Future II active (perfect stem + future of **esse** *to be*, except for the third person plural: **-erint** instead of -erunt):

monu-erō	*I will have warned*
monu-eris	*you will have warned*
monu-erit	*etc.*
monu-erimus	
monu-eritis	
monu-erint	

The perfect infinitive is **monu**-isse *to have warned*

For more information about the use and translation of the tenses, see the chapters on
▶ **Tenses** and **Temporal Relationships**.

Passive Tenses of the Perfect Stem

The passive tenses that are derived from the perfect stem always consist of two words in Latin: the **perfect passive participle (PPP)** and a form of **esse** *to be.*

The **PPP** is formed in various ways. Most **a-conjugation** verbs attach the ending **-tus** to the **present stem** to form the **PPP**, for example, **laudā-tus, -a, -um** *praised.* Many **e-conjugation** verbs add the ending **-itus** to the present stem (with deletion of the -e): **mon-itus** *warned.*

 The other verbs form the PPP in an **irregular way.** Like the irregular perfect forms, these participles must be memorized along with the word meanings, as one of the **principal parts.**

The tenses in detail (formation applies to all other verbs as well):

	INDICATIVE	CONJUNCTIVE
Perf.	laudātus + pres. ind. of **esse** **laudātus sum** *I have been praised*	**laudātus** + pres. subj. of **esse** **laudātus sim** (for translation, see Chapter 15)
Pluperf.	laudātus + imp. ind. of **esse** **laudātus eram** *I had been praised*	**laudātus** + imp. subj. of **esse** **laudātus essem** (for translation, see Chapter 15)
Fut. II	laudātus + future I of **esse** **laudātus erō** *I will have been praised*	

The PPP is declined like the **adjectives of the a- and o-declensions ending in -us, -a, -um.** In the passive tenses, the PPP behaves like an adjectival predicate nominative, agreeing with the word it modifies in **case, number, and gender;** that is, it agrees with the subject of the sentence.

Cunīculus albus ā fēle nigrā agitātus est.
The white rabbit was chased by the black cat.

The "agent," which in the example is **fēlis nigra** *black cat,* is always expressed in Latin by **ā/ab** plus the ablative.
▶ For more on this, see the section on the **ablative** in Chapter 17.

Sometimes the **PPP** and the form of **esse** that goes with it are **separated from each other** in Latin, and sometimes the form of **esse** is even omitted for stylistic reasons. Therefore, whenever you come across a participle, ask yourself whether it could be part of a predicate!

The **future active participle (FAP)** in combination with a finite form of **esse** conveys tense and is the equivalent of the future active infinite. It is formed by attaching **-ūrus, -a, -um** and, like the **PPP**, agrees with the **subject** of the sentence in **gender, number, and case.** This tense usually is translated with "about to" or "going to."

Fēlis cunīculum agitātūra est/erat.
The cat is/was about to chase the rabbit.

The infinitives that are formed from the perfect stem are:
laudātus, -a, -um esse *to have been praised*
laudātūrus, -a, -um esse *to be about to praise*

The **PPP** and the **FAP** also occur as **infinite verb forms without esse.**
▶ For more information on the use of participles, see Chapter 17.

12 Irregular Verbs

Some Latin verbs have distinctive forms and irregular conjugations. This category includes **esse** *to be,* **posse** *to be able (to),* **velle** *to wish, want,* **nōlle** *to be unwilling,* **mālle** *to prefer,* **ferre** *to carry,* **īre** *to go,* and **fierī** *to become, to be made.*

esse *to be*

The auxiliary verb **esse** occurs very frequently in various usages. Usually, in combination with a noun or a nominal form, it is part of a predicate. Rarely, it appears as a main verb, usually meaning *there is/are* or expressing belonging.

Mihi sunt cunīculus et fēlis.
I have a rabbit and a cat. (A rabbit and a cat belong to me.)

esse, sum, fui *to be*

PRESENT

INDICATIVE	SUBJUNCTIVE
1. sum	sim
2. es	sīs
3. est	sit
1. sumus	sīmus
2. estis	sītis
3. sunt	sint
I am	(see Chapter 15)

IMPERFECT

INDICATIVE	SUBJUNCTIVE
1. eram	essem
2. erās	essēs
3. erat	esset
1. erāmus	essēmus
2. erātis	essētis
3. erant	essent
I was	(see Chapter 15)

FUTURE I

IMPERATIVE I	IMPERATIVE II	
1. erō	–	
2. eris	es!	*be!*
	estō!	*you shall be!*
3. erit	estō!	*he shall be!*
1. erimus	–	
2. eritis	este!	*be!*
	estōte!	*you shall be!*
3. erunt	suntō!	*they shall be!*

Morphology

posse *to be able (to)*

Posse *to be able (to)* is a compound verb, derived from **pot-esse**. The first syllable always is **pot-** when the attached form of esse begins with a vowel; before a consonant, it changes to **pos-**.

posse, possum, potuī *to be able (to)*

PRESENT	
INDICATIVE	SUBJUNCTIVE
1. possum	possim
2. potes	possīs
3. potest	possit
1. possumus	possīmus
2. potestis	possītis
3. possunt	possint
I can (I am able to)	(see Chapter 15)

IMPERFECT	
INDICATIVE	SUBJUNCTIVE
1. poteram	1. possem
2. poterās	2. possēs
3. poterat	3. posset
1. poterāmus	1. possēmus
2. poterātis	2. possētis
3. poterant	3. possent
I was able to	(see Chapter 15)

FUTURE I
1. poterō
2. poteris
3. poterit
1. poterimus
2. poteritis
3. poterunt
I will be able to

The **perfect**, **pluperfect**, and **future II** are formed on the basis of the perfect stem, **potu-**:

PERFECT	
potuī ...	potuerim ...
I was/have been able to,	(see Chapter 15)
I could	

PLUPERFECT	
potueram ...	potuissem ...
I had been able to	(see Chapter 15)

FUTURE II	
potuerō ...	
I will have been able to	

> **!** Forms similar to **posse** are generated by the compound **prōd-esse** *to be useful,*
> *benefit, profit.* The syllable preceding a vowel is **prōd-**, which changes to **prō-** before
> a consonant. The present active indicative forms, for example, are **prōsum, prōdes,**
> **prōdest, prōsumus, prōdestis,** and **prōsunt.**

Morphology

velle, nōlle, mālle *to wish, want, to be unwilling (not want), to prefer*

	VELLE	NŌLLE	MĀLLE
Present Indicative	1. volō	nōlō	mālō
	2. vīs	nōn vīs	māvīs
	3. vult	nōn vult	māvult
	1. volumus	nōlumus	mālumus
	2. vultis	nōn vultis	māvultis
	3. volunt	nōlunt	mālunt
	I want	*I don't want*	*I prefer*
Present Subjunctive	1. velim	nōlim	mālim
	2. velīs	nōlīs	mālīs
	...	...	...
	(see Chapter 15)		
Imperfect Indicative	1. volēbam	nōlēbam	mālēbam
	2. volēbās	nōlēbās	mālēbās
	...	...	...
	I wanted	*I didn't want*	*I preferred*
Imperfect Subjunctive	1. vellem	nōllem	māllem
	2. vellēs	nōllēs	māllēs
	...	...	...
Future I	1. volam	nōlam	mālam
	2. volēs	nōlēs	mālēs
	...	...	...
	I will want	*I will not want*	*I will prefer*
Imperative I	–	nōlī! nōlīte!	–
Present Participle	volēns, entis	–	–
	wanting; one who wants		

The other tenses are regular and are derived from the perfect stems **volu-, nōlu-,** and **mālu-: voluī, nōluī, māluī.**

ferre *to carry*

ferre, ferō, tulī, lātum

	ACTIVE	PASSIVE
Present Indicative	1. ferō	feror
	2. fers	ferris
	3. fert	fertur
	1. ferimus	ferimur
	2. fertis	feriminī
	3. ferunt	feruntur
	I carry	*I am carried*
Present Subjunctive	1. feram	ferar
	2. ferās	ferāris
	...	...
Imperfect Indicative	1. ferēbam	ferēbar
	2. ferēbās	ferēbāris
	...	...
	I carried	*I was carried*
Imperfect Subjunctive	1. ferrem	ferrer
	2. ferrēs	ferrēris
	...	...
Future I	1. feram	ferar
	2. ferēs	ferēris
	...	...
	I will carry	*I will be carried*
Imperative I	fer! ferte! –	–
	carry!	
Imperative II	fertō! fertōte! feruntō!	–
	you, he, etc. shall carry!	
Infinitive	ferre	ferrī
	to carry	*to be carried*
Present Participle	ferēns, entis	–
	carrying, one who carries	

Only the forms of the present stem **fer-** are irregular. The other tenses are based on the perfect stem **tul-** and in the passive on the participial stem **lāt-: tulī, tulistī,** etc., and **lātus, -a, -um.**

Morphology

īre *to go*

In dealing with the present tense of **īre**, keep in mind that the **i-** becomes **e-** before the vowels **a**, **o**, and **u**.

	INDICATIVE	SUBJUNCTIVE
Present	1. eō	1. eam
	2. īs	2. eās
	3. it	3. eat
	1. īmus	1. eāmus
	2. ītis	2. eātis
	3. eunt	3. eant
	I go, etc.	(see Chapter 15)
Imperfect	ībam	īrem
	ībās	īrēs
	...	...
	I went, I was going	
Future I	ībō	
	ībis	
	...	
	I will go	
Imperative I	ī! īte!	
	go!	
Imperative II	ītō! ītōte! euntō!	
	you (sing.) shall go/he shall go!	
	you (pl.) shall go!	
	they shall go!	
PAP	iēns, euntis	
	going; one who is going	
FAP	itūrus, -a, -um	
	one who is about to go,	
	going to go	
Gerund	eundī, eundō ...	
	of going	
Gerundive	eundum (est)	
	one must go	

The perfect stem of **ire** is **i-**. From it are formed the following:

Perfect Indicative

1. iī	*I went/have gone,*
2. īstī	*you went,*
3. iit	*etc.*
1. iimus	
2. īstis	
3. iērunt	

Perfect Subjunctive

1. ierim	(see Chapter 15)
2. ieris	
3. ierit	
1. ierimus	
2. ieritis	
3. ierint	

Pluperfect Indicative

1. ieram	*I had gone*
2. ierās	*etc.*
3. ierat	
1. ierāmus	
2. ierātis	
3. ierant	

Pluperfect Subjunctive

1. īssem	(see Chapter 15)
2. īssēs	
3. īsset	
1. īssēmus	
2. īssētis	
3. īssent	

Future II

1. ierō	*I will have gone,*
2. ieris	*you will have gone,*
3. ierit	*etc.*
1. ierimus	
2. ieritis	
3. ierint	

As with other forms derived from the perfect stem (for example, in the pluperfect subjunctive), **ii-** becomes **ī-** before a vowel in the perfect infinitive: Accordingly, the perfect active infinitive is **īsse** *to have gone.*

The FAP is **itūrus, -a, -um**, *one who will go.* **Passive** forms exist only in the third person singular; then one speaks of an **impersonal passive**, as in **ītur** *one goes.*

fierī *to be done/made, become, happen*

Despite its passive infinitive form, **fierī** is not a deponent verb. In the present stem, it is conjugated like **audīre** (i-conjugation).

	INDICATIVE	SUBJUNCTIVE
Present	1. fīō	1. fīam
	2. fīs	2. fīās
	3. fit	3. fīat
	1. fīmus	1. fīāmus
	2. fītis	2. fīātis
	3. fīunt	3. fīant
	I am made	
Imperfect	1. fīēbam	1. fierem
	2. fīēbās	2. fierēs
	... ...	
	I was made	
Future I	1. fīam	
	2. fīēs	
	...	
	I will be made	
Imperative I	fī! fīte!	
	be made!	

In the perfect stem, some forms are replaced by forms of the verb **facere** *to make, to do*. The perfect passive, for example, is **factum est** *it was/has been done* or *has happened*. The gerundive, **faciendus, -a, -um**, is also derived from **facere**.

The FAP is replaced by **futūrus, -a, -um**, and the infinitive accordingly is **futūrum esse**.

Impersonal Verbs (verba impersōnālia)

Some **impersonal verbs,** for which no specific subject can be surmised, occur only in the third person singular:

decet (decuit)	*it befits, it suits*
libet (libuit, libitum est)	*it pleases*
licet (licuit, licitum est)	*it is permitted*
oportet (oportuit)	*it is necessary, proper*
mē paenitet (paenituit)	*I'm sorry, I regret*
mē pudet (puduit, puditum est)	*I'm ashamed*
mē taedet (pertaesum est)	*I'm tired, weary*

In the third person, these verbs can form different tenses and moods. The principal parts, some of which are irregular, are given in parentheses.

In addition, there are verbs that are **impersonal in a certain meaning:**

cōnstat (cōnstitit)	*it is agreed, it is certain*
iuvat (iūvit)	*it delights*
praestat (praestitit)	*it is better*
appāret (appāruit)	*it is evident*
ēvenit (ēvēnit)	*it happens*
accidit (accidit)	*it happens*
contingit (contigit)	*it befalls*
mē fallit (fefellit)	*it escapes me*
mē fugit (fūgit)	*it escapes me*
mē praeterit (praeteriit)	*it escapes me*

Morphology

Compound Verbs

A large part of the Latin vocabulary consists of **compounds** (**compōnere** *to bring all the parts together*). They are created by combining a **verb** with a **prefix**. The result is a new verb with a different meaning. English, too, has many compound verbs.

pōnere	*to put, place, lay*
dēpōnere	*to depose, put aside*
compōnere	*to compose, compile*

With some verbs, the consonant at the end of the prefix is **assimilated**; that is, the last letter of the prefix is dropped, as in **dimittere** (instead of **dismittere**) or the first letter of the root is doubled, as in **appōnere** (instead of **adpōnere**).

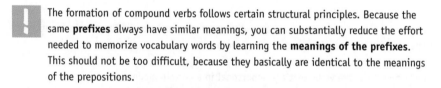 The formation of compound verbs follows certain structural principles. Because the same **prefixes** always have similar meanings, you can substantially reduce the effort needed to memorize vocabulary words by learning the **meanings of the prefixes**. This should not be too difficult, because they basically are identical to the meanings of the prepositions.

ab-, ā-, abs-, as- ab-	*away from, off, badly*	**ā-vocāre** *to call away,* **ab-dūcere** *to take away, remove*
ad-, ac-, af-, ag-, ap-, ar-, at- an-	*to, toward, against, intensely*	**ac-cēdere** *to approach,* **ad-esse** *to be present,* **ad-venīre** *to arrive*
ante-	*before, in front of, ahead of*	**ante-cēdere** *to go before,* **ante-pōnere** *to prefer*
circum-	*around*	**circum-dare** *to surround*
cōn-, co-, col-, com-, cor-	*with, together (or to intensify the basic meaning)*	**com-pellere** *to drive together,* **com-movēre** *to move, induce,* **cōn-firmāre** *to strengthen*
dē-, dī-, dif-, dir-	*down from, off, utterly (can imply removal or give a negative sense to the word)*	**dē-scendere** *to descend,* **dē-vincere** *to conquer,* **dī-mittere** *to send away, dismiss*
dis-	*apart, in different directions, at intervals (can also have negative force)*	**dis-cēdere** *to leave*

ē-, ex-, ef-	*out from, away, away from, off, thoroughly*	**ex-spectāre** *to expect,* **ef-fugere** *to escape*
in-, ig-, il-, im-, ir-	*in, into, toward, against*	**in-esse** *to be in, be there,* **ir-rumpere** *to irrupt, break in*
inter-	*among, between, mutually*	**inter-esse** *to concern, be of importance,* **inter-cēdere** *to intervene, go between,* **inter-rumpere** *to interrupt*
ne-, nec-, neg-	*negation*	**ne-scīre** *to not know,* **neg-legere** *to neglect*
ob-, obs- , oc-, of-, op-	*toward, against, opposite, for, intensely*	**ob-īre** *to go toward,* **oc-currere** *to run up to*
per-	*through, thoroughly (or to intensify the original meaning)*	**per-spicere** *to see through,* **per-terrēre** *to terrify*
prae-	*before, in advance of*	**prae-scrībere** *to write at the beginning, to lay down a rule,* **prae-portāre** *to carry in front*
praeter-	*past, beyond*	**praeter-īre** *to pass, go past,* **praeter-vehī** *to drive past*
prō-, prōd-	*forward, forth, instead of*	**prōd-ire** *to go, come forth,* **pro-ficīscī** *to set out, start*
re-, red-	*back, again, behind*	**red-īre** *to go back,* **re-sistere** *to resist*
sē-	*aside, apart, away*	**sē-cēdere** *to break away, go apart,* **sē-parāre** *to separate, part*
sub-, suc-, sup- sus-	*under, below, less than*	**sub-igere** *to subjugate, conquer,* **sub-dūcere** *to take or draw away*
super-	*over, across, above*	**super-fluere** *to overflow,* **super-esse** *to be in excess, to be left over*
trāns-, trā-	*across, beyond, through*	**trāns-gredī** *to cross, step over,* **trā-dere** *to hand over, hand down*

Deponent and Semideponent Verbs

Deponent (**dēpōnere** *to lay aside*) **verbs** are verbs that have only **passive forms** yet always have **active meanings**. They occur in all conjugations and are conjugated like the passive voice of other verbs in their group. In the dictionary, they are easily recognizable because they are listed in the **first person singular present passive indicative**, as here:

profisciscor	*to leave, set out*
versor	*to move around, to dwell*
sequor	*to follow, come after*
hortor	*to exhort, encourage*

The infinitives, like the passive infinitives of active verbs, end in **-(r)ī: profiscīscī, versārī, sequī,** and **hortārī.**

Despite their passive appearance, deponent verbs also have a few active forms:

PAP	**hortāns, -antis**
Gerund	**hortandī** (gen.)
FAP	**hortātūrus, -a, -um**
Future infinitive	**hortātūrum esse**

Verbs that have only **some deponent forms** (either the present or the perfect stem) are known as **semideponent verbs** (**semi** comes from Greek and means "halfway, in part").

There are only a few verbs that have only **active** forms in the **present stem**, only **passive** forms in the **perfect stem**, and are **exclusively active in meaning**. They are listed in the dictionary with their principal parts. The following, and their compounds, belong to this category:

audēre	**audeō (ausus sum)**	*to dare*
gaudēre	**gaudeō (gāvīsus sum)**	*to rejoice*
solēre	**soleō (solitus sum)**	*to be accustomed, used to*
fīdere	**fīdō (fīsus sum)**	*to trust, put confidence in*

The verb **revertī**, with the principal parts **revertor – revertī** *to return*, can be called a semideponent verb "in reverse." In the **present stem**, it has **passive** forms, but in the **perfect stem**, it has **active** forms.

"Defective" Verbs (verba dēfectīva)

There are only a few verbs that belong to this group. They are termed "defective" (**dēficere** *to lack*) because they lack **some forms**. Some verbs have only forms in the perfect tense system, while others have only a very few, isolated forms. Dictionaries generally list them as "verba dēfectīva."

Verbs that use only tenses of the perfect are **ōdisse**, **meminisse**, and **coepisse**:

ōdisse *to hate*			
ōdī	*I hate*	cum ōderim	*because I hate*
ōderam	*I hated*	ōdissem	*I would hate*
ōderō	*I will hate*	ōsūrus	*one who will hate*

meminisse *to remember, recall*			
meminī	*I remember*	cum meminerim	*because I remember*
memineram	*I remembered*	meminissem	*I would remember*
meminerō	*I will remember*	mementō(te)!	*remember!*

coepisse *to have begun*		
has forms in the present tense system, for example, **incipere** (PPP **coeptus** *begun*)		

The verbs **cōnsuēvisse** and **nōvisse** have a different meaning in the forms derived from the perfect stem:

cōnsuēvī (inf. cōnsuēvisse)	*I am accustomed* (actually, *I have become accustomed* as the perfect of **cōnsuēscō**)
nōvī (inf. nōvisse)	*I know* (actually, *I have become acquainted with* as the perfect of **nōscō**)

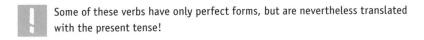

Some of these verbs have only perfect forms, but are nevertheless translated with the present tense!

Morphology

Verbs that have only a few isolated forms are **āiō** and **inquam**:

āiō	*I say*	Also: **aīs** *you say/said,* **ait** *he says/said* (also perfect in meaning), **āiunt** *they say,* **ut aiunt** *as is said,* **ain'** (in place of aisne)**?** *do you think?* Rarely used are these forms: **aiās, aiat,** and **aiant** (present subjunctive) and **aiēbam** etc. (imperfect active indicative). ▶ **inserted in indirect discourse** (see Chapter 18)
inquam	*I say*	Also: **inquis** *you say/said,* **inquit** *he says/said* (also with perfect meaning), **inquiunt** *they say,* **inquiēs** *you will say,* **inquiet** *he will say* ▶ **inserted in indirect discourse** (see Chapter 18)

These are isolated forms:

quaesō	*please (I ask, beseech)*	**salvē, avē**	*greetings!* (sing.)
quaesumus	*we ask, beseech*	**salvēte, avēte**	*greetings!* (pl.)

Special Verb Forms

In addition to the special verb forms already listed, Latin has the following special forms, which occur in Latin texts:

Supine I	The **first supine** occurs so **rarely** that it usually is given in the **notes** that usually accompany texts translated in schools. In form, it is identical to the nominative singular neuter of the PPP; for example, **laudātum.** The supine I is translated with *in order to* + infinitive, as in *"in order to praise."* It occurs exclusively after verbs of motions, such as *to come* or *to send.* **spectātum venīre** *to come **in order to** watch* **laudātum venīre** *to come **in order to** praise*

Supine II   The **second supine** ends in **-ū**. It is formed by dropping **-m** from the PPP, as in **laudatū**. It is translated with *to* + infinitive, as in *"to praise."* The supine ending in **-ū** is used only after certain adjectives or in fixed expressions, such as
facilis/difficilis dictū *easy/hard to say.*
The **supine II**, in connection with **īrī**, serves as the **future passive infinitive**:
spērō sē laudātum īrī *I hope he will be praised*
The **second supine** occurs so rarely that it usually is supplied by the editor of text editions for school students.

A **memory aid** for translating the supine: With the supine ending in **-um**, which expresses purpose, it should always be possible to use (*in order*) *to* in the translation; with the supine ending in **-ū**, *to* always is used.

Special short forms of verbs: With all verbs, in the **third person plural perfect indicative**, the ending **-ērunt** can be shortened to **-ēre** if this does not result in ambiguity; that is, **laudāvēre** instead of **laudāvērunt** is possible, but not **defendēre** (the spelling could lead to confusion with the infinitive).

In the entire **present tense system of the passive voice**, the ending **-ris** can be shortened to **-re** in the **second person singular**, unless it results in ambiguity. For example, **agitābāre** can replace **agitābāris**. **Note:** If a form ending in **-re** seems strange to you, always think of this possibility!

Before **-r-** and **-s-** in **perfect** forms using a **v**, such as **amāvērunt** or **audivissem**, the syllable **-ve-** or **-vi-** sometimes is omitted before the ending, unless ambiguity is the result. For example, **amāsti** can replace **amāvistī**.

In the **i-conjugation** and the **consonant conjugation**, **-v-** sometimes is omitted before **-ēr-**: **audivērunt = audiērunt**, **petivērunt = petiērunt**.

Special imperative forms without **-e** occur in these verbs: **dicere** *to say, tell,* **dūcere** *to lead,* **facere** *to make, to do,* and **ferre** *to carry;* they are **dīc! dūc! fac! fer!**

Frequently the uninflected form **fore** is used instead of **futūrum esse** as the future infinitive of **esse**.

Morphology

Principal Parts of Important Verbs

In the following list are found principal parts of important verbs; the list is not a complete one.

The so-called principal parts include these forms:
- **Infinitive** (such as **laudāre** *to praise*)
- **First person singular present indicative, active voice** (**laudō** *I praise*)
- **First person singular perfect indicative, active voice** (**laudāvī** *I praised*)
- **Neuter singular perfect passive participle** (**laudātum** *praised*)

A-CONJUGATION				
Perfect using v				
laudāre	laudō	laudāvī	laudātum	*to praise*
Perfect using reduplication				
stāre	stō	stetī	–	*to stand*
cōnstāre	cōnstō	cōnstitī	–	*to consist, to cost*
All compounds of **stāre** are conjugated like **cōnstāre**.				
dare	dō	dedī	datum	*to give*
Perfect using lengthening				
adiuvāre	adiuvō	adiūvī	adiūtum	*to help*

Principal Parts of Important Verbs

E-CONJUGATION

Perfect using v

dēlēre	dēleō	dēlēvī	dēlētum	*to destroy*

Perfect using u

habēre	habeō	habuī	habitum	*to have*
monēre	moneō	monuī	monitum	*to warn*
tenēre	teneō	tenuī	–	*to hold*
abstinēre	abstineō	abstinuī	–	*to abstain*

All compounds of **tenēre** are conjugated like **abstinēre**.

Perfect using s

iubēre	iubeō	iussī	iussum	*to order*

Perfect using reduplication

pendēre	pendeō	pependī	–	*to hang*

Perfect using lengthening

movēre	moveō	mōvī	mōtum	*to move*
vidēre	videō	vīdī	vīsum	*to see*

The compounds of this verb are also conjugated like **vidēre**.

I-CONJUGATION

Perfect using v

audīre	audiō	audīvī	audītum	*to hear*

Perfect using u

aperīre	aperiō	aperuī	apertum	*to open*

Perfect using s

sentīre	sentiō	sēnsī	sēnsum	*to feel*

Perfect using lengthening

venīre	veniō	vēnī	ventum	*to come*

CONSONANT CONJUGATION

Perfect using v

petere	petō	petīvī	petītum	*to seek, strive after*

All compounds of this verb are conjugated like **petere**.

Perfect using u

pōnere	pōnō	posuī	positum	*to set, lay, place*

All compounds of this verb are conjugated like **pōnere**.

Perfect using s

scrībere	scrībō	scrīpsī	scrīptum	*to write*
dūcere	dūcō	dūxī [x = k+s]	ductum	*to lead*

All compounds of this verb are conjugated like **dūcere**.

dīcere	dīcō	dīxī [x = k+s]	dictum	*to say*

All compounds of this verb are conjugated like **dīcere**.

regere	regō	rēxī [x = k+s]	rēctum	*to guide, direct*

All compounds of this verb are conjugated like **regere**.

vīvere	vīvō	vīxī [x = k+s]	–	*to live*
gerere	gerō	gessī	gestum	*to carry, bear*
mittere	mittō	mīsī	missum	*to send*

All compounds of this verb are conjugated like **mittere**.

Perfect using reduplication

cadere	cadō	cecidī	–	*to fall*
caedere	caedō	cecīdī	caesum	*to fell, to kill*
currere	currō	cucurrī	cursum	*to run, race*

Perfect using lengthening

agere	agō	ēgī	āctum	*to act, do*
legere	legō	lēgī	lēctum	*to read*
dēligere	dēligō	dēlēgī	dēlēctum	*to select*

All compounds of **legere** are conjugated like **dēligere**.

Perfect with no stem change

dēfendere	dēfendō	dēfendī	dēfēnsum	*to defend*
prehendere	prehendō	prehendī	prehēnsum	*to seize*

All compounds of this verb are conjugated like **prehendere**.

CONSONANT CONJUGATION (I-STEMS)				
Perfect using v				
cupere	cupiō	cupīvī	cupītum	*to wish, desire*
Perfect using u				
rapere	rapiō	rapuī	raptum	*to snatch, grab*
aspicere	aspiciō	aspexī [x=k+s]	aspectum	*to glimpse*
Perfect using lengthening				
capere	capiō	cēpī	captum	*to seize*
accipere	accipiō	accēpī	acceptum	*to accept*
All compounds of **capere** are conjugated like **accipere**.				
facere	faciō	fēcī	factum	*to make, do*
efficere	efficiō	effēcī	effectum	*to effect, cause*
Most compounds of **facere** are conjugated like **efficere**.				

By looking at the verbs of the consonant conjugation, it is impossible to tell whether they are so-called i-stem verbs or not (also verbs using lengthening with i). Only the first person singular (one of the principal parts) makes this clear: cup**iō**.

13 Tenses

Every speaker sees the event he or she is describing in a certain temporal context. Like English, Latin expresses these **time frames** by using various verb tenses.

Perfect tenses	**Cuniculus caesus est.**	*The rabbit was killed/has been killed.*
Present	**Cuniculus caeditur.**	*The rabbit is being killed.*
Future	**Cuniculus caedetur.**	*The rabbit will be killed.*

The Latin **present tense** denotes actions in the present or statements that apply to the present, while the **future** refers to a future action. There are various ways to express futurity in English, including *shall, will, to be going to, to be about to, to be to.*

 A distinctive feature is the **historical present (praesēns historicum)**: In narrative texts, the present may be used at especially suspenseful or dramatic moments, although the event being described took place in the past. In translating from Latin to English, it is best to render the historical present as a past tense, although English also can employ the historical present as a stylistic device.

Yesterday I was walking in town. All of a sudden a man comes up to me. I react with surprise. He stops and speaks to me... etc.

The **imperfect** (action continuing in the past) and **perfect** (action completed in the past) always appear side by side in Latin texts. The Latin **imperfect** is used for
- actions that the speaker began in the past but that affect the present: **linear imperfect** (**linea** *line*)
- actions that **were attempted in the past, but not completed: conative imperfect** (**conāri** *to attempt*)
- actions that were repeated again and again in the past: **iterative imperfect** (**iterāre** *to repeat*)

Because of these nuances of meaning that are expressed by the imperfect, this Latin sentence would make no sense:

Cunīculum caedēbam.
I used to kill the rabbit.

It is improbable
- that the speaker, at the time of the statement, was still engaged in killing the rabbit
- that he repeatedly attempted to kill the rabbit but did not succeed
- that he killed the rabbit several times in succession.

To clearly express killing carried out in the past, Latin uses the **perfect** (completed past). In contrast to the imperfect, the **perfect** describes events that took place once and have ended:

- The **present perfect** is used to describe past events that still concern the speaker at the moment of speaking and thus are directly connected with what has just been said.
- In the **historical perfect**, the speaker is relating events to another speaker, regardless of whether he or she feels affected at the moment.

PRESENT PERFECT (ALSO RESULTATIVE PERFECT)	
Cum cunīculō lūdere amāvī.	*I loved playing with the rabbit. (It is dead now.)* The speaker might make this statement in connection with a present expression of sadness at the rabbit's death.

HISTORICAL PERFECT	
Tum cunīculum cecīdit.	*Then he killed the rabbit.* The speaker tells what happened. It is up to him whether he comments or connects the event with the present.

The **perfect** is the preferred **narrative tense** in Latin. The perfect tense systems in Latin and English are similar and normally not a source of trouble for students.

 At certain points in a narrative, Latin uses the **historical infinitive** in place of the third person singular or plural of the perfect tense. It is employed as a stylistic device, to express suspense, amazement, confusion, or other states of mind.

Pater cunĭculum cecĭdit. Deinde flēre, clāmāre, mente aliēnārī.
The father killed the rabbit. Afterwards he wept, cried out, and was delirious.

If the temporal sequence of an action—as in the examples above—is depicted from the speaker's point of view, we speak of **absolute tense**.

14 Temporal Relationships

From the temporal perspective of the speaker, an event need not be viewed exclusively in an **absolute** way. Several actions can also be seen in relationship to one another. Then we speak of **relative tense**. Here the tense of the predicate in the subordinate clause is determined by the tense used in the main clause; thus a **temporal connection** is established between the events.

In Latin, the sequence of tenses follows strict rules, which differ for indicative and subjunctive subordinate clauses. Whether an **absolute** or a **relative** tense is selected depends on the type of subordinate clause.

Three temporal relationships can be expressed:

Anteriority	Simultaneity	Posteriority

Relative Use of Tense in Indicative Subordinate Clauses: Simultaneity

If the **simultaneous occurrence** (time contemporaneous) of two events is to be expressed, the same tense is used in both the main clause and the subordinate clause.

Dum pater cunīculum caedit, māter flet.
While the father kills the rabbit, the mother weeps.

 English does not always render the Latin future tense with the English future.

Māter dīxit: Sī cunīculum caedēs, eum edēmus.
The mother said: If you kill (are going to kill) the rabbit, we'll eat it.

Anteriority

If the action of the subordinate clause takes place **before** (time prior) the action of the main clause, the sequence of tenses is based on the predicate of the main clause.

Predicate of main clause	Predicate of subordinate clause (anterior state of affairs)
Present →	Perfect
Future →	Future II
Preterit →	Pluperfect

Some illustrations of temporal relationships:

PREDICATE IN (ANTERIOR) SUBORDINATE CLAUSE	PREDICATE IN MAIN CLAUSE
Perfect	Present
Quī cunīculum cecīdit, tristis est.	
Whoever killed a rabbit is sad.	
Future II	Future
Quī cunīculum cecīderit, tristis erit.	
Whoever has killed a rabbit will be sad.	
(literally: will have killed)	
Pluperfect	Imperfect
Quī cunīculum cecīderat, tristis erat.	
Whoever had killed a rabbit was sad.	

The Future II is not necessarily translated into English with the Future tense (as in the second example above).

Posteriority

The action of a subordinate clause can also take place **after** (time subsequent) that of the main clause. This temporal relationship is most common in clauses introduced by **antequam** or **priusquam**.

Antequam cunīculum caedētur, vitulum ēdero.
Before the rabbit is killed (literally: will be killed), I will have eaten the calf.

In translating sentences about posterior states of affairs, remember that English does not always render the Latin future as an English future.

Absolute Use of Tense in Indicative Clauses

In some subordinate clauses, the tense depends on the verb in the main (superordinate) clause. Absolute tense occurs in **temporal clauses** introduced by the following conjunctions:

cum *when all of a sudden* (only in this meaning)	**cum prīmum** *as soon as*
postquam *after*	**dum** *while*
ut *when, as*	**dōnec** *while, as long as, until*
ubī *as soon as*	**quoad** *as far as, as long as*

This use becomes irritating to us especially when the predicate of the main clause is in the past. Here, too, the present is used to express simultaneity and the perfect to express anteriority:

Dum cunīculum caeditur, **librum lēgī.**
While the rabbit was being killed, I read a book.

Postquam cunīculum caesum est, liberī cum ave lūdēbant.
After the rabbit had been killed, the children played with the bird.

 In subordinate clauses introduced by *after,* English uses the pluperfect or past, not the present perfect, when a past tense form is used in the main clause.

In addition, the independent use of tense is also found in clauses that express comments (especially in relative and causal clauses).

Tum liberī cum cunīculō lūserant, quī, ut scītis, caesus est.
At that time the children played with the rabbit, which, as you know, has been killed.

Although the rabbit was killed after the children played with it, the posteriority of the action in the subordinate clause is not expressed in Latin.

Relative Use of Tense in Subjunctive Clauses

The sequence of tenses in subordinate clauses with the subjunctive is governed by strict rules. What is important here is whether the predicate of the main clause is a **primary tense** or a **historical tense**. The primary tenses are the present, future, and present perfect; the historical tenses are all other forms of the past (except the present perfect).

MAIN CLAUSE	DEPENDENT CLAUSE		
	Anteriority	**Simultaneity**	**Posteriority**
Present/Future	Perfect	Present	**-ūrus sim**
Past tense	Pluperfect	Imperfect	**-ūrus essem**

Because there is no Latin future subjunctive, posteriority is expressed by the paraphrased future.

Liberī quaerunt, cūr pater cunīculum caesūrus sit.
The children ask why the father is going to kill the rabbit.

Liberī quaerunt, cūr pater cunīculum cecīderit.
The children ask why the father killed the rabbit.

Liberī quaerunt, cūr pater cunīculum caedat.
The children ask why the father is killing the rabbit.

Special feature:
Posteriority usually is taken into account only in dependent questions and clauses that are introduced with **nōn dubitō quīn** *there is no doubt that*. Other subordinate clauses are treated as simultaneous (time contemporaneous). The relationship to the future often is expressed by adverbs of time, such as **mox** *soon* or **brevī (tempore)** *within a short time*.

▶ In the individual sections on **subordinate (dependent) clauses**, you will learn when the subjunctive is used in the various types of clauses.

15 The Moods

Latin, like English, has **three verb moods**. It is the attitude of the speaker toward his or her statement that determines whether a verb is in the **indicative**, **subjunctive**, or **imperative mood**. The subjunctive is not always easily distinguished in English, however.

- If a speaker views what he says as **factual**, he uses the **indicative**.
- If a speaker views his statement as **possible**, **not factual**, or if he is expressing a wish, the **subjunctive** is used.
- The **imperative** is used to express a **command** addressed to a person or group of persons (in the second person singular or plural, rarely in the third person).

▶ This chapter deals with the use of the indicative and the subjunctive in Latin. To learn how to form and use the **imperative**, see the appropriate section in Chapter 11 and the section on independent commands and wishes in Chapter 18.

The Indicative

The use of the indicative in Latin is comparable to English usage. The following points should be noted:

- Latin uses the indicative for nonfactual events with expressions such as **can**, **should**, **must** and for expressing **evaluations**.

  Decuit eum cunīculum caedere.
  It was fitting that he killed the rabbit.
  or
  It would have been fitting that he kill the rabbit.

Similar subjunctive variants also occur with the following verbs and expressions:

possum/poteram	*I could/I could have*
dēbeō/dēbēbam, dēbuī	*I had to/I would have had to*
oportet/oportēbat, oportuit	*It would be proper/it would have been proper*
tuum/meum est	*it would be your/my task*

- Latin uses the indicative when a factual event is evaluated as unexpected: **numquam putāvi** *I never would have thought*

- The indicative is also used in rhetorical questions that contain a certain statement: **quis dubitat...?** *Who would doubt...?*

The Subjunctive

The Latin subjunctive expresses the idea that an event is perceived as **possible, desirable,** or **nonfactual.**

It is also used in a subordinate clause in **indirect discourse,** to indicate that the opinion expressed is not that of the speaker.

Paul said he (John) cut class because of a physics test.

In a main clause, it expresses a condition that is **contrary to fact.**

If Paul were to use his free time to study more, he would really be a good student.

In addition, the subjunctive is used in many other contexts in Latin. The following table will give you an overview of the various types of subjunctives in a **main clause**, with an equivalent in English.

PRESENT SUBJUNCTIVE

aliquis dīcat
someone could say

Potential subjunctive (potestās *power*) of the present: expresses a **supposition or assumption.**

eāmus!
let's go!
(always first person plural)

Hortative subjunctive (hortārī *to urge, exhort*): used to **urge** (exhort); addressed to the **first person plural.**

abeat!
let him go!
(always third person)
abeant!
let them go!

Jussive subjunctive (iubēre *to order, command:* used for **commands** addressed to the **third person singular** or **plural.**

quid faciam?
What should I do?

Deliberative or Dubitative subjunctive (dēliberāre *to deliberate, ponder,* **dubitāre** *to doubt, hesitate*) of the present; used to **formulate a consideration or a doubt** addressed to oneself.

(utinam) salvus redeat!
May he come back safely!

Optative subjunctive (optāre *to wish*) of the present: expresses a **fulfillable wish in the present.**

IMPERFECT SUBJUNCTIVE

dīceret aliquis
someone could have said
crēderēs/dīcerēs
one could have believed/said

Potential subjunctive of the past: expresses a possibility in the past.

facerem
I would act

Irreal subjunctive of the present: formulates a **consideration** that will not become a reality.

quid facerem?
What should I have done?

Deliberative/Dubitative subjunctive of the past: formulates a deliberation or a doubt addressed to oneself concerning a matter that is in the past.

(utinam) pater vīveret!
If only my father were still alive!

Optative subjunctive (imperfect subjunctive): expresses an unfulfillable present wish.

PERFECT SUBJUNCTIVE	
dīxerit aliquis *someone could say*	**Potential subjunctive** of the present (identical in meaning to present subjunctive)
nē dubitāveris! *don't doubt!*	**Prohibitive subjunctive:** negated imperative.
(utinam) salvus redierit! *I hope he has come back safely!*	**Optative subjunctive:** expresses a fulfillable wish in the past.

PLUPERFECT SUBJUNCTIVE	
fēcissem *I would have acted*	**Irreal subjunctive** of the past: expresses a missed opportunity to act in the past.
(utinam) pater vīdisset! *If only my father could have seen it!*	**Optative subjunctive:** unfulfilled wish in the past.

 The **subjunctive** plays an important role in Latin subordinate clauses. The English helping verbs (could, would, should, might, etc.) are frequently used to translate Latin subjunctives.

- The subjunctive appears in dependent irreal conditional clauses, dependent clauses expressing a wish or desire, dependent interrogative clauses, dependent adverbial clauses, and some relative clauses.
- Some Latin conjunctions require the subjunctive, which then is not translated as such: **ut/ut nōn** *that (not), in order that (not), so that (not),* **nē** *that... not,* **cum** *when, as, after, although, whenever.*

▶ For additional information on the use of the subjunctive in clauses and ways to translate it, see the sections on the various kinds of **subordinate clauses**.

PART II: SYNTAX

The first part of this grammar book tells you how the different forms of nouns and verbs are put together, what function they have, and approximately how they can be translated into English. The focus is on individual words and their meaning. In the part that follows, we are concerned not with **semantics** but with **syntax.** Here you will learn something about the function of the individual word within a sentence, the various **elements of a sentence**, and the structural principles of the Latin language.

In the introduction to the chapter on verbs, we have already pointed out that a finite verb alone can constitute a grammatically complete sentence. This is true in Latin because the predicate contains information about not only the tense, mood, and voice (active or passive) of the verb, but also the person or thing that is the subject of the sentence.

The **subject** and the **predicate** are the cornerstones of a sentence, both in Latin and in English. Many sentences, however, are amplified by additional information, provided by the **oblique cases** (genitive, dative, accusative, ablative), adverbs, **prepositional phrases, nominal forms of the verb, subordinate clauses, relative clauses**, or **adjuncts.**

abl.abs., PC, AcI, NcI...

These and other abbreviations are commonly used by Latin teachers, but you may find them strange and puzzling. That will change as you make your way through Part II.

Among the topics covered here is the variety of possible objects of a sentence, a special feature of Latin. In some respects, of course, they resemble the objects of an English sentence. But there are certain differences too, which may initially seem strange and complicated to us, though on closer inspection and with a bit of practice, they are not at all difficult to translate.

Chapter 17 begins with possibilities for **using case to indicate object.** Such elements are generally easier to translate than so-called **coherent (sentential) constructions**, which are described in the subsequent section.

16 Elements of a Sentence

The **subject** and the **predicate** are the basic elements of a simple sentence. In Latin, the subject is contained in the predicate, indicated by the personal form of the verb; therefore, a finite verb form can stand alone as a complete sentence.

Appropinquō. *I approach.*

In many Latin sentences, the subject is named, in addition, by a word in the nominative case. This syntactic function can be taken on by the following: substantives, substantivized adjectives, pronouns, quantifiers (numerals), substantivized infinitives, participles, AcI, NcI, and subordinate clauses. If the verb in question is an impersonal one, the subject goes unnamed.

Iuvat. *It is pleasing.*

In addition to **simple predicates** (as in the preceding two examples), there also exist **compound predicates**, which consist of an **auxiliary** (helping) **verb** (such as **esse** *to be* or **manēre** *to stay, remain*) and a **predicate nominative**. Usually a noun or adjective in the nominative case takes the role of predicate nominative.

Animal cunīculus est. *The animal is a rabbit.*
Cunīculus albus est. *The rabbit is white.*

Gerundives and participles can also serve as predicate nominatives.

Puer laudandus est. *The boy must be praised (literally: is one to be praised).*
Puer laudātus est. *The boy was praised.*

Whether a sentence that consists of a subject and a predicate (like the last four examples) is grammatically complete depends on the **valency** (number of arguments controlled by a verbal predicate) of the verb. Most verbs require **two sentence elements**: a subject and an object.

Fēlis cunīculum persequitur. *The cat chases the rabbit.*

Without the accusative object **cunīculum**, this sentence would be incomplete. There even exist verbs that require **three objects**.

Pater puerō cunīculum dōnat. *The father gives the boy a rabbit.*

The verb **dōnāre** *to give* leads us to expect not only the naming of the person receiving the gift in the **dative** (answering the question *to whom?*), but also the mentioning of the gift in the **accusative** (answering the question *whom/what?*).

▶ For more on objects as indicated by case, see the sections on the individual cases in this chapter.

17 Possible Objects and Complements

A distinction is made between necessary elements, the **objects of a sentence**, and additional, **nonrestrictive information**, without which the sentence still would be grammatically complete.

The following can serve as objects and added information: **case forms**, **prepositional phrases**, **nominal forms of the verb**, **dependent clauses**, **adjuncts**, and **adverbials**.

Adjuncts or Attributes

Adjuncts or **attributes** (**attribuere** *to bestow*) are sentence elements that are not dependent on the predicate, but belong with a **noun** and modify or qualify it. **Adjectives**, **pronouns**, **quantifiers**, and **nominal forms of the verb** can serve as attributes. They answer the question *what kind of?* or *which?* and **agree** with their antecedents in **case, number, and gender**.

A noun in the same case that appears as an attribute is known as an **appositive** (**appōnere** *to add to*). It usually is set off by commas.

Caesar, fēlis puerī, cunīculum album persequitur.
Caesar, the boy's cat, chases the white rabbit.

Genitive attributes, ablative attributes, and prepositional attributes, however, do **not agree** with their antecedent in case, number, and gender.

fēlis puerī	*the boy's cat*	(genitive attribute)
cunīculus summā pulchritūdine	*a rabbit of extreme beauty*	(ablative attribute)
remōtus ā culpā esse	*to be free from guilt*	(prepositional attribute)

111

An adjective used as an attribute can also modify several nouns. If the antecedents differ in gender, then the adjective agrees with the nearest antecedent in case, number, and gender.

vir summā pulchritūdine et fortitūdine
a man of extraordinary beauty and bravery

▶ A relative clause frequently provides more information about a noun. For more on this topic, see the section on **Relative Clauses**.

The Predicative

As a predicative, a noun or adjective describes the **state or condition** of a person or a thing **at the time of the verb's action**. In Latin, it agrees with its antecedent in case, number, and gender.

Cunīculus *inopīnāns* **ā patre caesus est.**
The rabbit, unsuspecting, was killed by the father.

The following adjectives frequently have a predicative function:

absēns, -ntis	*absent*	**libēns, -entis**	*ready, willing*
praesēns, -ntis	*present*	**inopīnāns, -ntis**	*unsuspecting*
nūdus, -a, -um	*nude, naked*	**vīvus, -a, -um**	*alive*
miser, -a, -um	*sad*	**sōlus, -a, -um**	*alone*

If a substantive is used as a predicative, the English translation sometimes requires the addition of "as."

Pater *senex* **multōs cunīculōs cecīdit.**
As an old man, the father killed many rabbits.

Official titles such as **cōnsul** *consul,* **dictātor** *dictator,* or other designations of persons such as **senex** *old man* or **iuvenis** *young man* are frequently used in this way.

Possible Objects and Complements

Objects in Various Cases

The cases perform **syntactic functions** in a sentence. By **syntactic function**, we mean the role that the given case can play within a sentence as a **sentence element**. Thus the case is not viewed in isolation, but in terms of its interaction with the other sentence elements and its function in the sentence context.

The nominative, or **cāsus rēctus** (**rēctus** *straight*), is set apart from the genitive, dative, accusative, and ablative, because it is the only case that can occur alone in a sentence. The other cases, known as the **cāsūs oblīquī** (**oblīquus** *bent*), in contrast, require at least one other case.

CASE	SYNTACTIC FUNCTION
Nominative *Who? What?*	**subject** or **predicate nominative**
Genitive *Whose?*	**object**, **predicate nominative**, or **attribute/adjunct**
Dative *To/for whom?*	**object**, **predicate nominative**, or **adverbial**
Accusative *Whom? What? Where to?*	**object**, **predicate nominative**, or **adverbial modifier** (rarely: with prepositions as **attribute/adjunct**)
Ablative *With what? By what? From where? Where? Why? About what?*	**object**, **predicate nominative**, **adverbial**, or **attribute**

Accusative

The accusative very frequently is used as the object of a sentence. It can refer to a person or thing that is the object of an action (*whom? what?*), to an expanse of space and time (answering the question *how wide? how far? how old? how tall? how deep?*), or to the goal of movement (*where to?*). There are verbs that require an accusative object on the basis of their meaning.

In a sentence, the accusative performs the function of an **object**, but it can also occur as a **predicate nominative (predicative)** or **adverbial complement**.

Accusative Object Designating a Person or Thing

* Answers the question *whom? what?*

Verbs that require an accusative object because of their **valency** are called **transitive verbs**:

alloquī *to address*	**aggredī** *to attack*
circumīre *to go around*	**trānsīre** *to cross, go across*

They form a **personal passive**, with the **accusative object** becoming the **subject**. **Intransitive verbs**, by contrast, cannot take an accusative object and form an **impersonal passive**.

Transitive:

fēlis flūmen (acc.) **trānsit**	*the cat crosses the river*
flūmen (nom.) **ā fēle trānsitur**	*the river is crossed by the cat*

Intransitive:

scelestus filiō nocet	*the criminal does harm to the son*
filiō ā scelestō nocētur	*harm is done to the son by the criminal*

The following fixed expressions with the accusative have a special meaning:

adīre ōrāculum/ amīcum	*to turn to an oracle/ to a friend*	**inīre foedus**	*to enter into an alliance*
but: **adīre ad amīcum**	*to walk up to a friend*	but: **inīre in domō amīcī**	*to go into the house of friends*
obīre prōvinciam	*to travel through a province*		
obīre mortem	*to die*		

 Some Latin verbs construed as **transitive** have English equivalents that may be **intransitive**.

fugere	*to flee from*	**hostem fugere**	*to flee from the enemy*
effugere	*to escape*	**mortem effugere**	*to escape death*
adiuvāre	*to help*	**amīcum adiuvāre**	*to help the friend*
sequī	*to follow*	**fēlem sequī**	*to follow the cat*
ulcīscī	*to take revenge*	**hostem ulcīscī**	*to take revenge on the enemy*

IMPERSONAL (TRANSITIVE) LATIN EXPRESSIONS			
mē fugit	*it escapes me*	**mē piget**	*it annoys me/I regret*
mē fallit	*I don't know*	**mē pudet**	*it shames me/I am ashamed*
mē iuvat	*I'm glad, it pleases me*	**mē paenitet**	*I regret/it annoys me*
mē decet	*It is proper for me*	**mē taedet**	*it disgusts me*

Some verbs (such as verbs expressing a frame of mind) can be used both as intransitive verbs with another case and as transitive verbs with the accusative.

dolēre mortem/morte/dē morte *to suffer from the death*

The accusative of content reinforces the content of the action expressed by the verb and is used with verbs that usually are intransitive, such as **id studeō** *I'm giving it my attention.*

Note that the expression **Cavē canem!** *Beware of the dog!* is **transitive**.
In the meaning *to shun, avoid* it is **intransitive**, as in **Cavē ā perīculīs!**
Avoid dangers!

Syntax

Verbs with a Double Accusative

There are transitive verbs that, because of their meaning, even require two accusative objects. The following table lists some of the verbs used with a **double accusative**.

docēre *to teach* and **cēlāre** *to conceal*	
id tē cēlō	*I conceal this from you*
id tē doceō	*I teach you this*
poscere *to request, demand*, and **flāgitāre** *to demand earnestly*	
amīcum cunīculum poscō	*I nag my friend for a rabbit*
ōrāre *to request, ask*, and **rogāre** *to ask, beseech* or **interrogāre** if the direct object is a neuter pronoun	
id/haec amīcum rogō	*I ask my friend for it/for these things*
Verbs meaning *to have, to take, to give*	
aliquem amīcum habēre	*to have someone as a friend*
comitem aliquem sūmere	*to take someone as a companion*
habēre, putāre, exīstimāre, dūcere, arbitrārī and **iūdicāre** meaning *to consider (as)*	
tē amīcum habuī	*I considered you my friend*
cunīculus fēlicem fortem exīstimat	*the rabbit thinks the cat is strong*
praebēre and **praestāre** *to prove (to be something)*	
fortem sē praebēre/praestāre	*to prove (to be) brave*
trāicere *to bring across*, **trādūcere** *to lead across*, and **trānsportāre** *to bring across*	
exercitum flūmen trādūcere	*to lead an army across the river*

Possible Objects and Complements

Accusative of Direction

- Answers the question: *where to?*

The accusative indicates direction with the names of **cities** and **small islands**. It performs not only the syntactic function of a direct object, but also that of an **adverbial modifier** denoting place. It is used with or without a preposition.

Rōmam *to Rome*
Dēlum proficīscī *to set out toward Delos*

With larger islands and names of countries, the preposition **in** + the accusative is used.

in Crētam mittere *to send to Crete*

 Note the frequently occurring terms **domum** *home, homeward* and **rūs** *(in)to the countryside.*

Accusative of Extent

- Answers the question *how tall? how deep? how long? how wide? how old? how far?*

The accusative of extent performs not only the role of an accusative object in a sentence, but also the syntactic function of an **adverbial modifier** indicating time or dimensions.

 Memorize the following:
The accusative is always used to answer these questions:
How long? How wide? How old? How far? How tall? How deep?

ducentōs pedēs altus/longus/lātus	*200 feet high/deep/long/wide*
trīgintā annōs	*30 years long*

Verbs such as **trāicere** *to bring across,* **trādūcere** *to lead across,* and **trānsportāre** *to bring across* indicate direction and are followed by the accusative.

exercitum flūmen trādūcere *to lead an army across the river*

Syntax

Accusative as Predicate Nominative

A noun in the accusative case can, along with verbs meaning *to make, to choose,* and *to name/appoint,* be a **predicate nominative (nominal)**.

aliquem cōnsulem facere/creāre *to make/elect someone consul*
aliquem imperātōrem appellāre/nōmināre/dēclārāre/dīcere *to name someone commander*
aliquem fēlīcem dīcere *to characterize someone as happy*

 Note this fixed expression, which occurs frequently:
aliquem certiōrem facere dē aliquā rē *to inform someone about something*

Dative

The dative case indicates a person or thing that is the recipient of an action (*to/for whom?*), the person on whose behalf an action takes place (*for whom?*), or the purpose of an action (*for what purpose, to what end?*).

In a sentence, it has the function of an **object**, but like the accusative, it can also be an **adverbial** or a **predicate nominative**.

Verbs with Dative Object

In addition to verbs that are used with the accusative, there are also verbs that require the dative case. The following table will provide an overview of such verbs.

TRANSITIVE VERBS			
alicui dōnum dare	*to give someone a present*	**coniugī vērum dīcere**	*to tell the wife the truth*
amīcum urbī mittere	*to send the friend to the city*	**amīcae adventum coniugis nūntiāre**	*to announce to the girlfriend the husband's arrival*
amīcae sēcrētum crēdere	*to confide a secret to the girlfriend*	**amīcae dīvortium suādēre**	*to suggest divorce to the girlfriend*

Possible Objects and Complements

INTRANSITIVE VERBS			
adulterō nocēre	*to harm the adulterer*	**coniugī īrāscī**	*to anger the husband*
amīcae servīre	*to serve a friend (f.)*	**scelestō appropinquāre**	*to approach the criminal*

COMPOUNDS OF ESSE			
adesse amīcō	*to help a friend*	**dēesse amīcīs**	*to be lacking to the girlfriends*
prōdesse cīvibus	*to benefit the citizens*	**praeesse exercituī**	*to command the army*

IMPERSONAL VERBS			
accidit	*it befalls*	**contingit**	*it falls to (someone's) lot*
libet	*it pleases*	**placet**	*it pleases*
licet	*it is permitted*		

 Some Latin verbs that take a dative object are rendered in English with a direct (accusative) object.

litterīs studēre	*to pursue knowledge eagerly*	**coniugī parcere**	*to be lenient to the husband*
<u>but:</u> **id studēre**	*to be striving for something*		
amīcae favēre	*to favor the friend (f.)*	**amīcō invidēre**	*to envy the friend*
coniugī miserae persuādēre	*to persuade the sad wife*	**virō nūbere**	*to marry the man*

Syntax

Dative of Benefit or Harm (dativus commodī or incommodī)

- Answers the question *for whom? for what?*

This dative denotes a person or thing for whose **benefit (dativus commodī)** or **harm (dativus incommodī)** something is done.

Nōn scholae, **sed** vītae **discimus.**
We learn not just for school, but for life.

Some verbs are used with the dative of benefit when they have the meaning *to look after, be concerned about, take care of.* With an accusative object, their meaning is different.

cōnsulere cīvibus	to look after the citizens	timēre lībertātī	to be concerned about freedom
but: cōnsulere senātum	to consult the senate	but: adulterium timēre	to fear adultery
amīcīs prōvidēre	to take care of the friends (f.)		
but: rēs futūrās prōvidēre	to foresee the future		

Dative of Agent (dativus auctōris)

- Answers the question: *by whom (is something done)?*

This dative appears primarily in **gerundive constructions**. With a gerundive (rarely also with the passive voice), this dative denotes the "perpetrator."

Cunīculus mihi caedendus est.
The rabbit must be killed by me.

It appears only very rarely in other constructions.

Dative of Possession (dativus possessivus)

- Answers the question *to whom (does something belong)?*

In connection with **esse**, the dative of possession denotes the person who is in possession of something. This dative performs the syntactic function of a predicate nominative.

Mihi cuniculī et fēlēs sunt.
(literally: to me are rabbits and cats) I have/own rabbits and cats.

Dative of Purpose (dativus finālis)

- Answers the question *to/for whom (is something useful, etc.)*

In this usage, the dative occurs with **esse** and indicates an effect or a purpose. It performs the syntactic function of a **predicate nominative**.

amicō ūsuī/dētrimentō/honōrī/cūrae/ cordī esse	*to be of use/detriment to the friend, to bring honor to the friend, to be of concern to the friend, to be close to the friend's heart*

In connection with verbs such as **venīre** *to come,* **tribuere** *to divide, assign,* **relinquere** *to relinquish, abandon,* and **dare** *to give,* the dative of purpose performs the syntactic function of an **adverbial**.

Puer cuniculō auxiliō **venit.**
The boy comes to the aid of the rabbit.

Cuniculō is the dative object, and **auxiliō** is an adverbial. Often the dative, when used adverbially, is rendered with a **prepositional phrase** in English.

Note the following fixed expressions:
alicui aliquid crīminī dare *to reproach someone for something*
alicui aliquid vitiō dare *to hold something against someone*
alicui aliquem auxiliō mittere *to send someone someone to help*

Syntax

Genitive

The genitive tells us that one person or thing belongs to another (*whose?*) or gives more information about a noun (*what kind of?*). It usually performs the syntactic function of an **adjunct (attribute)**, modifying a noun, and sometimes functions as a **predicate nominative**. It can also qualify the meaning of verbs, and then it takes on the function of an **object** or an **adverbial**.

In English, the genitive, or possessive case, is represented by the preposition *of* or by the enclitic *-'s/s'* (sing./pl.): *the friend of my brother/my brother's friend, the friend of my brothers/my brothers' friend.*

Genitive as Noun Modifier

• Answers the question *whose?*

It appears as the **genitive attribute** of a noun and describes it in greater detail. In English, a free translation sometimes seems best.

poena mortis *(the penalty of death) the death penalty*
nōmen Hannibalis *(the name of Hannibal) the name Hannibal, Hannibal's name*
pōculum vīnī *a cup of wine*

As with the accusative and dative, there are various types of genitives, depending on the field of application.

Subjective and Objective Genitive (genitīvus subiectīvus and obiectīvus)

• Answers the question *whose? directed at whom or what?*

This genitive modifies a noun and denotes either the "perpetrator" or the "victim" of an act. The terms **subiectīvus** and **obiectīvus** are somewhat confusing. The following example may illustrate the difference between the subjective and objective usages.

amor parentum

This Latin expression can be viewed either as **genitivus subiectivus** or as **genitivus obiectivus** and translated in different ways. The former sees the genitive **parentum** as the subject, the agent of the action, which is expressed by the antecedent: *the love of parents (for their children, for rabbits, etc.)*. The **genitivus obiectivus**, on the other hand, sees the genitive **parentum** as the object, the recipient of the action. Accordingly, the translation might be *love for/of (one's) parents*.

If both possible translations make sense, you will have to rely on the context to decide which one is appropriate.

GENITĪVUS SUBIECTĪVUS			
victōria Rōmānōrum	*the Romans' victory*	**invidia amīcī**	*the friend's envy*
epistula Plīniī	*Pliny's letter*	**lēx nātūrae**	*the law of nature*
GENITĪVUS OBIECTĪVUS			
victōria Rōmānōrum	*the victory over the Romans*	**invidia amīcī**	*the envy of the friend*
epistula Plīniī	*the letter to Pliny*	**spēs salūtis**	*the hope of rescue*

With personal pronouns, only one translation is possible. **Amor vestri** is generally translated as *love for you*. If *your love* were intended, this would be expressed by using the possessive pronoun: **amor vester**. The **genitivus obiectivus** is frequently used with adjectives or participles that require translation with a prepositional phrase, such as **cupidus** *greedy (for)*, **studiōsus** *striving/eager (for)*, **perītus** *expert (in)*, **memor** *in memory (of)*, **cōnscius** *privy (to)*, **appetēns** *covetous (of)*, or **patiēns** *patient (under)*.

Syntax

Partitive Genitive (genitīvus partitīvus)

- Answers the question *of what?*

This genitive refers to a **whole**, of which the antecedent denotes a part: *a great part of our circle of acquaintances.*

Therefore, it occurs after nouns that state a **quantity**, after **pronouns that are used substantively**, and after **comparatives** and **superlatives**.

NOUNS			
pars cunĭculōrum	*part of the rabbits*	**magna cōpia frūmentī**	*a large quantity of grain*

ADJECTIVES OF QUALITY, COMPARATIVES AND SUPERLATIVES			
(only in the nom. sing. neuter or acc. sing. neuter, without a preposition!			
multum, plūs, plūrimum, nimium carnis	*much, more, most, too much meat*	**paulum, minus, minimum carnis**	*little, less, very little meat*
maior cunĭculōrum	*the older of the rabbits*	**satis auxiliī**	*enough help*

SUBSTANTIVIZED PRONOUNS			
quis cunĭculōrum?	*which of the rabbits?*	**nēmō cunĭculōrum caesōrum**	*none of the rabbits that were killed*
altera amīcārum	*one (of the two) girlfriends*	**quis nostrum/ vestrum?**	*which of us/of you*
quid cōnsiliī?	*which decision?*		

FIXED EXPRESSIONS			
ubi terrārum?	*where in the world?*	**quō gentium?**	*(to) where in all the world? to what part of the world?*

Possible Objects and Complements

Genitive of Quality (genitīvus quālitātis)

• Answers the question *what kind of?*

The **genitīvus quālitātis** denotes a property or characteristic of its antecedent. Therefore, it almost always is accompanied by an adjective, pronoun, or quantifier. Usually these genitives indicate number, dimensions, type, and value.

vir magnī animī	*a man of noble mind*	**puer decem annōrum**	*(a boy of 10 years), a 10-year-old boy*
rēs eius modī	*things of this kind*		

The genitive of quality frequently appears in the syntactic function of a **predicate nominative**.

Cunīculī excellentis pulchritūdinis fuērunt.
The rabbits were of extraordinary beauty.
▶ To state physical and mental characteristics, Latin can also use the **ablātīvus quālitātis**. For more information, see the appropriate section.

Genitive of Price (genitīvus pretiī)

• Answers the question *how much?*

This genitive, in combination with **esse**, functions as a predicate nominative, stating the value of a person or the price of a thing.

magnī, plūris, plūrimī esse	*to be worth much, more, (the) most*
parvī, minōris, minimī esse	*to be worth little, less, (the) least*
tantī, quantī, nihilī esse	*to be worth so much, how much, nothing*

It sometimes occurs as an **adverbial** with verbs such as **aestimāre** *to estimate,* **dūcere** *to consider, regard,* **facere** *to make, do,* **emere** *to buy,* and **vendere** *to sell.*

Cunīculum magnī vendit.
He is selling the rabbit for a lot of money.

Syntax

Genitive of Possession (genitīvus possessīvus)

- Answers the question *whose?*

The genitive that is most common in English indicates **ownership**. It can be expressed by using the preposition *of* or by adding -'s, as is frequently done in colloquial speech.

the parents of Mark or *Mark's parents*

Depending on the application, the genitive of possession performs the syntactic function of an **attribute (adjunct)** or **predicate nominative**.

Attribute			
cunīculus amīcī	*the friend's rabbit*	**timor cunīculōrum**	*the fear of rabbits*

Predicate nominative with esse, fierī, habērī and putārī			
patris esse	to belong to the father/be the father's	**amīcī fierī**	to become the friend's property
alicuius habērī/ putārī	to be regarded as someone's property		

The genitīvus possessīvus emphasizes the **owner** (*father, friend*) of a thing. In contrast, the datīvus possessīvus (for example, **mihi est cunīculus** *I have a rabbit/the rabbit belongs to me*) emphasizes the possession (*the rabbit*).

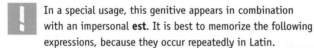 In a special usage, this genitive appears in combination with an impersonal **est**. It is best to memorize the following expressions, because they occur repeatedly in Latin.

cōnsulis est	*it is the consul's task/duty*
meum, tuum, nostrum, vestrum, eōrum eius est	*it is my, your, our, your, their, his/her/its task/duty*
magnī virī est	*it is the characteristic of a great man*

All these expressions can be used not only with **est**, but also with **vidētur** or **putātur** *it seems*, as in this example: **cōnsulis vidētur** *it seems to be the consul's duty.*

Possible Objects and Complements

Genitive as Complement of the Verb

Some verbs need a genitive object as a complement.

Verbs of remembering, mentioning, and forgetting			
amicōrum meminisse	*to remember friends*	**iniūriārum oblivīscī**	*to forget injustices*

With impersonal expressions of feeling (piget, pudet, paenitet, taedet), the person who feels something is in the accusative, while the object of the feeling itself is in the genitive:			
mē paenitet iniūriae	*I regret the injustice*	**mē piget stultitiae meae**	*I'm annoyed at my stupidity*

but: With neuter pronouns, the object of the feeling is the subject, as in **id mē paenitet** *I regret it.*

With interest and rēfert *it is important, it matters*	
eius māximē interest/rēfert	*it is especially important to him*

With verbs reflecting the language of the courts			
aliquem accūsāre sceleris	*to accuse someone of a crime*	**aliquem damnāre reī capitālis**	*to convict someone of a capital offense*
aliquem absolvere prōditiōnis	*to acquit someone of a charge of high treason*		

Ablative

 The ablative is a special feature of Latin. English has no ablative case as such; instead it uses prepositions—such as *by, with,* and *from*—where Latin makes uses of the ablative.

In the ablative, three formerly independent Latin cases now are merged. This explains why there are so many ways to translate the ablative. Originally, this case denoted a **separation** (**ablātīvus sēparātīvus**) from something and answered the question *from where? from what?* That was the origin of its name (ablative comes from **auferre – abstulī – ablātum** *to take*

away). Later, two other cases merged with the ablative, the **locative** (*where? when?*) and the **ablative of means** (**ablātīvus instrumentālis**: *with what? by what?*). In light of the linguistic origins of the case, a distinction essentially continues to be made among these three meanings. There are, however, some subcategories, which are listed below under their common names.

Usually the ablative is translated by using prepositions.

The ablative generally takes on the syntactic function of an **adverbial**. With a very few verbs, it is used as an **object** complement. Rarely, it is used **attributively** or **predicatively**.

Ablative of Separation (ablātīvus sēparātīvus)

* Answers the question *from where? from what?*

The ablative of separation, which is sometimes called the **separative** (**sēparāre** *to separate*) because of its Latin name, is the true ablative. It denotes **movement away from a certain point** and is used with verbs expressing the ideas of **taking away and doing without**. If it is used to denote ancestry or social position, we speak of the **ablātīvus orīginis** (**orīgō** *origin, ancestry, birth*). The ablative of comparison, too (**ablātīvus comparātiōnis**), is a subcategory of the separative.

To denote the **point of origin** of movement, the ablative is used with the names of cities, villages, and smaller islands. It answers the question *from where?*

▶ To indicate direction, in answer to the question *to where?* the accusative is used; in answer to the question *where?* the **ablative of place** is used. To learn more about this, see the appropriate sections later in this chapter.

| **Rōmā, Athēnīs, Dēlō** | *from Rome, from Athens, from Delos* | | |
| **domō** | *from home* | **rūre** | *from the country(side)* |

As with the accusative of direction, a preposition is used before the case (**ā/ab** or **ē/ex**) when speaking of larger islands and names of countries. With other nouns, too, and when used attributively, a preposition is added.

Possible Objects and Complements

ā Graeciā/ex urbe Rōmā *away from Greece/from the city of Rome*
dē montibus *down from the mountains*

For statements of place (for example, *in Rome*), there exist **locative** forms for names of cities and towns: **Rōmae** *in Rome*. For more on this topic, see the section on the ablative of place later in this chapter.

The following are examples of statements of place that answer the question *from where?*—whereas English would regard them as answering the question *where?*

ā fronte	*in front (from the front)*	**ex omnibus partibus**	*on all sides*
ā latere	*on/at the side (from the side)*	**ā tergō**	*in the rear (from the rear)*

The **ablātīvus orīginis** is a subcategory. In combination with **nātus** and **ortus**, it indicates origin.

parentibus humilibus nātus/ ortus	*of humble parentage*	**Apollō Iove nātus**	*Apollo, Jupiter's son*
nātus/ortus nōbilī genere	*of noble birth*	**equestrī locō ortus**	*from the knightly class*

The **ablative of separation** (**ablātīvus sēparātīvus**) is used with verbs of taking away and doing without, such as **prīvāre, spoliāre, exuere** *to rob, deprive of*, **nūdāre** *to lay bare*, **fraudāre** *to defraud of*, **līberāre** *to free, liberate*, **levāre** *to raise, lighten* **solvere** *to loosen*, **vacāre** *to be free of*, **carēre** *to be without*, and **egēre** *to need, be in need of*. It answers the question *of/from what?* Sometimes (especially with persons), the meaning of the ablative is supplemented with a preposition such as **ā/ab**, **dē**, or **ē/ex**.

līberāre cūrīs (Thing)	*to free from cares*	**spoliāre vītā**	*to deprive of life*
but: līberāre ā tyrannō (Person)	*to free from a tyrant*	**vacāre (ā) cūrīs**	*to be free from cares*
auxiliō egēre	*to need/require help*	**arcēre (ā) forō**	*to keep away from the Forum*
līberāre captivitāte	*to free someone from captivity*	**prīvāre omnī spē**	*to deprive of all hope*

Ablative of Comparison (ablātīvus comparātiōnis)

- Answers the question *than who? than what?*

The ablative of comparison is a subcategory of the separative. It follows comparatives and denotes the **object of comparison**. The **ablātīvus comparātiōnis** takes the place of a construction using **quam** *than* + nominative or accusative.

Construction with quam	ablātīvus comparātiōnis
Fēlis fortior quam cunīculus est. *The cat is stronger than the rabbit.*	**Fēlis fortior cunīculō est.** *The cat is stronger than the rabbit.*
Fēlem fortiōrem quam cunīculum pūtō. *I think the cat is stronger than the rabbit.*	**Fēlem fortiōrem cunīculō pūtō.** *I think the cat is stronger than the rabbit.*

Ablative of Means (ablātīvus īnstrumentālis)

- Answers the question *with what? by what?*

The ablative of means, which is sometimes referred to as the **instrumental (īnstrūmentum** *instrument, tool*), states the means by which or instrument with which something takes place.

gladiō pūgnāre *to fight with a sword*

Frequently, a freer translation works better in English:

manū tenēre	to hold in the hand (with the hand)	**memoriā tenēre**	to hold in memory
proeliō lacessere	to challenge to a fight	**viā Appiā proficīscī**	to travel on the Appian Way

Possible Objects and Complements

The instrumental, used as an **attribute**, often occurs in combination with the following verbs and adjectives:

complēre	to fill up, to equip	implēre	to fill up, fill in
ōrnāre, īnstruere	to ornament, to equip	abundāre, redundāre	to be in abundance, be rich in something, fill
afficere	to provide with	praeditus, -a, -um	equipped, provided with something
contentus, -a, -um	contented with something	(in)dignus, -a, -um	(un)worthy of a thing
frētus, -a, -um	relying on something	cōnfīsus, -a, -um	trusting in something

With a few verbs, it acts as a complementary **object**. These verbs are **ūtī** to make use (of), **fungī** to occupy oneself (with), **fruī** to enjoy, have the benefit (of), and **potīrī** to become powerful (through).

fruī vītā to enjoy life
ūtī auctōritāte to use one's influence

The impersonal expression **opus est** there is need, it is necessary is used with the ablative. The thing that is needed is in the **instrumental**; the person in need is in the dative.

Nōbīs frūmentō opus est.
We need grain.

Ablative of Manner (ablātīvus modī)

• Answers the question with what? through what?

The ablative of manner is a subcategory of the **instrumental**. Like the latter, it answers the question with what? or through what? but indicates the **attending circumstances** of the action rather than a thing. It is used with or without the preposition **cum**. The preposition usually is absent when an attribute accompanies the noun.

cum dīligentiā colere	to cultivate with diligence	cum misericordiā caedere	to kill with mercy
(cum) summō studiō	with the greatest enthusiasm	(cum) magnō perīculō	in great danger

 Memorize the following fixed terms and phrases, which occur frequently.

cāsū/forte	by chance, accidentally	nōmine	in the name of
iūre	justly, rightly	suā/meā sponte	of his/my own will, voluntarily
iniūriā	unjustly, wrongly	mōre maiōrum	by the custom of the fathers/ancestors
iussū	at the command of, by order of	eōdem modō	in the same way
hāc condiciōne	on condition	aequō animō	with equanimity

Ablative of Cause (ablātīvus causae)

- Answers the question *why? for what reason?*

Like the **ablātīvus modī**, it is a subcategory of the instrumental. It states the reason for or cause of an event (*why?*) and is used primarily with verbs and adjectives expressing **affect or emotion**.

It often is rendered in English with a prepositional construction.

cōnficī morbō	weakened by an illness	gaudēre victōriā	to rejoice at the victory
cōnfīdere virtūte	to rely on the capability	maestus cunīculō caesō	sad about the rabbit that was killed

The **ablātīvus causae** can be used with a participle, which often can be omitted in English translation.

amōre adductus *out of love, moved by love*
metū coāctus *compelled by fear, out of fear*

Possible Objects and Complements

Ablative of Quality (ablātīvus quālitātis)

• Answers the question *what is it like?*

This ablative, too, is regarded as a subcategory of the instrumental. The **ablātīvus quālitātis** (**quālitās** *quality*) denotes a **property or quality**: **vir magnā audāciā** *a man of great boldness*.

It appears in the syntactic function of an **attribute** or **predicate nominative**.

ATTRIBUTIVE USAGE	
mōns magnā altitūdine	*a mountain of great height/altitude*

PREDICATE NOMINATIVE	
bonō animō esse	*to be in good spirits*

The genitive of quality can also be used in these instances, with no difference in meaning.

Ablative of Price (ablātīvus pretiī)

• Answers the question *how much?*

It can also be regarded as a detailed variant of the **ablātīvus quālitātis**, since it, too, indicates the quality of something but is limited to the **price** (**pretium** *price*) of a thing. You need to memorize the following fixed terms, because they occur frequently in connection with a statement of price.

magnō, plūrimō, parvō, minimō emere/ vendere/stāre/cōnstāre	*to buy/sell at a high price, at a very high price, cheaply, very cheaply; to cost a lot, quite a lot, little, very little*

Ablative of Specification (ablātīvus limitātiōnis)

- Answers the question *to what extent? in what way?*

It is used **attributively** or **predicatively** and modifies a noun or a verbal action.

| māior nātū | older (older in terms of birth) | aeger pedibus | footsore |
| minor nātū | younger | excellere dīgnitāte | to stand out in terms of personal significance |

Ablative of Measure (ablātīvus mēnsūrae)

- Answers the question *by how much?*

The **ablātīvus mēnsūrae** (**mēnsūra** *measure*) also indicates by how much something differs from something else. It defines measurement or dimension and is used **attributively** or **predicatively**.

multō facilius	much lighter	multō praestāre amīcīs	to far exceed the friends
paulō post brevī post	a little later	multō mālle	to much prefer
mīlle passibus ab hoste	one mile from the enemy		

Ablative of Place (ablātīvus locī)

- Answers the question *where? in what place?*

The ablative of place replaces the forms of the **locative**, which at one time was a separate case. It is used with the names of cities and smaller islands.

Carthāgine, Athēnīs, Delphīs vīvere *to live in Carthage, Athens, Delphi*

Possible Objects and Complements

With larger islands or countries, the preposition **in** + ablative is used (as with the accusative of direction).

in Italiā, Crētā vīvere *to live in Italy, on Crete*

▶ To state a direction (*where to?*), the **accusative of direction** is used; to state a **point of origin** (*where from?*), the corresponding **ablative** is used. Read the appropriate chapters and sections to learn more about this.

In addition, the ablative of place frequently is used with **locus** *place* in combination with an attribute (**inīquō locō** *in an unfavorable place*), with nouns along with **tōtus** (**tōtō orbe terrārum** *in the entire world/all over the world*) and in the following fixed expressions:

terrā marīque	*on sea and on land*	**dextrā (manū)**	*on the right*
ūnā cum	*together with*	**sinistrā (manū)**	*on the left*
rēctā (viā)	*straight ahead*		

! A few **locative forms** have been preserved. This is true for some names of cities and islands of the a- and o-declensions and a few fixed expressions. Therefore, you need to memorize the following. The locative forms are **phonetically** equivalent to the **genitive singular**:

Rōmae	*in Rome*	**domī**	*at home*
Corinthī	*in Corinth*	**rūrī**	*in the country(side)*
Tarentī	*in Tarentum*	**domī militiaeque/ domī bellīque**	*in war and in peace*
Dēlī	*on Delos*	**humī**	*on the ground*

Syntax

Ablative of Time (ablātīvus temporis)

- Answers the question *when? at what time?*

The **ablātīvus temporis** refers to a point in time or a period of time.

vēre	*in the spring*	**posterō diē**	*(on) the following day*
initiō, prīncipiō	*at the beginning*	**memoriā nostrā**	*in our times*
prīmā lūce	*at daybreak*	**tertiā vigiliā**	*in the third night watch*
paucīs annīs	*within a few years*	**brevī (tempore)**	*in a short time*

Circumstances are indicated by using the **ablātīvus temporis + in**:

in bellō/in pāce	*in war(time)/in peace(time)*	**in pueritiā/in senectūte**	*in childhood/in old age*
in praesentiā	*at the present*	**in tempore**	*at the right time, on time*
in rēbus secundīs	*in good fortune*	**in rēbus adversīs**	*in ill fortune*

> **!** The following statements of time are still old **locatives**, and this provides evidence that this ablative was derived from the ablative of place:

vesperī	*in the evening*	**cottīdiē**	*daily, every day*
herī	*yesterday*	**noctū**	*at night*
prīdiē	*the day before*	**diū**	*for a long time*
postrīdiē	*the following day*		

Complements Using Prepositional Expressions

▶ Of course, sentences can also have prepositional phrases as complements. In the chapter on prepositions in the first part of this grammar book, you will find an overview of the various prepositions and the cases with which they are used.

Complements Using Nominal Forms of the Verb and Coherent Constructions

In Latin, as in English, verbs can be substantivized, or used as nouns. This results in **verbal nouns** and **verbal adjectives** that have features of a noun and of a verb. They are formed from verbs, declined like nouns, and treated as **nominal constituents**. In the following section, you will learn how to form them and in what context they occur.

When an agent (person or thing) to which the verbal information applies is named in addition to the nominal form of the verb, we speak of **coherent constructions**. They are called **"coherent"** because they can take on the function of **clauses** and frequently are translated as such. Their special characteristic is that they consist of only a few words in Latin, and the speaker of Latin can express a great deal with these few words.

Cunīculum caesūrum esse sciō.
I know that the rabbit is to be killed.

These **coherent constructions** with the infinitive are known as **AcI (accusātīvus cum infinitīvō)**.

In general, **coherent constructions** include expressions with **participles (participium coniūnctum** and **ablātīvus absolūtus), gerunds,** and **gerundives,** or with the **infinitive (AcI** and **NcI, nominātīvus cum infinitīvō).** They are a special feature of Latin. Generally they cannot be literally translated into English.

The Gerund as Verbal Noun

The **gerund** is a **substantivized infinitive**, an infinitive used as a noun. Gerunds occur both in Latin and in English, where they are known as the *-ing* form of the verb: ***Learning** is fun* or ***the wearing** of the green.*

The substantivized infinitive, like any other Latin noun, can be declined.

Nom.	(the) praising
Gen.	of (the) praising
Dat.	to/for (the) praising
Acc.	(the) praising

Because Latin has no definite or indefinite articles, it resorts to the use of **verbal nouns**. They are declined like **neuter nouns of the o-declension** (in the singular) and often translated with the English gerund:

Nom.	infinitive	**laudāre**	(the) praising
Gen.	gerund	**laudandī**	of (the) praising
Dat.	gerund	**laudandō** (very rare)	to/for (the) praising
Acc.	infinitive/gerund	**laudāre/(ad) laudandum**	(the) praising
Abl.	gerund	**laudandō**	by/through (the) praising

If the **verbal noun** occurs **as a subject or object** (in the nominative or accusative), the infinitive itself is used.

Errāre (Nom.) **hūmānum est.**
To err is human.

Fēlis lūdere (acc.) **quam cantāre** (acc.) **māvult.**
The cat prefers singing to dancing.

For all other cases, the gerund is formed by adding **-nd- +** a case ending to the present stem to create a verbal noun. The form **laudandum** occurs only in combination with the preposition **ad.**

 Verbs of the consonant conjugation and the i-conjugation add an **-e-** between the present stem and **-nd-** to form the gerund, as here: **audiendī** (gen.). The gerund of **īre** is **eundī** (gen.).

The Use of the Gerund

The gerund occurs as an attribute in the **genitive** following nouns that require a complement or modifier or with adjectives that are used with the genitive, such as **cupidus, -a, -um**, or with **causā** and **grātiā**.

In the genitive	**ars scribendī**	*the art of writing*
In the genitive with an object	**cupiditās librōs scribendī**	*the desire to write books*
With adjectives	**scribendī cupidus**	*eager to write*
With **causā** and **grātiā**	**scribendī causā/grātiā**	*in order to write/for the sake of writing*

The **dative** of the gerund occurs only very rarely, as a dative of purpose (**datīvus fīnālis**) in fixed combinations, such as **scribendō adesse** *to be there for the purpose of writing* or **solvendō nōn esse** (*"not to be there for the purpose of paying"*) *to be unable to pay*.

In the **accusative**, the gerund occurs only as a prepositional object with the preposition **ad** (rarely, also after **in** or **ob**), as in **ad scribendum** *in order to write, while writing*.

The **ablative** of the gerund is used with or without a preposition.

Without a preposition	**docendō discimus**	*We learn by teaching.*
	iniūriās ferendō	*by suffering insults*
With the prepositions **in** and **dē**, more rarely **ex** and **ab**	**dē bene vīvendō disputāre**	*to talk about a good life*

Despite its use as a noun, the gerund is treated as a verb and, like verbs, can be complemented by **objects** and **adverbs** (as seen in several previous examples).

Infinitive	**bene** (adv.) **scrībere**	*to write well, writing well*
Gerund	**ars bene scribendī** (gen.)	*the art of writing well*
Infinitive	**librōs** (acc. object) **scrībere**	*writing books, to write books*
Gerund	**ad librōs scribendum**	*while/for writing books*

Syntax

Gerundive and Participle as Verbal Adjectives

Verbal adjectives are adjectives derived from verbs. Like the gerund, they are treated as **nouns** and are **declined**. Because they are adjectives and as such agree with their antecedent in **case, number, and gender**, they have forms in all genders.

Verbal adjectives include **participles**   **laudāns, -ntis** (PAP)
                                             laudātus, -a, -um (PPP)
                                             laudātūrus, -a, -um (FAP)

and the **gerundive**   **laudandus, -a, -um**

Gerundive as Verbal Adjective

The gerundive is formed by adding **-nd-** and the ending **-us, -a**, or **-um** to the present-tense stem. For verbs of the consonant conjugation and the i-conjugation (as for the gerund), an **-e-** is added **audiendus, -a, -um**). The gerundive of **ire** *to go* is **eundus, -a, -um**.

The gerundive agrees in **case, number, and gender** with its antecedent, is declined like an adjective of the **a-/o-declension**, and has forms in all genders. It is a **verbal adjective** with a **passive meaning** and denotes obligation or necessity: an action that must or is to be performed (negated: that must not be performed).

cuniculus amandus	*(literally: a rabbit that is to be loved) a rabbit that must be loved = a lovable rabbit*
facinus laudandum	*(literally: a deed that is to be praised) a deed that must be praised = a praiseworthy deed*

 Because English does not have a gerundive construction, we often translate it with the passive infinitive or with equivalents such as *must* or *should*. Another possibility is an impersonal construction: *one must/should …*

The gerundive is used in various ways. It is **rarely** used as an **attribute** (as in the two examples above). Most frequently, it serves as a **predicate adjective**, agreeing in case, number, and gender with a noun in one of the cases. Then it expresses a simultaneous verbal action (or one that is intended and therefore subsequent).

Possible Objects and Complements

Cunĭculus amandus est.
(literally: the rabbit is one that is to be loved). The rabbit must be loved/is lovable.

In part, the gerund and the gerundive are used in overlapping ways. The gerundive is more common in the ablative and genitive.

gerundive	**cōnsilium relinquendae Italiae**	*the plan to leave Italy*
gerund	**cōnsilium Italiam relinquendī**	*the plan to leave/for leaving Italy*
gerundive	**gaudēre cunĭculō caedendō**	*to be glad about the rabbit that is to be killed*
gerund	**gaudēre cunĭculum caedendō**	*to be glad about the rabbit that is to be killed*

While the gerundive occurs rather seldom in the dative, it is often combined with a preposition that is followed by the accusative.

Ad caedendum cunĭculum parāta sum.
I am ready to kill the rabbit.

The gerundive can also be used in the **nominative** (or in AcI in the accusative) as a **predicate nominative**, together with the helping verb **esse**, to constitute the **predicate** of a sentence. This predicate expresses a **necessity** or a **goal** (when negated, a **prohibition** or a **restriction**). It behaves like an adjectival predicate nominative in that it agrees with the subject in case, number, and gender.

Cunĭculus caedendus nōn est.
The rabbit must not be killed.

The best-known example of this use is a quote from Cato, who allegedly spoke these words as he called repeatedly for the destruction of Carthage:

Cēterum cēnseō Carthāginem esse dēlendam.
Furthermore, I think Carthage must be destroyed.

▶ This example contains an **AcI**. For more on this construction, see the appropriate section in this chapter.

The person who must do something or is forbidden to do something is always in the **dative (datīvus auctōris)**.

Cunīculus mihi caedendus nōn est.
The rabbit must not be killed by me.
Better: *I must not kill the rabbit.*

Impersonal constructions may often be translated with *one must/should not.*

Philosophandum est.
One must philosophize.

Cunīculum caedendum nōn est.
The rabbit must not be killed.

In combination with some verbs, such as **concēdere** *to relinquish, yield,* **permittere** *to allow, to let go,* **dare** *to give,* **relinquere** *to leave behind,* and **trādere** *to surrender, to hand down,* the gerundive expresses an intention or a purpose. Below is an example of how this can be translated into English.

Cunīculum caedendum tibi trādō.
I'm giving you the rabbit, so that you can kill it./I'm giving you the rabbit to be killed.

Participles

The participles (like the gerund and gerundive) are **nominal forms of the verb.** They are **declined**, have forms in all genders, and, as **verbal adjectives**, **agree in case**, **number**, **and gender** with the word to which they refer.

cunīculus dormiēns	*a sleeping rabbit*
cunīculus caesus	*a dead rabbit (a rabbit that has been killed)*
cunīculus moritūrus	*a rabbit that will die/is about to die*

Participles used predicatively as a **participium coniūnctum** (conjunct participle or participle in agreement) or **ablātīvus absolūtus** (ablative absolute) are far more common than participles used attributively (as in the preceding examples). Both constructions are special features of Latin, and they allow the speaker to express trains of thought in a very compressed way. They are **coherent constructions** and take the place of a clause.

The **present active participle** (PAP) is declined like adjectives of the third declension ending in **-ns** (such as **prūdēns, -entis**). The ending **-e** also occurs in the ablative singular, along with **-ī**. The **perfect passive participle** (PPP) and **future active participle** (FAP) follow the a-/o-declension.

▶ On the formation of the participles, see the sections of this book dealing with verb conjugations in Chapter 11.

The Conjunct Participle (participium coniūnctum)

Every participle can be used as a **participium coniūnctum** (PC). It frequently is in the nominative, but can occur in all cases. Therefore, every participle in the nominative, genitive, dative, or accusative—and, after a preposition, also in the ablative—that is linked with a noun by **agreement in case, number, and gender** is a PC. Participles that appear in the ablative with a congruent noun **without a preposition** are not PCs, but **ablative absolutes** (▶ see the following section).

The special characteristic of the PC is that the antecedent alone (without the participle) performs a syntactic function in the sentence. That is, it can be the subject, object, etc. If the participle were to be deleted, the sentence still would be grammatically complete. The participle, as an **attribute**, modifies the integrated noun, and thus it is directly linked (**coniūnctum**) with the sentence.

Līberī cunīculum ā patre caesum ēdērunt.
The children ate the rabbit (that was) killed by the father.

The **PC** can be translated in various ways. A literal translation may be possible, but undesirable for stylistic reasons.

Syntax

relative clause	*The children ate the rabbit, which was killed by the father.*
subordinate clause	*After the rabbit had been killed by the father, the children ate it.*
prepositional expression	*The children ate the rabbit after its killing by the father.*
coordinate clauses	*The rabbit was killed by the father and then it was eaten by the children.*

Modifiers (objects, adverbs, etc.) that are used with the PC (in the examples above, **ā patre**) are placed between the antecedent and the participle, which are separated for emphasis (hyperbaton).

The PC expresses a **temporal relationship** to the main action.

perfect participle	**Cunīculum caesum ēdērunt.** *After the rabbit had been killed, they ate it.*	**participle of anteriority**
present participle	**Pater caedens flēvit.** *While the father was doing the killing, he wept.*	**participle of simultaneity**
future participle	**Pater caesūrus flēvit.** *The father, who was about to kill, wept.*	**participle of posteriority**

 The nominal antecedent does not need to be stated with the PC if it is contained in the predicate as the subject of the sentence.

Ā patre caesus ā līberīs ēsus est.
It was eaten by the children after it was killed by the father.

Possible Objects and Complements

The Ablative Absolute (ablātīvus absolūtus)

In addition to the **participium coniūnctum**, Latin has a second participial construction: the **ablātīvus absolūtus**. All participles whose antecedent is in the **ablative** (without a preposition) form an **ablātīvus absolūtus** that agrees with the antecedent in gender, number, and case.

With the **participium coniūnctum**, the antecedent of the participle alone (without the participle) has a function in the sentence, but the antecedent in the ablative absolute (**abl. abs.**) plays no role in the sentence. It could not be translated so as to make sense in the sentence context without the accompanying participle. Through the **abl. abs.**, an additional statement is added to the main statement of the sentence. The construction thus is **loosened from (absolūtus)** the sentence. It can be inserted into the sentence as an adverbial modifier and often requires a subordinate clause in English.

Cunīculō ā patre caeso līberī flēvērunt.
The children wept after the rabbit had been killed by the father.

The main statement of the example sentence is that the children were crying. The **ablative absolute** explains why the children are so sad: Their beloved rabbit has been killed.

Because English has no comparable construction, the **ablative absolute** cannot be translated literally. It is rendered as a **coherent construction** by means of a subordinate clause in which the antecedent becomes the subject and the participle becomes the predicate.

As with the PC, the participle in the **abl. abs.** expresses a temporal relationship to the action that is performed in the sentence in which the **abl. abs.** is embedded.

perfect participle	Cunīculō ā patre caeso līberī flēvērunt. *After the rabbit had been killed by the father, the children wept.*	participle of anteriority
present participle	Patre caedente māter flēvit. *While the father did the killing, the mother wept.*	participle of simultaneity

In most instances, **ablative absolutes** contain a **PPP**. Constructions with the **PAP** are less common. The **FAP** is never an element of an **abl. abs.**

Tips on translating the abl. abs.: If the participle is a **PPP**, you can form a subordinate clause introduced by **"after,"** in which the antecedent is the subject and the participle becomes the predicate. If the participle is a **PAP**, you can form a subordinate clause introduced by **"while."** Thus, you can readily decode the content of the construction. Then you can consider whether a different conjunction (such as *although* or *as*) would be more suitable in the context.

Note the following special feature:

Because Latin lacks a **PAP for esse**, sentences such as **Hannibal dux erat**. **Cicerō cōnsul est**, etc. appear as incomplete nominal **ablative absolutes**:

Hannibale duce	*under Hannibal's leadership*
Cicerōne cōnsule	*during Cicero's consulate, when Cicero was consul*
mē duce	*under my leadership*
tē absente/praesente	*in your absence/presence*
mē invītō	*against my will*
patre vīvō	*during father's lifetime*

Possible Objects and Complements

Constructions Using the Infinitive

Latin has sentences in which the **infinitive** acts as the **subject**. These constructions also occur in English. They present no problems with regard to their translation.

Cunīculum caedere opus est.
It is necessary to kill a rabbit.

The subject question *"Who* or *what* is necessary?"* is answered by the infinitive **caedere** *to kill.*

The infinitive appears as the subject in combination with **impersonal expressions:**

facile est	*it is easy*	**decet**	*it is proper*
tempus est	*it is time*	**iuvat**	*I am glad (it makes me happy)*
mōs est	*it is the custom*	**prōdest**	*it benefits*
cōnsuētūdō est	*it is the practice*	**praestat**	*it is better*
turpe est	*it is shameful*	**libet**	*it pleases*
nōn ferendum est	*it is unbearable*	**piget mē**	*it displeases me*
ūtile est	*it is useful*	**interest**	*it is important*
scelus est	*it is a crime*	**opus est**	*it is necessary*
pār est	*it is appropriate*	**oportet**	*it is fitting*
etc.			

▶ Impersonal expressions like the foregoing can also introduce an **AcI.** Read more on this topic in the section dealing with AcI later in this chapter.

If the subject infinitive consists of a helping verb + predicate nominative, the predicate nominative is in the accusative.

Iūcundum esse iuvat. *I am glad to be popular.*

The **infinitive** can also take on the function of an **object.** This happens with verbs that need an infinitive as a complement.

Pater cunīculum caedere non cūnctātus est.
The father did not hesitate to kill the rabbit.

velle	*to want*	**statuere**	*to set up, establish*
nōlle	*to not want*	**audēre**	*to dare*
mālle	*to prefer*	**incipere**	*to start*
cupere	*to wish*	**dēsinere**	*to stop*
studēre	*to strive for*	**pergere**	*to proceed*
posse	*to be able, can*	**solēre**	*to be accustomed*
dēbēre	*to have to, must*	**cōnsuēvisse**	*to be accustomed*
cōnārī	*to try*	**cūnctārī**	*to hesitate*

! Only a very few Latin infinitives are part of a construction with the "pure" infinitive. Most are part of an **AcI** or an **NcI**. Therefore, you always need to ask yourself whether the construction in question might be an **AcI** or an **NcI**.

▶ For more on the **AcI** and **NcI**, see the following chapters.

Accusative with Infinitive (AcI)

Most Latin infinitives (around 90 percent!) are not part of an infinitive construction, but of an **AcI** (**accūsātivus cum īnfīnītīvō** *accusative with infinitive*) or (much more rarely) an **NcI** (**nōminātivus cum īnfīnītīvō** *nominative with infinitive*). This happens because Latin prefers to work with greatly compressed phrases. Along with participial constructions (**participium coniūnctum** and **ablātīvus absolūtus**) and predicative constructions with gerunds and gerundives, the **AcI** and **NcI** are common ways of achieving that goal.

A sentence construction that is comparable to **AcI** also occurs in English. Often it is used with verbs of sensory perception.

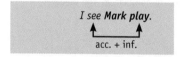

*I see **Mark play**.*
acc. + inf.

This construction would be a commonly occurring one in Latin. It would be expressed as follows:

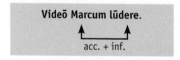

Videō Marcum lūdere.
acc. + inf.

Possible Objects and Complements

In a sentence, the **AcI** depends on a superordinate verb (a "head verb," concerning the senses). In our example, it is the verb **videō**. In English, the **AcI** also can be rendered with a clause introduced by *that* without changing the meaning.

> *I see that Mark is playing.*

In Latin, some statements using the **AcI** can be translated into English only with a *that* clause and not with an infinitive construction. The agent of the action, which is the subject of the **AcI** in terms of content, is always in the accusative in Latin (**"accusative subject"**). The predicate of the **AcI** is formed by an infinitive (**"infinitive predicate"**). The **AcI** subject and the **AcI** predicate can be expanded.

Videō Marcum semper cum amīcō Gāiō lūdere.
I see that Marcus always plays with his friend Gaius.

The **AcI** answers the question *whom or what* does Marcus see? It takes on the syntactic role of an **object**.

 Note that the **AcI** is not set off by commas; it is treated not as a subordinate clause, but as a sentence **element** (coherent construction) that is embedded in the sentence context. This makes it more difficult to spot an **AcI** quickly.

If the subjects of the "head verb" and the **AcI** are identical, it is replaced in both singular and plural by the reflexive pronoun **sē**.

Marcus dīcit sē semper cum amīcō Gāiō lūdere.	*Marcus says that he always plays with his friend Gaius.*
Marcus et Gāius dīcunt sē semper inter sē lūdere.	*Marcus and Gaius say that they always play with one another.*

If the subject of the superordinate clause differs from the subject of the **AcI**, the reflexive pronoun **sē** is replaced by the non-reflexive personal pronouns **eum** or **eōs/eās**.

Claudius scit eōs (Marcus et Gāius) semper lūdere.
Claudius knows that they (Marcus and Gaius) are always playing.

Depending on the **temporal relationship** between the action expressed in the **AcI** and the superordinate clause, the **predicate infinitive** is selected. With respect to the **predicate of the main clause**, it can express anteriority (earlier in time), simultaneity (same time), or posteriority (later in time).

> **Perfect infinitive = anteriority**
> **Present infinitive = simultaneity**
> **Future infinitive = posteriority**

Earlier time	**Līberī sciunt** patrem **cunīculum** cecidisse. *The children know that the father killed the rabbit.*
Same time	**Līberī sciunt** patrem **cunīculum** caedere. *The children know that the father is killing the rabbit.*
Later time	**Līberī sciunt** patrem **cunīculum** caesurum esse. *The children know that the father will kill the rabbit.*

In Latin, there are certain verbs that often are followed by the **AcI** as an object.

It follows verbs of saying and thinking (**verba dīcendī et sentiendī**) or occurs with verbs of feeling and expression of emotion (**verba affectūs**), such as these:

dīcere	*to say*	**vidēre**	*to see*
negāre	*to deny*	**putāre**	*to think, believe*
iubēre	*to order*	**audīre**	*to hear*
nuntiāre	*to report, announce*	**mirārī**	*to wonder*
clamāre	*to call, cry out*	**querī**	*to complain*
scīre	*to know*	**dolēre**	*to regret*
intellegere	*to recognize, understand*	**gaudēre**	*to rejoice, be glad*

The AcI often follows **impersonal expressions**:

cōnstat	*it is certain*	**necesse est**	*it is necessary*
appāret	*it is apparent*	**fāma est**	*it is rumored*
mē fugit	*it escapes me*	**oportet**	*it is fitting, proper*

Esse can be omitted if the predicate infinitive consists of a compound form of **esse**.

The **AcI** is sometimes not altogether easy to find, as it is not set off by commas and the sentence order is not fixed.

> **Mundum** Stoici censent **regi numine deorum, eumque esse quasi communem urbem et civitatem hominum et deorum, et unumquemque nostrum eius mundi esse partem;** ex quo illud natura consequi, ut communem utilitatem nostrae anteponamus. (Cicero, de finibus III 63)
>
> *The Stoics think **that the world is ruled by the workings of the gods and that it is, so to speak, a common city and citizenry of men and gods, and that each one of us is a part of this world;** from this it follows naturally that we prefer the well-being of the community to our own good.*

Nominative with Infinitive (NcI)

With some transitive verbs, when the conversion to the **passive** takes place, the **AcI** is replaced by an **infinitive construction with a nominative**, which is simultaneously the subject of the superordinate clause.

Cuniculi dicuntur animalia domita esse.
Rabbits are said to be tame animals./It is said that rabbits are tame animals.

Like the AcI, the NcI often can be rendered in English with a *that* clause. The **predicate nominative**, if there is one, is also in the **nominative case**.

 English, like Latin, also has the NcI pattern, consisting of a passive verb or a cognition/perception verb followed by an infinitive with *to* (as in the example above).

The **NcI** appears with **vidēri** *to seem*, **dīci** *to be said*, **putāri** *to be regarded as*, and similar verbs in all persons, both singular and plural. With **trādere** and **ferre** in the meaning *to pass down, to report*, it occurs only in the **third person** singular or plural of the passive voice.

Dīcor cunīculum amāvisse.
I am said to have loved the rabbit.

Līberī trāduntur cum cunīculīs lūsisse.
The children are reported to have played with rabbits.

In addition, it is used with **iubērī** *to order,* **sinī** *to permit,* **vetārī** *to forbid,* **cōgī** *to be forced,* and verbs with similar meanings in all persons, both singular and plural.

Pater iubētur cunīculum caedere.
The father was ordered to kill the rabbit.

▶ The **temporal relationship** of the infinitives to the superordinate verb is governed in the **NcI** just as it is in the **AcI**. For more, see the preceding section.

18 Types of Sentences

English has **four types of sentences**. Their names derive from the meaning they convey.

- **Declarative sentences** are used to make statements.
- **Interrogative sentences** express a question.
- **Imperative sentences** are used for commands.
- **Conditional sentences** indicate a dependent relationship between events or conditions.

In addition, there are **main clauses** and **subordinate clauses** (dependent clauses). **Subordinate clauses** take on the function of a **sentence element** and therefore cannot appear without a **main clause**. Subordinate clauses are introduced by a subordinating conjunction, a pronoun, an adverb, or an interrogative word.

After the rabbit had been killed, the father took it to the butcher.

▶ An overview of the types of subordinate clauses can be found in the section on **complex sentences** later in this chapter.

Latin has the same types of sentences. In the following material, you will find more information about main clauses and subordinate clauses in Latin. It is most important to know something about the use of **mood**, as Latin makes far greater use of the subjunctive than English.

▶ Latin has various ways to "compress" or "condense" information that English expresses at greater length. For more about these possibilities, see the section on **coherent constructions**.

Declarative Sentences

Mood	Declarative sentences generally are in the **indicative** mood of all tenses, unless they express a possibility or make an assertion that does not correspond to reality. Then the **subjunctive** is used.
Negation	**nōn**
	<u>rarely</u>: **nihil** *nothing,* **numquam** *never,* **nūllō modō** *by no means,* **minimē** *not at all*
	Double negation equals reinforced assertion:
	nēmō nōn *everyone,* **nōn ignōro** *I am certain,* **nōnnumquam** *sometimes*
	Negations do not cancel each other out if they do not follow each other immediately:
	neque – neque *neither – nor,* **nē – quidem** *not once*

Syntax

Overview of the use of moods in declarative sentences:

Present indicative The event is depicted as → **real**.	**Līberī tristēs sunt, sī cunīculus caeditur.** *The children are sad if the rabbit is being killed.*
Present subjunctive Weakens the degree of reality to a possibility (potentialis of the present)	**Līberī tristēs sint, sī cunīculus caeditur.** *The children probably are sad if the rabbit is being killed.*
Perfect subjunctive Identical in meaning to the present subjunctive. → **potentialis of the present**	**Nēmō laetātus erit cunīculum caesum esse.** *No one ought to be glad that the rabbit was killed.*
Imperfect subjunctive Expresses a possibility in the past. → **potentialis of the past** It is limited to certain expressions such as **crēderēs**, **dīcerēs** *one could have said* or **vidērēs** *one could have seen.*	**Nōn facile discernerēs, utrum cunīculus an bōs caesus esset.** *It would not have been easy to decide whether the rabbit or the cow should be killed.*
The speaker assumes something that in reality has not taken place. → **Irrealis of the present**	*The children would cry whether the rabbit or the cow was killed.*
Pluperfect subjunctive Expresses an assumption about an event in the past. → **Irrealis of the past**	**Līberī nōn flēvissent, sī cunīculus nōn caesus esset.** *The children would not have cried if the rabbit had not been killed.*

Independent Interrogative Clauses

The material below deals with interrogative clauses that are **independent**. This means that they occur as main clauses and are not dependent on a superordinate clause.

Mood	The use of mood in independent interrogative clauses corresponds to that in declarative sentences. An additional type of subjunctive is the **deliberative**, which expresses question involving doubt and addressed to oneself. **quid fāciam?** *what shall I do?* **quid fācerem?** *what should I have done?*
Negation	Independent interrogative clauses are negated like declarative sentences.

Overview of the various types of interrogative sentences:

<u>Word question</u>: Question about a person, a thing, or a specific circumstance. Introduced by an **interrogative pronoun** or **interrogative adverb** such as **quis?** *who?*, **quid?** *what?*, **quandō?** *when?*, **ubī?** *where?*, and **cūr?** *why?*

Quandō cunĩculus caedētur?
When will the rabbit be killed?

<u>Sentence question</u>: Question about a situation. The questions are not asked with an introductory question word, but with an entire sentence. It is the **answer expected** that determines which **interrogative particle** (usually not translated) is used:

-ne: usually attached to the word being stressed, leads one to expect the answer **yes** or **no**

Vidēsne patrem?
Do you see the father?

nōnne (approximately) *not*: The answer **yes** is expected

Nōnne patrem vidēs?
Don't you see the father?

num: The answer **no** is expected

Num patrem vidēs?
You don't see the father, do you?

<u>Decision question:</u> It offers a choice between two possibilities and is expressed with **utrum -an**, **-ne -an**, or a simple **...-an.**

(Utrum) patrem an mātrem vidēs?
Do you see father or mother?

<u>Rhetorical question</u>: This is a question only in formal terms; in terms of content, it is a **declaration** or **statement**, and no answer is expected.

Quid est pulchrius cunĩculō?
What is more beautiful than the rabbit?
→ The speaker does not really want to know what is more beautiful than the rabbit; he wants to say that the rabbit is extraordinarily beautiful.

Syntax

Independent Commands and Wishes

The following material deals with commands and wishes that are **independent**; that is, they occur as main clauses and are not dependent on a superordinate clause.

Mood	**imperative** or **subjunctive**
Negation	**nē**
	<u>more rarely</u>: **nihil** *nothing,* **numquam** *never*

Overview of the various types of sentences expressing wishes and commands:

Commands
The **first imperative** is used to address a command to the second person. It can **not** be combined with a **negation**.

Vocā patrem!
Call the father!

Prohibition
A prohibition/negated command is expressed with **nē + perfect subjunctive (prohibitive)** or **nōlī** (singular) or **nōlīte** (plural) **+ infinitive.**

Nē vocāveris patrem!
Don't call the father!
Nōlī patrem vocāre!
Don't call the father!
Nōlīte patrem vocāre!
Don't call the father!

Requests
The **hortative** is used to address requests or demands to the first person plural in the **present subjunctive.**

Eāmus domum!
Let's go home!

Those addressed to the third person singular and plural are expressed in the present subjunctive (**iussive**).

Patrem vōcet!
Let him call the father!

Wishes
Wishes are expressed with the subjunctive (**optative**). Wishes that the speaker regards as **fulfillable** are in the **present subjunctive** (present) or **perfect subjunctive** (fulfillable wishes in the past). Those regarded as **unfulfillable** are expressed with the **imperfect subjunctive** (present) and **pluperfect subjunctive** (past).

(Utinam) vocet patrem!
I hope he calls the father!

(Utinam) vocāvisset patrem!
If only he had called the father!

Compound Sentences (Parataxis)

Most Latin sentences are compound; that is, they consist of one or more independent clauses and may possibly contain dependent clauses. Latin distinguishes between a **compound sentence (parataxis)** and a **complex sentence (hypotaxis)**.

The term "compound sentence" indicates that two **clauses of equal value are joined together**. Two or more independent clauses form a so-called **parataxis**. They can be linked by a **conjunction** or can use **asyndetic coordination**, with no coordinating conjunction present between the clauses. **Asyndeton** (absence of linkage by a conjunction) frequently is used as a stylistic means. It lends a dramatic effect to an event and serves to create a sense of expectation in the listener.

Vēnī, vidī, vīcī.
I came, I saw, I conquered.

In English translation, the word *and* sometimes is inserted before the last element. Latin has various ways to connect compound sentences by using **conjunctions**. The following table gives an overview of the most important conjunctions, which can connect independent clauses as well as sentence elements:

et, -que, atque *and*	
In Latin, **et** frequently is used between all the members of a series that are to be linked. In English, *and* generally appears only before the last member of the series. Take this into account when you translate.	**Pater cunīculum cecīdit et māter tristis fuit et līberī flēvērunt.** *The father killed the rabbit, the mother was sad, and the children wept.*
Individual terms (not clauses) are linked with **-que** if they are **closely related**. Frequently these are words that are similar (**synonyms**) or opposite (**antonyms**) in meaning. Note that **-que** is never added to the first member of a series.	**terrā marīque** *on land and sea* **senātus populusque Rōmānus** *the Senate and the Roman people*
atque also is used mostly to link terms that go together and places emphasis on the word that follows.	**Idem velle atque idem nōlle, ea dēmum firma amīcitia est.** *To like the same things and not like the same things, only this is a strong friendship.*

OTHER CONJUNCTIONS			
etiam	also, even	**neque (nec)**	and not, nor
quoque	also, too	**nē – quidem**	not even
aut	or	**-ve**	or
vel	or	**sīve**	or
sed	but	**vērum**	but
autem	however, moreover	**at**	but, mind you
tamen	nevertheless, still	**vērō**	however, indeed
nam	for	**enim**	for, in fact, truly
itaque	and so, therefore	**igitur**	therefore
ergō	therefore	**proinde**	then, hence
et – et	both – and	**aut – aut**	either – or
neque – neque	neither – nor	**vel – vel**	either – or
cum – tum	both – and	**nōn modo/sōlum – sed etiam**	not only – but also

Complex Sentences (Hypotaxis)

A **complex sentence (hypotaxis)** is the term used for a construction that consists not only of principal clauses, but also of **dependent, subordinate clauses.** The clauses are referred to as dependents because they cannot occur alone; they must be part of a complex sentence, which consists of at least one independent clause and any number of dependent clauses.

The following types exist:
- **Dependent clauses of the first degree**, which are dependent on a main or principal clause.
- **Dependent clauses of the second degree**, which are dependent on a dependent clause of the first degree.
- **Dependent clauses of the third degree**, which are dependent on a dependent clause of the second degree.

The following table provides an overview of the various types of dependent clauses.

Type of clause/syntactic function	"Signal word"	Example
Subject clause/subject (answers the question *who* or *what?*)	*that, whether,* or *interrogative pronoun*	It is not nice **that** the rabbit was killed.
Object clause/object (answers the question *whom* or *what?*)	*that, whether,* or *interrogative pronoun*	I asked you **whether** you wanted to become my wife.
The following types of clauses perform the function of an **adverbial**:		
Temporal clauses (answer the question *when?*)	*when, after, while,* etc.	**After** I had come from school, I ate dinner.
Conditional clauses (answer the question *under what circumstances?*)	*if, in case*	**If** you are my friend, you will support me.
Concessive clauses (contain a **restriction**)	*although, even if*	I am sad, **although** the rabbit tasted good.
Causal clauses (answer the question *why?*)	*because*	You are diligent, **because** you spend time studying Latin grammar.
Modal clauses (answer the question *how?*)	*by, through*	**By** engaging in sports, we keep fit.
Comparative clauses (contain a **comparison**)	*than*	It is better to starve **than** to eat the rabbit.
Adversative clauses (contain a **contrast**)	*while, whereas*	I at least make an effort, **while** you don't even try at all.
Final (purposive) clauses (answer the question *for what purpose?*)	*so that*	A salesperson travels **so that** he can get away from his office.
Consecutive clauses (contain a **consequence**)	*so that*	I quit my job, **so that** I could study.
Local clauses (answer the question *where? to where?*)	*where*	I live **where**(ever) I please.
Relative clauses/attribute (contain a modifier of a noun, a thing, or a situation)	*relative pronoun* (*who, which, that,* etc.)	The teacher, **who** was on vacation, never came back.
Predicative clauses/predicative (contain a modifier of the events expressed in the predicate)	*Interrogative pronoun* (*how, which,* etc.)	Our vacation is just **as** we imagined it.

Syntax

The following material presents the types of clauses and their characteristics. We are not concerned here with the sequence of tenses; the focus now is on the **general theme of the types of dependent clauses** and the **use of mood in dependent clauses**.

▶ To learn about the sequence of tenses in indicative and subjunctive dependent clauses, see the section on the sequence of tenses.

Indirect Interrogative Clauses

MOOD	SUBJUNCTIVE
Translation	depends on context: frequently the subjunctive is not translated.
Negation	**nōn**
Dependent on	expression of saying, asking, knowing, such as **nescīre** *to not know,* **dubitāre** *to doubt,* **rogāre** *to ask*
Introduced by	**interrogative pronoun** or **interrogative adverb** ▶ more in the chapter on interrogative sentences
Differentiates between	**word questions**, **sentence questions**, and **double questions** ▶ more in the chapter on interrogative sentences
Syntactic function	**subject**, **object**, or **predicate**

Examples:

Nesciō, quid respondeam.
I don't know what answer to give.

Quid est (causae), cūr cunīculus caesus sit?
What is the reason why the rabbit was killed?

Dubitō, an cunīculus nōn caesus sit.
I doubt that (whether) the rabbit was killed.

Dēlīberandum est, utrum cunīculus an bōs caedendus sit.
One must consider whether the rabbit or the cow should be killed.

In Latin, the subjunctive indirect interrogative sentence is preferable after verbs of saying, etc.

Temporal Clauses

Temporal clauses (**tempus** *time*) contain a **time designation.**

MOOD	SUBJUNCTIVE OR INDICATIVE
Translation	The subjunctive is not translated.
Negation	**nōn**
Introduced by	**cum** *when, since, although, whenever,* **postquam** *after,* **antequam** *before,* etc.
Syntactic function:	**adverbials**

Whether the indicative or the subjunctive is used in a temporal clause depends on the introductory conjunction of the dependent clause. A popular conjunction in temporal dependent clauses is the Latin **cum**. Depending on the meaning, it is used with the **indicative** or with the **subjunctive**. When you are translating a sentence in which **cum** appears, you must also keep in mind the mood of the predicate.

In the following table, you will gain an overview of which Latin conjunctions require the indicative, and which require the subjunctive.

CONJUNCTIONS WITH THE INDICATIVE	
cum *then, when, after, since* (**cum temporāle**) It emphasizes the time of an action and is used with the indicative of all tenses.	**Māter eō tempore librum lēgit, cum pater cunīculum cecīdit.** *The mother was reading a book when the father killed the rabbit.*
cum *when (suddenly)* (**cum inversīvum**) It connects two events that occurred in rapid succession.	**Pater cunīculum cecīdit, cum māter vēnit.** *The father was killing the rabbit when the mother suddenly came.*
cum *whenever, every time* (**cum iterātīvum**) In addition, **quotiēns** and **quotiēnscumque** have the same meaning.	**Cum pater cunīculum cecīdit, māter vēnit.** *Every time the father killed a rabbit, the mother came.*
postquam *after* It is used with the **perfect indicative**.	**Postquam cunīculus caesus est, līberī flēvērunt.** *After the rabbit was killed, the children wept.*

Syntax

ut (prīmum), cum (prīmum), ubi (prīmum), simul *as soon as, once*
The **perfect indicative** is used with these conjunctions.

Ut cunīculus caesus est, līberī flēvērunt.
As soon as the rabbit was killed, the children wept.

dum, dōnec, quoad, quamdiū *while (when), as long as*
They link two actions occurring at the same time.

Māter domum pūrgāvit, dum pater cunīculōs cecīdit.
The mother was cleaning the house while the father was killing the rabbit.

dum *while*
It is always used with the **present indicative**.

Māter domum pūrgāvit, dum pater cunīculōs caedit.
The mother cleaned the house, while the father killed the rabbit.

CONJUNCTIONS WITH THE SUBJUNCTIVE

cum *when, as*
(**cum nārrātīvum** or **historicum**)
Like the **cum temporāle**, it contains a time designation, but it also has causal significance. This use of **cum** derives its name from its frequent appearance in **stories** (**nārrāre** *to narrate, tell*).

Līberī flēvērunt, cum cunīculus caesus sit.
The children wept when the rabbit was killed.

Conjunctions with the Indicative or the Subjunctive

antequam, anteāquam, priusquam *before*
These conjunctions occur with the indicative, unless the dependent clause they introduced has a final (purposive) meaning.

Pater secūrem comparāverat, antequam cunīculum cecīderit.
The father had acquired an ax before he killed the rabbit.
The dependent clause has a secondary final meaning, because it can be assumed that the father acquired the ax in order to kill the rabbit with it.

dum, dōnec, quoad *until*
They are used with the indicative, unless the dependent clause they introduce has a secondary meaning.

 dum in the meaning of *as long as* is always used with the indicative.

Domum pūrgāvī, dum cunīculum cecīderim.
I cleaned the house until I killed the rabbit.
The dependent clause has a secondary meaning, because it can be assumed that the person stopped cleaning in order to kill the rabbit.

Conditional Clauses

Conditional clauses (**condiciō** *condition*) contain a condition with regard to the statement of the superordinate clause.

Mood	indicative or subjunctive
Translation	If the subjunctive is used, it is translated as such.
Negation	**nisi** *if...not, unless, except*
Introduced by	**sī** *if,* **quod sī** *but if,* **dum** *if only*
Syntactic function	**adverbial**

Depending on the speaker's intention, conditional clauses use the indicative or the subjunctive. The indicative is used if the statement is regarded as feasible (**realis**).

Sī pater cunīculum caedit, eum edimus. Nisi eum caedit, non edimus.
If the father kills the rabbit, we'll eat it. If he doesn't kill it, we won't eat it.

If the conditional clause contains an intellectual game; that is, if the speaker regards a condition and its consequence as realistic but not inevitable, then the **potentialis** (**present subjunctive** or **perfect subjunctive**) is used.

Sī pater cunīculum caedat, līberī flēbunt.
If the father kills the rabbit, the children will weep.

If the speaker expresses a condition that he knows will not become reality, the **irrealis** (**imperfect subjunctive** or **perfect subjunctive**) is used.

Sī pater cunīculum caederet, līberī flērent.
If the father were to kill the rabbit, the children would weep.

CONJUNCTIONS IN A CONDITIONAL CLAUSE			
nisi forte	*unless, if...not*	**sīn, sīn autem**	*but if*
sīve – sīve	*on the one hand, but if, if ... or if*	**seu – seu**	*on the one hand, but if, if...or if*
nōn – nisi	*only*	**nihil – nisi**	*nothing but, only*
nēmō – nisi	*only*	**nihil aliud – nisi**	*only*

The conjunctions **dum, modo**, and **dummodo** *if only* introduce a wish, are negated with **nē**, and are always used with the subjunctive.

Flēverint, dum cunīculum caedere possim.
Let them go ahead and cry, if I can only kill the rabbit.

Some conjunctions containing **sī** are used to express a mere assumption. The conjunctions **quasi, tamquam (sī), velut sī** *as if* are always used with the subjunctive (**irrealis**).

Concessive Clauses

Concessive clauses name a **counterargument** to the content of the superordinate clause.

Mood	Indicative or subjunctive
Translation	The subjunctive is not translated.
Negation	**nōn**
Introduced by	**quamquam, etsī, cum** *although*, etc.
Syntactic function	**adverbial**

Whether the subjunctive or the indicative is used in concessive clauses depends on the introductory conjunction. The table below indicates which concessive clauses are used with the indicative and which are used with the subjunctive.

CONCESSIVE CONJUNCTIONS WITH THE INDICATIVE			
quamquam	*although*	**tametsī**	*even if, even though*
etsī	*even if, even though*	**etiamsī**	*even if, even though*
CONCESSIVE CONJUNCTIONS WITH THE SUBJUNCTIVE			
cum (**cum concessīvum**)	*although*	**quamvīs**	*although, however much*
ut (**ut concessīvum**)	*assuming that*	**licet**	*may ... be*

Examples:

Tamen cuniculus caesus est, quamquam līberī cum eō lūdēbant.
Nonetheless the rabbit was killed, although the children played with it.

Cunīculum caedam, cum līberī eum ament.
I will kill the rabbit, even though the children love it.

Causal Clauses

Causal (**causa** *reason, cause*) dependent clauses give the **reason** for the action of the superordinate clause.

Mood	indicative or subjunctive
Translation	The subjunctive is not translated
Negation	**nōn**
Introduced by	**cum, quia, quod** *because, since*
Syntactic function	**adverbial**

Causal clauses are in the **indicative** when they name an **actual cause**. If the causal independent clause designates an **imaginary cause**, the **subjunctive** is used. **Different conjunctions** are used for both moods in Latin.

CONJUNCTIONS WITH THE INDICATIVE			
quod	*because, since*	**quoniam**	*since*
quia	*because, since*		
CONJUNCTIONS WITH THE SUBJUNCTIVE			
cum	*because, since*	**quippe cum**	*since*
(cum causāle)			
praesertim cum	*especially as*		

Pater tristis est, cum cunīculum cecīderit.
The father is (definitely) sad because he killed the rabbit.

Tristis sum, quia cunīculus caesus est.
I am sad because the rabbit was killed.

Adversative Clauses

Adversative clauses (**adversārī** to oppose) express a contrast to the statement of the superordinate clause.

Mood	subjunctive
Translation	The subjunctive is not translated.
Negation	**nōn**
Introduced by	**cum** while; whereas **(cum adversātīvum)**
Syntactic function	**adverbial**

Example:

Pater cunīculum cecīdit, cum māter eum vīvere volūerit.
The father killed the rabbit, while the mother wanted it to live.

Final (Purposive) Clauses

Final clauses (**finālis** having to do with purpose) denote an **intention** or a **desire**.

Mood	subjunctive
Translation	The subjunctive is usually not translated, depending on context.
Negation	**nē**
Dependent on	verbs of demanding, requesting, wishing, and caring such as **postulāre** to demand, **imperāre** to command, **optāre** to wish, and **cūrāre** to care or verbs of fearing such as **timēre** or **metuere** to fear
Introduced by	**ut** that or **nē** that ... not
Syntactic function	**adverbial**

Examples:

Māter imperat, nē cunīculus caedātur.
The mother orders that the rabbit not be killed.

Rogō, ut domum veniās.
I ask that you come home.

Id eō cōnsiliō fēcī, ut amīcōs delectārem.
I did this in order to please my friends.

After verbs of fearing, such as **timēre, metuere, verērī** *to fear* or after **perīculum est** *there is a danger*, **nē** is used in the meaning of **ut**. The negation is **nē nōn**.

Vereor, nē cunīculus (nōn) caedātur.
I fear that the rabbit will (not) be killed.

Consecutive Clauses

Consecutive clauses (**cōnsequī** *to follow, achieve*) denote an actual or possible **consequence**.

Mood	subjunctive
Translation	The subjunctive is not translated.
Negation	**nōn, nēmō, nihil**, etc.
Dependent on	impersonal expressions of happening, such as **fit** *it happens,* **est** *it is the case,* **mōs est** *it is customary,* demonstratives such as **ita** *so,* **adeō** *so far, so much,* etc., **tantus** *so large*
Introduced by	**ut** *(so) that,* **ut nōn** *(so) that ... not,* **ut nēmō** *that no one,* etc.
Syntactic function	**adverbial**

Examples:

Cōnsuētūdō est, ut cunīculī (nōn) caedantur.
It is customary that rabbits are (not) killed.

Nēmō tam stultus est, ut suā sponte cunīculum caedat, quem amat.
No one is so stupid that he voluntarily kills a rabbit that he loves.

Subjunctive Clauses with quīn

Subjunctive clauses with **quīn** *that* follow negated principal clauses.

Mood	subjunctive
Translation	The subjunctive is not translated.
Negation	**nōn**
Dependent on	negated expressions of doubting, such as **dubitāre** *to doubt,* verbs of preventing and resisting, such as **recūsāre** *to decline, refuse* and **impedīre** *to hinder,* or after other negated verbs
Introduced by	**quīn** *that,* **quīn nōn** *that ... not*
Syntactic function	**adverbial**

Nōn dubitō, quīn amīcus certus es.
I don't doubt that you are a reliable friend.

Relative Clauses

Mood	subjunctive or indicative
Translation	The subjunctive may be translated or not, depending on context.
Negation	**nōn**
Introduced by	relative pronouns such as **quī** *which* or relative adverbs such as **ubī** *where* or **quandō** *when*
Syntactic function	**attribute**

Indicative relative clauses contain a **purely objective attributive modifier** or follow generalizing relative pronouns such as **quisquis** *whoever* or **ubicumque** *wherever.*

Tuī reminīscor, ubicumque es.
I think of you wherever you are.

Relative clauses are in the **subjunctive** if they have a **consecutive, final, causal, concessive,** or **adversative general theme.**

Pater cunīculum cecīdit, quem ederent. *The father killed the rabbit, which they wanted to eat.*	The relative clause contains the **goal** with which the killing is connected and thus has a **secondary final (purposive) meaning.** The relative clause can also be regarded as **causal** or **consecutive**, because it mentions the reason for or consequence of the killing.
Pater cunīculum cecīdit, quem nōn ederent. *The father killed the rabbit, which they did not want to eat.*	The relative clause contains a **secondary concessive meaning:** The father killed the rabbit **although** they were not planning to eat it.

 You can detect the secondary meaning of a relative clause by inserting a conjunction, such as *because, although*, etc., in place of the relative pronoun, as a test.

The father killed the rabbit because they wanted to eat it.
= **secondary causal meaning**

In addition, relative clauses are in the **subjunctive** if they depend on an **indefinite antecedent** in the principal clause and have an **explanatory (explicative) meaning.**

Sunt, quī cunīculōs nōn caedant.
There are people who do not kill rabbits.

Additional expressions that are followed by relative clauses in the subjunctive are:

nēmō est, quī	*there is no one who*	**(nōn) est, quod**	*there is a (no) reason that/for*
nēmō est, quīn	*there is no one who ... not*	**nōn habeō, quod**	*I have no reason for*

One special feature is that relative clauses can also be **restricted** by a dependent clause, a participial construction, or a coherent construction. This means that they are subordinated to a dependent clause and the relative pronoun conforms to the construction in question.

Cunĭculus, quĭ quantī aestimāveris sciō, mortuus est.
The rabbit that I know you loved so much is dead.

The relative pronoun can, for example, also be an **accusative subject** in an AcI. The relative clause that is restricted by the AcI must then be translated freely, to link it with the superordinate clause.

Cunĭculum doleō, quem ā patre caesum esse sciō.
I mourn the rabbit, which I know to have been killed/was killed by the father.

If a form of **quī, quae, quod** or of another relative pronoun stands at the **beginning of a principal clause**, it is a **relative linkage.** This is true if the relative pronoun refers to a word in the preceding sentence. In such a case, it is translated as a **demonstrative** or **personal pronoun.**

Cunĭculus caesus est. Quī summā pulchritūdine erat.
The rabbit was killed. It was of extraordinary beauty.

Indirect Discourse

When a speaker reproduces statements made by someone else, he expresses them in indirect discourse (**ōrātiō oblīqua**). Latin has various ways of rendering indirect discourse, and we present them in the material below.

Declarative sentences in indirect discourse depend on **verba dīcendī** and are in **AcI**.

Hic narrāvit patrem cunīculum cecīdisse.
This man said (that) the father killed the rabbit.

In indirect discourse, it is common for several **AcI to appear in a series** without any need for a finite verb to be present. The finite verb is mentioned only at the beginning of the portion in indirect discourse.

Pater narrāvit sē cunīculum cecīdisse; puerum flēvisse, mātrem librum lēgisse; sē ipsum cunīculum ēdisse.
The father said he had killed the rabbit; the son cried, the mother read a book; he himself ate the rabbit.

In indirect discourse, imperative clauses are in the subjunctive mood. They are negated with **nē**.

Līberī ā patre postulāvērunt: Nē cunīculum cecīderit, nē eum ēderit, cum tristēs essent.
The children demanded of the father: He must not kill the rabbit, must not eat it, or else they would be sad.

Similarly, dependent clauses in indirect discourse—like the dependent clause introduced by **cum** in the example above—are formed with the **subjunctive**.

▶ To learn about questions in indirect discourse, see the section on **indirect interrogative sentences**.

Glossary

Ablative

The ablative is the so-called sixth case in Latin and has no equivalent in English. It can perform various functions and must then be translated in different ways. The ablative of separation (**ablativus separativus)** is the true ablative. It designates the point at which a movement originates and is used with verbs meaning *to deprive* and *to lack*. A subcategory of the **separative** is the ablative of comparison (**ablativus comparationis**). To denote motion from some point, the ablative is used with the proper names of cities, villages, and small islands. It answers the question *from where?* As an instrumental, the ablative also answers the questions *by/with/what?*

Ablative absolute/abl. abs.

Typical Latin participial construction, in which the antecedent and (usually) a participle are in the ablative case.

Absolute tense

The tense in the dependent clause is not dependent on the verb of the superordinate clause.

Accusative

The accusative can designate a person or thing that is the object of an action (*whom? what?*), an expanse of space or time (answering the questions *how wide? how far? how long? how old? how tall? how deep?*), or the goal of a movement (*to what place?*). There are verbs that require an accusative object because of their meaning. In a sentence, the accusative performs the

syntactic function of an object, but it can also occur as a predicate nominative or an adverbial modifier.

AcI/accusativus cum infinitivo (accusative with infinitive)

The AcI answers the question *whom or what?* In a sentence, it depends on a superordinate verb ("head verb," that is, a verb of feeling, speaking, expressing an opinion, etc.).

Adjective

Adjectives are words that describe the quality of a thing, a person, or a circumstance. They can modify nouns.

Adverb

Adverbs supplement the meaning of a verb (*ad + verbum*, "to" + "word"). More rarely, an adverb also serves to modify an adjective, a participle, or another adverb. Adverbs are classified as particles and can be neither declined nor conjugated.

Adverbial, adverbial modifier (adverbial phrase)

A type of adjunct or complement that is grammatically not essential to a sentence; it answers questions about the action of the verb (*how? where? when? why? with what? for what purpose?*).

Agreement

Agreement or concord refers to changes in form that indicate which word another word relates to. It affects case, number, and gender.

Glossary

Apposition (*apponere* to add to)
This is an element that is not mandatory in terms of content; it usually defines or modifies a noun. This construction is set off by commas.

Asyndeton
This stylistic means omits conjunctions between words, phrases, or clauses.

Attribute (*attribuere* to allocate to)
Sentence element that does not depend on the predicate, but on a noun, which it modifies. Adjectives, pronouns, quantifiers, and nominal forms of the verb can act as attributes. They answer the question *what kind of?* and agree in case, number, and gender with the word they modify.

Case
The case indicates the role a word plays within a sentence. It determines its syntactic function.

Casus obliqui/oblique cases
All cases except the nominative or the vocative are unable to appear without a sentence element in the nominative. They must "lean against" another element in the sentence and thus are "oblique."

Casus recti
The nominative and the vocative are "straight cases" (*casus recti*). The other cases cannot occur without a sentence element in the nominative case.

Coherent constructions
If, in addition to the nominal form of the verb, a person or thing performing an action is named, and the verbal information refers to it, we speak of "coherent constructions." These constructions can perform the function of dependent clauses, and sometimes they are translated as such. Their special feature is that they consist of only a few words, which the speaker of Latin can use to great advantage.

Comparative
Second degree of comparison of an adjective or adverb.

Comparative sentence
Such sentences contain a comparison.

Comparison
The making of comparisons between two or more beings or objects by using different forms or "degrees" (positive, comparative, superlative) of adjectives or adverbs.

Conjugation
Every verb can be assigned to one of five conjugations (conjugation classes), depending on the ending of the present-tense stem. The present stem is obtained by removing the infinitive ending.

Conjugations/conjugational classes
a-conjugation (1st conjugation), *lauda-re*; e-conjugation (2nd conjugation), *mone-re*; I-conjugation (4th conjugation), *audi-re*; consonant conjugation (3rd conjugation), *ag-ere*; mixed conjugation (also: consonant conjugation with i-enhancement), *cap-ere*.

Conjunction
Part of speech that connects words, phrases, or clauses.

Correlative pronouns
Indicate a mutual relationship: *talis – qualis,*
etc.

Dative
The dative denotes the person or thing
affected by the action of the verb (*to whom/
what?*), or the person on whose behalf an
action occurs (*for whom/what?*), or the
purpose of an action (*for what purpose?*). It
performs the function of an object in the
sentence, but like the accusative, it can also
be an adverbial or a predicate nominative.
Declension (*declinare* to bend, decline)
All nouns, adjectives, and participles can be
declined. The declensional ending reflects
the case and number (often the **gender** as
well). With adjectives and participles, the
gender is also taken into account.

"Defective" verbs (*verba defectiva*)
These verbs are called "defective" (*deficere*
to lack) because they lack some forms.

Demonstrative pronouns
Identify a noun or pronoun.

Deponent verbs (*deponere* to put down)
These verbs have only passive forms but
have active-voice meaning. They occur in
all conjugations and are conjugated like the
passive voice of other verbs in their group.
In the dictionary, they are listed under
the first person singular present passive
indicative.

Gender
Grammatical genders: masculine (m.), feminine (f.), neuter (n.).

Genitive
This case indicates that a person or
thing belongs to another person or thing
(*whose?*). As genitives qualitatis, it modifies
a noun (*what kind of?*). It usually performs
the syntactic function of a noun attribute,
and sometimes that of a predicate nominative. It can also qualify the meaning of
verbs, and then it assumes the function of
an object or an adverbial.

Genus verbi
Tells whether an action occurs in the active
or is performed in the passive.

Gerund
A verbal noun; as such, it can be declined in
the singular.

Gerundive
English has no exact equivalent; it sometimes uses a passive infinitive to achieve
the same effect. Sometimes the gerundive
can be translated with an adjective: *a rabbit
that is to be loved = a lovable rabbit.* The
Latin gerundive is defined as a verbal
adjective.

Head verb
Superordinate verb on which the AcI
depends.

Hortative (*hortari* to exhort, urge)
The hortative is used to express requests or
exhortations addressed to the first person
plural. (*Let's go home!*)

Hyperbaton
Figure of speech involving deliberate separation of words that go together; its purpose

is to lend emphasis or achieve a certain effect.

Hypotaxis (complex sentence)
Construction that consists not only of independent main clauses, but also of dependent, subordinate clauses. They are called dependent because they cannot stand alone but must be part of a complex sentence, which consists of at least one principal clause and any number of subordinate clauses.

Imperative (First, Second) (*imperare* to command)
Latin has two types of imperatives. The more common **first imperative** is used for requests, commands, or suggestions. It directly addresses the second person singular or plural, but without using a personal pronoun (*veni!* or *venite!* Come on!). A wish or command that is to be carried out in the near or distant future is expressed by using the **second imperative**. It is less common than the first imperative, and it is used primarily for general regulations, laws, and instructions. It addresses the second or third person singular or plural.

Indefinite pronouns
They replace nouns but without being specific or exact.

Indicative
The indicative is one of the three moods of the verb (along with the subjunctive and the imperative). If the speaker believes that what he/she says is factual, the verb form is in the indicative.

Inflection (*flectere* to bend)
The grammatical function of a word within a sentence is marked in several ways, one of which is its inflection (conjugation for verbs, declension for nouns, adjectives, and pronouns).

Instrumental
A historic proto-Indo-European grammatical case that merged with the Latin ablative. It answers the question *with what?* or *by what means?*

Interjection
A word added to express emotion.

Interrogative pronouns
Used in order to ask a question.

Intransitive verbs
Unlike transitive verbs, intransitive verbs cannot take an accusative object, and they form an impersonal passive.

Irrealis of the past
This irrealis mood indicates that a situation or action did not occur in the past.

Irrealis of the present
This irrealis mood expresses a situation or action that will not occur.

Jussive (*iubere* to order, assign)
The jussive is used to express commands addressed to the second and third persons singular and plural in the present subjunctive. (*Let him call the father!*)

Kind of action
Distinction between active and passive.

Locative
One of the classic Indo-European cases, which merged in part with the ablative. It answers the question *where?*

Mood (*modus, -i* m. manner, mode)
Describes the relationship of the statement to reality:
Indicative (mood of reality)
Subjunctive (mood of perception)
Imperative (command form)

NcI/nominativus cum infinitivo (nominative with infinitive)
With some transitive verbs, when the passive voice is formed, an infinitive construction with a nominative takes the place of the AcI. The nominative is simultaneously the subject of the superordinate clause.

Nominal form of the verb
The so-called nominal forms of verbs are created by substantivizing verbs. These forms include verbal nouns and verbal adjectives, which have properties of a noun and a verb. They are made up of verbs but are declined like nouns and treated as nominal elements of a sentence.

Nominals (*nomen, -inis* m. name)
All nominals can be declined. They include nouns (substantives), adjectives, pronouns, and numerals (quantifiers).

Nominative
Case that answers the question *who or what?* The nominative, as casus rectus,

is distinguished from the genitive, dative, accusative, and ablative, because it is the only case that can appear alone (without another case) in a sentence.

Numerals (quantifiers)
Cardinal numerals (cardinalia) *one, two, three ...*
Ordinal numerals (ordinalia) *first, second, third ...*
Distributives (distributive) *one each, two each, three each ...*
Multiplicatives (multiplicativa) *once, twice, thrice/three times ...*

Number (*numerus, -i* m. number)
There are two grammatical numbers, **singular** and **plural**. Some nouns, because of their meaning, occur only in the singular (singularia tantum) or only in the plural (pluralia tantum).

Object (complement)
The person or thing affected by the action described in the predicate.

Optative (*optare* to wish)
A mood of the verb that denotes wishes or possibilities.

Parataxis
Construction in which independent clauses are juxtaposed without conjunctions. A parataxis consists of two or more principal clauses.

Participal stem/supine stem
Third principal part, used to form the perfect, pluperfect, and future II in the passive, as well as the perfect passive participle

(PPP), future active participle (FAP), perfect passive infinitive and future active infinitive, as well as the supines I and II (hence the name "supine stem").

Participium coniunctum/PC (*coniunctum* joined, linked)
All participles can be used as participium coniunctum. The special feature of the PC is that the antecedent alone (without the participle) performs a syntactic function in the sentence; that is, it can be the subject, object, etc. If the participle were to be deleted, the sentence still would be grammatically complete. The participle, as an attribute, describes or modifies the integrated noun and thus is directly linked with the sentence (*coniunctum*).

Participle
Participles (like the gerund and the gerundive) are nominal forms of the verb. They are declined, have forms in all genders, and as verbal adjectives must agree in case, number, and gender with their antecedent.

Particles (*particula, -ae* f. small part)
Words that cannot be inflected: adverbs, prepositions, conjunctions and subjunctions, interjections, modal particles (filler words), and negative particles (such as "not").

Perfect stem
Second principal part; used for all forms of the perfect tense, including the perfect active infinitive, all forms of the pluperfect, and all forms of the future II in the active voice.

Personal pronouns
Pronouns that take the place of proper or common nouns.

Pluralia tantum
Nouns that, because of their meaning, occur only in the plural.

Positive
First degree of comparison of an adjective or adverb.

Possessive pronouns
Take the place of possessive adjectives, nouns, or noun phrases.

Potentialis of the past (*potestas* possibility)
Expresses a possibility in the past.

Potentialis of the present (*potestas* possibility)
Expresses an assumption or supposition.

Predicate
The predicate is the central unit of a sentence. It consists of at least one finite verb. It tells which action is performed at a certain time.

Predicate nominative/nominal
The predicate nominative is a part of the predicate. It can be a noun in the nominative case, a pronoun, an adjective, an adverb, or an infinitive. It occurs with a form of *esse* or another linking verb.

Predicative
The predicative combines the syntactic functions of an adverb and an attribute. Nouns, adjectives, and participles can be

predicatives. A predicative is used to specify the verbal action or describe it in greater detail, along with the antecedent, with which it agrees in case, number, and gender. *Cuniculus salvus viam transit.* The rabbit crossed the street unharmed. Here we are concerned with the moment at which the rabbit crosses the street. The rabbit's condition in the past and future is of no concern.

Predicative clause
Such clauses contain more information about the action of the predicate.

Prefix
Affixed before the stem of a word.

Prepositions (*praepositus* placed in front)
Classed as particles; cannot be inflected.

Present stem
First principal part, used in all forms of the present tense, including the infinitive, all forms of the imperfect, and all forms of the future I in the active and passive voices, as well as the present active participle (PAP), the gerund and gerundive, and the imperative.

Principal parts
Verb forms used to form the tenses. They include the present and perfect active forms in the first person singular indicative and, if one exists, the perfect passive participle of a verb. Example: facere – facio – feci – factum.

Pronominal adjectives
Certain adjectives are known as pronominal adjectives because their case endings in the genitive singular (-ius) and dative singular (-i) and their meaning indicate that they are closely related to pronouns. Examples: unus, -a, -um, solus, -a, -um, totus, -a, -um.

Pronouns
Take the place of nouns or noun phrases.

Reflexive pronouns
Indicate that the object is the same as the subject.

Relative clause
Such clauses contain more information about a noun, a thing, or a circumstance.

Relative pronouns
Refer to a previously mentioned noun and add more information about it.

Semantics
The study of meaning.

Semideponent verbs
Verbs that are similar to deponent verbs in that they are passive in form and active in meaning, but only in the present stem or the perfect stem.

Separative (*separare* to separate)
The ablative of separation, often known as the separative because of its Latin name, is the true ablative.

Singularia tantum
Nouns that, because of their meaning, occur only in the singular.

Glossary

Subject
Basic element of every sentence; essential to the predicate. It generally is in the nominative case.

Subjunctive
One of the three moods of the verb (along with the indicative and the imperative).
If a speaker believes his statement to be possible or irreal, or if he is expressing a wish, Latin uses the subjunctive mood of the verb form.

Suffix
Affix placed after the stem of a word.

Superlative
Third (and highest) degree of comparison of adjectives and adverbs.

Syntactic function
Tells which grammatical function a word performs within the sentence.

Syntax
Study of the rules for combining elements for grammatical sentences.

Temporal clause (*tempus, -oris* n. time)
Tells when an action is performed. Latin has six tenses: present, imperfect, future I and II, perfect, and pluperfect.

Transitive verbs
Verbs that, because of their valency, require an accusative object are called transitive verbs. They form a personal passive.

Valency
Refers to the number of sentence elements required by a verb. Most verbs require a subject and an object.

Verb
Verbs are the second large group (nouns being the first) of words that can be inflected. They are conjugated (*coniugare* to link). There are various conjugational classes.

Verba defectiva/defective verbs
These verbs are called "defective" (*deficere* to be lacking) because they lack certain forms.

Verbal adjectives/verbal nouns
By substantivizing verbs, we obtain verbal nouns and verbal adjectives, which have the properties of a noun and a verb. They are formed from verbs, but declined like nouns and treated as nominal elements of the sentence.

Vocative
Form of address (*vocare* to call, name)
This case is not listed in the tables of declensions, because its grammatical forms are identical to the nominative. Only words of the o-declension that end in -us and -ius have different forms.

Verb Tables

How to use the verb tables

The sequence of the tables of regular verbs in the respective verb conjugations is always the same: first the juxtaposition of the active and passive forms using the present stem, then the forms derived from the perfect stem or the participial stem, and finally the present and perfect forms of one of the deponent verbs in this conjugational class.

The table of principal parts of important verbs (page 236) is arranged by conjugational class and method of forming the perfect tense.

An alphabetical list of verbs is found on page 255.

Structure of the Conjugation Tables and Principal Parts

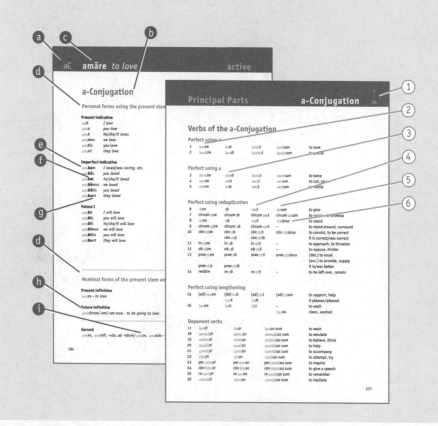

How to use the verb tables

(a) Abbreviation for the conjugational class: for example, **aC** = a-Conjugation, **aD** = deponent verb of the a-conjugation, **mC** = mixed conjugation; or for the irregular verbs, **iV**

(b) Conjugation (conjugational class)

(c) Example

(d) General arrangement: at the top, the personal forms, that is, those that name the person(s) performing the action; below, the nominal forms, that is, forms that are not based on the person (infinitive, participles, gerunds, gerundives)

(e) Stem: present, perfect, and participal stems (for the PPP, the root): marked in blue

(f) Indicators of tense and mood: emphasized in boldface. For the compound passive forms and the forms of esse, however, the tense and mood indicators are not in boldface, for reasons of clarity

(g) Personal ending: in roman type

(h) The future participle and the future infinitive, derived from this participle, are derived from the participial stem, but because of their active meaning, they are always placed with the forms using the present stem

(i) Two alternatively used accusative forms of the gerund: ad amandum *or* amāre

(1) Indication of the number of principal parts on this page

(2) Present infinitive

(3) 1st person singular of the present active indicative

(4) 1st person singular of the perfect active indicative

(5) Neuter of the perfect passive participle (PPP)

(6) If the PPP is not in common use, the future participle

a-Conjugation

Personal forms using the present stem

Present indicative
amō	*I love*
amās	*you love*
amat	*he/she/it loves*
amāmus	*we love*
amātis	you love
amant	*they love*

Imperfect indicative
amābam	*I loved/was loving,* etc.
amābās	*you loved*
amābat	*he/she/it loved*
amābāmus	*we loved*
amābātis	*you loved*
amābant	*they loved*

Future I
amābō	*I will love*
amābis	*you will love*
amābit	*he/she/it will love*
amābimus	*we will love*
amābitis	*you will love*
amābunt	*they will love*

Present subjunctive
(Note that there is no single general rendering for Latin subjunctives. Only one possibility is given here.)
amem	*I may love,* etc.
amēs	*you may love*
amet	*he/she/it may love*
amēmus	*we may love*
amētis	*you may love*
ament	*they may love*

Imperfect subjunctive
amārem	*I might love,* etc.
amārēs	*you might love*
amāret	*he/she/it might love*
amārēmus	*we might love*
amārētis	*you might love*
amārent	*they might love*

Imperative
amā	*love!*
amāte	*love!*

Future imperative
amātō	*you shall love!*
amātō	*he/she/it shall love!*
amātōte	*you shall love!*
amantō	*they shall love!*

Nominal forms of the present and participial stems

Present infinitive
amāre – *to love*

Future infinitive
amātūrum/-am/-um esse – *to be going to love*

Present participle
amāns, amantis – *loving; one who loves*

Future participle
amātūrus/-a/-um – *one who will love*

Gerund
amāre, amandī, -ndo, ad -ndum/amāre, amando – *loving, of loving, to/for loving,* etc.

a-Conjugation

Personal forms using the present stem

Present indicative

amor	*I am loved*
amāris	*you are loved*
amātur	*he/she/it is loved*
amāmur	*we are loved*
amāminī	*you are loved*
amantur	*they are loved*

Imperfect indicative

amā**bar**	*I was loved*
amā**bā**ris	*you were loved*
amā**bā**tur	*he/she/it was loved*
amā**bā**mur	*we were loved*
amā**bā**minī	*you were loved*
amā**ba**ntur	*they were loved*

Future I

amā**bor**	*I will be loved*
amā**be**ris	*you will be loved*
amā**bi**tur	*he/she/it will be loved*
amā**bi**mur	*we will be loved*
amā**bi**minī	*you will be loved*
amā**bu**ntur	*they will be loved*

Present subjunctive

(Note that there is no single general rendering for Latin subjunctives. Only one possibility is given here.)

amer	*I may be loved, etc.*
am**ē**ris	*you may be loved*
am**ē**tur	*he/she/it may be loved*
am**ē**mur	*we may be loved*
am**ē**minī	*you may be loved*
amentur	*they may be loved*

Imperfect subjunctive

amā**rer**	*I would be loved*
amā**rē**ris	*you would be loved*
amā**rē**tur	*he/she/it would be loved*
amā**rē**mur	*we would be loved*
amā**rē**minī	*you would be loved*
amā**re**ntur	*they would be loved*

Imperative

–

Future imperative

–

Nominal forms of the present and participial stems

Present infinitive
amā**rī** –to be loved

Future infinitive
amā**t**um **īrī** – *to be going to be loved*

Present participle
–

Future participle
–

Gerundive
ama**ndus**/-a/-um – *lovable; one who must be loved*

a-Conjugation

Personal forms using the perfect stem

Perfect indicative

amāvī	*I loved/have loved, etc.*
amāvistī	*you loved*
amāvit	*he/she/it loved*
amāvimus	*we loved*
amāvistis	*you loved*
amāvērunt	*they loved*

Pluperfect indicative

amāveram	*I had loved*
amāverās	*you had loved*
amāverat	*he/she/it had loved*
amāverāmus	*we had loved*
amāverātis	*you had loved*
amāverant	*they had loved*

Future II

amāverō	*I will have loved*
amāveris	*you will have loved*
amāverit	*he/she/it will have loved*
amāverimus	*we will have loved*
amāveritis	*you will have loved*
amāverint	*they will have loved*

Perfect subjunctive

(Note that there is no single general rendering for Latin subjunctives. Only one possibility is given here.)

amāverim	*I may have loved*
amāveris	*you may have loved*
amāverit	*he/she/it may have loved*
amāverimus	*we may have loved*
amāveritis	*you may have loved*
amāverint	*they may have loved*

Pluperfect subjunctive

amāvissem	*I might have loved*
amāvissēs	*you might have loved*
amāvisset	*he/she/it might have loved*
amāvissēmus	*we might have loved*
amāvissētis	*you might have loved*
amāvissent	*they might have loved*

Nominal forms of the perfect stem

Perfect active infinitive

amāvisse – *to have loved*

Perfect active participle

–

a-Conjugation

Personal forms using the participial stem

Perfect indicative

amātus/-a/-um sum   *I have been loved*
amātus/-a/-um es   *you have been loved*
amātus/-a/-um est   *he/she/it has been loved*
amātī/-ae/-a sumus   *we have been loved*
amātī/-ae/-a estis   *you have been loved*
amātī/-ae/-a sunt   *they have been loved*

Pluperfect indicative

amātus/-a/-um eram   *I had been loved*
amātus/-a/-um erās   *you had been loved*
amātus/-a/-um erat   *he/she/it had been loved*
amātī/-ae/-a erāmus   *we had been loved*
amātī/-ae/-a erātis   *you had been loved*
amātī/-ae/-a erant   *they had been loved*

Future II

amātus/-a/-um erō   *I will have been loved*
amātus/-a/-um eris   *you will have been loved*
amātus/-a/-um erit   *he/she/it will have been loved*
amātī/-ae/-a erimus   *we will have been loved*
amātī/-ae/-a eritis   *you will have been loved*
amātī/-ae/-a erunt   *they will have been loved*

Perfect subjunctive
(Note that there is no single general
rendering for Latin subjunctives.
Only one possibility is given here.)

amātus/-a/-um sim   *I may have been loved*
amātus/-a/-um sīs   *you may have been loved*
amātus/-a/-um sit   *he/she/it may have been loved*
amātī/-ae/-a sīmus   *we may have been loved*
amātī/-ae/-a sītis   *you may have been lovded*
amātī/-ae/-a sint   *they may have been loved*

Pluperfect subjunctive

amātus/-a/-um essem   *I might have been loved*
amātus/-a/-um essēs   *you might have been loved*
amātus/-a/-um esset   *he/she/it might have been loved*
amātī/-ae/-a essēmus   *we might have been loved*
amātī/-ae/-a essētis   *you might have been loved*
amātī/-ae/-a essent   *they might have been loved*

Nominal forms of the participial stem

Perfect passive infinitive
amātum/-am/-um esse –
to have been loved

Perfect passive participle
amātus/-a/-um – *one who has been loved*

Deponent Verbs of the a-Conjugation

Personal forms using the present stem

Present indicative
hortor	*I urge*
hortāris	*you urge*
hortātur	*he/she/it urges*
hortāmur	*we urge*
hortāminī	*you urge*
hortantur	*they urge*

Imperfect indicative
hortā**bar**	*I urged, was urging,* etc.
hortā**bā**ris	*you urged*
hortā**bā**tur	*he urged*
hortā**bā**mur	*we urged*
hortā**bā**minī	*you urged*
hortā**ban**tur	*they urged*

Future I
hortā**bor**	*I will urge*
hortā**ber**is	*you will urge*
hortā**bit**ur	*he will urge*
hortā**bim**ur	*we will urge*
hortā**bim**inī	*you will urge*
hortā**bun**tur	*they will urge*

Present subjunctive
(Note that there is no single general rendering for Latin subjunctives. Only one possibility is given here.)
hort**ēr**	*I may urge,* etc.
hort**ēr**is	*you may urge*
hort**ē**tur	*he may urge*
hort**ē**mur	*we may urge*
hort**ē**minī	*you may urge*
hortentur	*they may jurge*

Imperfect subjunctive
hortā**rer**	*I might urge,* etc.
hortā**rē**ris	*you might urge*
hortā**rē**tur	*he might urge*
hortā**rē**mur	*we might urge*
hortā**rē**minī	*you might urge*
hortā**ren**tur	*they might urge*

Imperative
hortāre	*urge!*
hortāminī	*urge!*

Future imperative
hortātor	*you shall urge!*
hortātor	*he/she/it shall urge!*
–	
hortāntor	*they shall urge!*

Nominal forms of the present and participial stems

Present infinitive
hortārī – *to urge*

Present participle
hortāns, hortantis – *urging; one who urges*

Future infinitive
hortāt**ū**rum/-am/-um esse – *to be going to urge*

Future participle
hortāt**ū**rus/-a/-um – *one who will urge*

Gerund and Gerundive
hortārī, hortandī – *(the) urging,* etc.; hortandus/-a/-um – *one who is urged/must be urged*

Deponent Verbs of the a-Conjugation

Personal forms using the participial stem

Perfect indicative
hortātus/-a/-um sum   *I urged/have urged*
hortātus/-a/-um es   *you urged*
hortātus/-a/-um est   *he/she/it urged*
hortātī/-ae/-a sumus   *we urged*
hortātī/-ae/-a estis   *you urged*
hortātī/-ae/-a sunt   *they urged*

Pluperfect indicative
hortātus/-a/-um eram   *I had urged*
hortātus/-a/-um erās   *you had urged*
hortātus/-a/-um erat   *he/she/it had urged*
hortātī/-ae/-a erāmus *we had urged*
hortātī/-ae/-a erātis *you had urged*
hortātī/-ae/-a erant   *they had urged*

Future II
hortātus/-a/-um erō   *I will have urged*
hortātus/-a/-um eris   *you will have urged*
hortātus/-a/-um erit   *he/she/it will have urged*
hortātī/-ae/-a erimus *we will have urged*
hortātī/-ae/-a eritis *you will have urged*
hortātī/-ae/-a erunt   *they will have urged*

Perfect subjunctive
(Note that there is no single general
rendering for Latin subjunctives.
Only one possibility is given here.)
hortātus/-a/-um sim   *I may have urged*
hortātus/-a/-um sīs   *you may have urged*
hortātus/-a/-um sit   *he/she/it may have urged*
hortātī/-ae/-a sīmus   *we may have urged*
hortātī/-ae/-a sītis   *you may have urged*
hortātī/-ae/-a sint   *they may have urged*

Pluperfect subjunctive
hortātus/-a/-um essem *I might have urged*
hortātus/-a/-um essēs *you might have urged*
hortātus/-a/-um esset *he/she/it might have urged*
hortātī/-ae/-a essēmus *we might have urged*
hortātī/-ae/-a essētis *you might have urged*
hortātī/-ae/-a essent *they might have urged*

Nominal forms of the participial stem

Perfect infinitive
hortātum/-am/-um esse – *to have urged*

Perfect Participle
hortātus/-a/-um – *one who has urged*

e-Conjugation

Personal forms using the present stem

Present indicative

moneō	*I warn*
monēs	*you warn*
monet	*he/she/it warns*
monēmus	*we warn*
monētis	*you warn*
monent	*they warn*

Imperfect indicative

monēbam	*I warned/was warning*
monēbās	*you warned*
monēbat	*he/she/it warned*
monēbāmus	*we warned*
monēbātis	*you warned*
monēbant	*they warned*

Future I

monēbō	*I will warn*
monēbis	*you will warn*
monēbit	*he/she/it will warn*
monēbimus	*we will warn*
monēbitis	*you will warn*
monēbunt	*they will warn*

Present subjunctive

(Note that there is no single general rendering for Latin subjunctives. Only one possibility is given here.)

moneam	*I may warn*
moneās	*you may warn*
moneat	*he/she/it may warn*
moneāmus	*we may warn*
moneātis	*you may warn*
moneant	*they may warn*

Imperfect subjunctive

monērem	*I might warn*
monērēs	*you might warn*
monēret	*he/she/it might warn*
monērēmus	*we might warn*
monērētis	*you might warn*
monērent	*they might warn*

Imperative

monē	*warn!*
monēte	*warn!*

Future imperative

monētō	*you shall warn!*
monētō	*he/she/it shall warn!*
monētōte	*you shall warn!*
monentō	*they shall warn!*

Nominal forms of the present and participial stems

Present infinitive

monēre – *to warn*

Future infinitive

monitūrum/-am/-um esse – *to be going to warn*

Present participle

monēns, monentis – *warning; one who warns*

Future participle

monitūrus/-a/-um – *one who will warn*

Gerund

monēre, monendī, -ndo, ad -ndum/monēre, monendo – *(the) warning, of (the) warning,* etc.

e-Conjugation

Personal forms using the present stem

Present indicative

moneor	*I am warned*
monēris	*you are warned*
monētur	*he/she/it is warned*
monēmur	*we are warned*
monēminī	*you are warned*
monentur	*they are warned*

Imperfect indicative

monēbar	*I was warned, was being warned, etc.*
monēbāris	*you were warned*
monēbātur	*he/she/it was warned*
monēbāmur	*we were warned*
monēbāminī	*you were warned*
monēbantur	*they were warned*

Future I

monēbor	*I will be warned*
monēberis	*you will be warned*
monēbitur	*he/she/it will be warned*
monēbimur	*we will be warned*
monēbiminī	*you will be warned*
monēbuntur	*they will be warned*

Present subjunctive

(Note that there is no single general rendering for Latin subjunctives. Only one possibility is given here.)

monear	*I may be warned*
moneāris	*you may be warned*
moneātur	*he/she/it may be warned*
moneāmur	*we may be warned*
moneāminī	*you may be warned*
moneantur	*they may be warned*

Imperfect subjunctive

monērer	*I might be warned*
monērēris	*you might be warned*
monērētur	*he/she/it might be warned*
monērēmur	*we might be warned*
monērēminī	*you might be warned*
monērentur	*they might be warned*

Imperative

–

Future imperative

–

Nominal forms of the present and participial stems

Present infinitive

monērī – *to be warned*

Future infinitive

monitum īrī – *to be going to be warned*

Present participle

–

Future participle

–

Gerundive

monendus/-a/-um – *one who is being warned/must be warned*

e-Conjugation

Personal forms using the perfect stem

Perfect indicative

monuī	*I warned, have warned, etc.*
monuistī	*you warned*
monuit	*he/she/it warned*
monuimus	*we warned*
monuistis	*you warned*
monuērunt	*they warned*

Pluperfect indicative

monueram	*I had warned*
monuerās	*you had warned*
monuerat	*he/she/it had warned*
monuerāmus	*we had warned*
monuerātis	*you had warned*
monuerant	*they had warned*

Future II

monuerō	*I will have warned*
monueris	*you will have warned*
monuerit	*he/she/it will have warned*
monuerimus	*we will have warned*
monueritis	*you will have warned*
monuerint	*they will have warned*

Perfect subjunctive

(Note that there is no single general rendering for Latin subjunctives. Only one possibility is given here.)

monuerim	*I may have warned*
monueris	*you may have warned*
monuerit	*he/she/it may have warned*
monuerimus	*we may have warned*
monueritis	*you may have warned*
monuerint	*they may have warned*

Pluperfect subjunctive

monuissem	*I might have warned*
monuissēs	*you might have warned*
monuisset	*he/she/it might have warned*
monuissēmus	*we might have warned*
monuissētis	*you might have warned*
monuissent	*they might have warned*

Nominal forms of the perfect stem

Perfect active infinitive
monuisse – *to have warned*

Perfect active participle
–

e-Conjugation

Personal forms using the participial stem

Perfect indicative

monitus/-a/-um sum	*I have been warned*
monitus/-a/-um es	*you have been warned*
monitus/-a/-um est	*he/she/it has been warned*
monitī/-ae/-a sumus	*we have been warned*
monitī/-ae/-a estis	*you have been warned*
monitī/-ae/-a sunt	*they have been warned*

Pluperfect indicative

monitus/-a/-um eram	*I had been warned*
monitus/-a/-um erās	*you had been warned*
monitus/-a/-um erat	*he/she/it had been warned*
monitī/-ae/-a erāmus	*we had been warned*
monitī/-ae/-a erātis	*you had been warned*
monitī/-ae/-a erant	*they had been warned*

Future II

monitus/-a/-um erō	*I will have been warned*
monitus/-a/-um eris	*you will have been warned*
monitus/-a/-um erit	*he/she/it will have been warned*
monitī/-ae/-a erimus	*we will have been warned*
monitī/-ae/-a eritis	*you will have been warned*
monitī/-ae/-a erunt	*they will have been warned*

Perfect subjunctive

(Note that there is no single general rendering for Latin subjunctives. Only one possibility is given here.)

monitus/-a/-um sim	*I may have been warned*
monitus/-a/-um sīs	*you may have been warned*
monitus/-a/-um sit	*he/she/it may have been warned*
monitī/-ae/-a sīmus	*we may have been warned*
monitī/-ae/-a sītis	*you may have been warned*
monitī/-ae/-a sint	*they may have been warned*

Pluperfect subjunctive

monitus/-a/-um essem	*I might have been warned*
monitus/-a/-um essēs	*you might have been warned*
monitus/-a/-um esset	*he/she/it might have been warned*
monitī/-ae/-a essēmus	*we might have been warned*
monitī/-ae/-a essētis	*you might have been warned*
monitī/-ae/-a essent	*they might have been warned*

Nominal forms of the participial stem

Perfect passive infinitive

monitum/-am/-um esse – *to have been warned*

Perfect passive participle

monitus/-a/-um – *warned; one who has been warned*

Deponent Verbs of the e-Conjugation

Personal forms using the present stem

Present indicative
vereor	_I fear, am fearing, etc._
verēris	_you fear_
verētur	_he/she/it fears_
verēmur	_we fear_
verēminī	_you fear_
verentur	_they fear_

Imperfect indicative
verēbar	_I feared, am fearing, etc._
verēbāris	_you feared_
verēbātur	_he/she/it feared_
verēbāmur	_we feared_
verēbāminī	_you feared_
verēbantur	_they feared_

Future I
verēbor	_I will fear_
verēberis	_you will fear_
verēbitur	_he/she/it will fear_
verēbimur	_we will fear_
verēbiminī	_you will fear_
verēbuntur	_they will fear_

Present subjunctive
(Note that there is no single general rendering for Latin subjunctives. Only one possibility is given here.)
verear	_I may fear_
vereāris	_you may fear_
vereātur	_he/she/it may fear_
vereāmur	_we may fear_
vereāminī	_you may fear_
vereantur	_they may fear_

Imperfect subjunctive
verērer	_I might fear_
verērēris	_you might fear_
verērētur	_he/she/it might fear_
verērēmur	_we might fear_
verērēminī	_you might fear_
verērentur	_they might fear_

Imperative
verēre	_fear!_
verēminī	_fear!_

Future imperative
verētor	_you shall fear!_
verētor	_he/she/it shall fear!_
–	
verēntor	_they shall fear!_

Nominal forms of the present and participial stems

Present infinitive
verērī – _to fear_

Future infinitive
veritūrum/-am /-um esse – _to be going to fear_

Present participle
verēns, verentis – _fearing; one who fears_

Future participle
veritūrus/-a/-um – _one who will fear_

Gerund and Gerundive
verērī, verendi , etc. – _(the) fearing, etc._; verendus/-a/-um – _one who is feared/must be feared_

Deponent Verbs of the e-Conjugation

Personal forms using the participial stem

Perfect indicative

veritus/-a/-um sum	*I feared, have feared, etc.*
veritus/-a/-um es	*you feared*
veritus/-a/-um est	*he/she/it feared*
veritī/-ae/-a sumus	*we feared*
veritī/-ae/-a estis	*you feared*
veritī/-ae/-a sunt	*they feared*

Pluperfect indicative

veritus/-a/-um eram	*I had feared*
veritus/-a/-um erās	*you had feared*
veritus/-a/-um erat	*he/she/it had feared*
veritī/-ae/-a erāmus	*we had feared*
veritī/-ae/-a erātis	*you had feared*
veritī/-ae/-a erant	*they had feared*

Future II

veritus/-a/-um erō	*I will have feared*
veritus/-a/-um eris	*you will have feared*
veritus/-a/-um erit	*he/she/it will have feared*
veritī/-ae/-a erimus	*we will have feared*
veritī/-ae/-a eritis	*you will have feared*
veritī/-ae/-a erunt	*they will have feared*

Perfect subjunctive

(Note that there is no single general rendering for Latin subjunctives. Only one possibility is given here.)

veritus/-a/-um sim	*I may have feared*
veritus/-a/-um sīs	*you may have feared*
veritus/-a/-um sit	*he/she/it may have feared*
veritī/-ae/-a sīmus	*we may have feared*
veritī/-ae/-a sītis	*you may have feared*
veritī/-ae/-a sint	*they may have feared*

Pluperfect subjunctive

veritus/-a/-um essem	*I might have feared*
veritus/-a/-um essēs	*you might have feared*
veritus/-a/-um esset	*he/she/it might have feared*
veritī/-ae/-a essēmus	*we might have feared*
veritī/-ae/-a essētis	*you might have feared*
veritī/-ae/-a essent	*they might have feared*

Nominal forms of the participial stem

Perfect infinitive

veritum/-am/-um esse – *to have feared*

Perfect participle

veritus/-a/-um – *one who has feared*

i-Conjugation

Personal forms using the present stem

Present indicative
audiō	*I hear*
audīs	*you hear*
audit	*he/she/it hears*
audīmus	*we hear*
audītis	*you hear*
audiunt	*they hear*

Imperfect indicative
audiēbam	*I heard, was hearing,* etc.
audiēbās	*you heard*
audiēbat	*he/she/it heard*
audiēbāmus	*we heard*
audiēbātis	*you heard*
audiēbant	*they heard*

Future I
audiam	*I will hear*
audiēs	*you will hear*
audiet	*he/she/it will hear*
audiēmus	*we will hear*
audiētis	*you will hear*
audient	*they will hear*

Present subjunctive
(Note that there is no single general rendering for Latin subjunctives. Only one possibility is given here.)
audiam	*I may hear*
audiās	*you may hear*
audiat	*he/she/it may hear*
audiāmus	*we may hear*
audiātis	*you may hear*
audiant	*they may hear*

Imperfect subjunctive
audīrem	*I might hear*
audīrēs	*you might hear*
audīret	*he/she/it might hear*
audīrēmus	*we might hear*
audīrētis	*you might hear*
audīrent	*they might hear*

Imperative
audī	*hear!*
audīte	*hear!*

Future imperative
audītō	*you shall hear!*
audītō	*he/she/it shall hear!*
audītōte	*you shall hear!*
audiuntō	*they shall hear!*

Nominal forms of the present and participial stems

Present infinitive
audīre – *to hear*

Future infinitive
audītūrum/-am/-um esse – *to be going to hear*

Present participle
audiēns, audientis – *hearing; one who hears*

Future participle
audītūrus/-a/-um – *one who will hear*

Gerund
audīre, audiendī, -ndo, ad -ndum/audīre, audiendo – *(the) hearing, of (the) hearing,* etc.

i-Conjugation

Personal forms using the present stem

Present indicative

audior	*I am heard*
audīris	*you are heard*
audītur	*he/she/it is heard*
audīmur	*we are heard*
audīminī	*you are heard*
audiuntur	*they are heard*

Imperfect indicative

audiēbar	*I was heard, was being heard, etc.*
audiēbāris	*you were heard*
audiēbātur	*he/she/it was heard*
audiēbāmur	*we were heard*
audiēbāminī	*you were heard*
audiēbantur	*they were heard*

Future I

audiar	*I will be heard*
audiēris	*you will be heard*
audiētur	*he/she/it will be heard*
audiēmur	*we will be heard*
audiēminī	*you will be heard*
audientur	*they will be heard*

Present subjunctive

(Note that there is no single general rendering for Latin subjunctives. Only one possibility is given here.)

audiar	*I may be heard*
audiāris	*you may be heard*
audiātur	*he/she/it may be heard*
audiāmur	*we may be heard*
audiāminī	*you may be heard*
audiantur	*they may be heard*

Imperfect subjunctive

audīrer	*I might be heard*
audīrēris	*you might be heard*
audīrētur	*he/she/it might be heard*
audīrēmur	*we might be heard*
audīrēminī	*you might be heard*
audīrentur	*they might be heard*

Imperative

–

Future imperative

–

Nominal forms of the present and participial stems

Present infinitive
audīrī – *to be heard*

Future infinitive
audītum īrī – *to be going to be heard*

Present participle
–

Future participle
–

Gerundive
audiendus/-a/-um – *worth hearing; one who must be heard*

197

i-Conjugation

Personal forms using the perfect stem

Perfect indicative
audīvī	*I heard, have heard, etc.*
audīvistī	*you heard*
audīvit	*he/she/it heard*
audīvimus	*we heard*
audīvistis	*you heard*
audīvērunt	*they heard*

Pluperfect indicative
audīveram	*I had heard*
audīverās	*you had heard*
audīverat	*he/she/it had heard*
audīverāmus	*we had heard*
audīverātis	*you had heard*
audīverant	*they had heard*

Future II
audīverō	*I will have heard*
audīveris	*you will have heard*
audīverit	*he/she/it will have heard*
audīverimus	*we will have heard*
audīveritis	*you will have heard*
audīverint	*they will have heard*

Perfect subjunctive
(Note that there is no single general rendering for Latin subjunctives. Only one possibility is given here.)
audīverim	*I may have heard*
audīveris	*you may have heard*
audīverit	*he/she/it may have heard*
audīverimus	*we may have heard*
audīveritis	*you may have heard*
audīverint	*they may have heard*

Pluperfect subjunctive
audīvissem	*I might have heard*
audīvissēs	*you might have heard*
audīvisset	*he/she/it might have heard*
audīvissēmus	*we might have heard*
audīvissētis	*you might have heard*
audīvissent	*they might have heard*

Nominal forms of the perfect stem

Perfect active infinitive
audīvisse – *to have heard*

Perfect active participle
–

i-Conjugation

Personal forms using the participial stem

Perfect indicative

audītus/-a/-um sum   *I have been heard*
audītus/-a/-um es   *you have been heard*
audītus/-a/-um est   *he/she/it has been heard*
audītī/-ae/-a sumus *we have been heard*
audītī/-ae/-a estis   *you have been heard*
audītī/-ae/-a sunt   *they have been heard*

Pluperfect indicative

audītus/-a/-um eram *I had been heard*
audītus/-a/-um erās *you had been heard*
audītus/-a/-um erat *he/she/it had been heard*
audītī/-ae/-a erāmus *we had been heard*
audītī/-ae/-a erātis *you had been heard*
audītī/-ae/-a erant *they had been heard*

Future II

audītus/-a/-um erō *I will have been heard*
audītus/-a/-um eris *you will have been heard*
audītus/-a/-um erit *he/she/it will have been heard*
audītī/-ae/-a erimus *we will have been heard*
audītī/-ae/-a eritis *you will have been heard*
audītī/-ae/-a erunt *they will have been heard*

Perfect subjunctive

(Note that there is no single general rendering for Latin subjunctives. Only one possibility is given here.)

audītus/-a/-um sim *I may have been heard*
audītus/-a/-um sīs   *you may have been heard*
audītus/-a/-um sit   *he/she/it may have been heard*
audītī/-ae/-a sīmus *we may have been heard*
audītī/-ae/-a sītis *you may have been heard*
audītī/-ae/-a sint   *they may have been heard*

Pluperfect subjunctive

audītus/-a/-um essem *I might have been heard*
audītus/-a/-um essēs *you might have been heard*
audītus/-a/-um esset *he/she/it might have been heard*
audītī/-ae/-a essēmus *we might have been heard*
audītī/-ae/-a essētis *you might have been heard*
audītī/-ae/-a essent *they might have been heard*

Nominal forms of the participial stem

Perfect passive infinitive

audītum/-am/-um esse – *to have been heard*

Perfect passive participle

audītus/-a/-um – *heard; one who has been heard*

Deponent Verbs of the i-Conjugation

Personal forms using the present stem

Present indicative

largior	*I give*
largīris	*you give*
largītur	*he/she/it gives*
largīmur	*we give*
largīminī	*you give*
largiuntur	*they give*

Imperfect indicative

largiēbar	*I gave, was giving,* etc.
largiēbāris	*you gave*
largiēbātur	*he/she/it gave*
largiēbāmur	*we gave*
largiēbāminī	*you gave*
largiēbantur	*they gave*

Future I

largiar	*I will give*
largiēris	*you will give*
largiētur	*he/she/it will give*
largiēmur	*we will give*
largiēminī	*you will give*
largientur	*they will give*

Present subjunctive

(Note that there is no single general rendering for Latin subjunctives. Only one possibility is given here.)

largiar	*I may give*
largiāris	*you may give*
largiātur	*he/she/it may give*
largiāmur	*we may give*
largiāminī	*you may give*
largiantur	*they may give*

Imperfect subjunctive

largīrer	*I might give*
largīrēris	*you might give*
largīrētur	*he/she/it might give*
largīrēmur	*we might give*
largīrēminī	*you might give*
largīrentur	*they might give*

Imperative

largīre	*give!*
largīminī	*give!*

Future imperative

largītor	*you shall give!*
largītor	*he/she/it shall give!*
–	
largiuntor	*they shall give!*

Nominal forms of the present and participial stems

Present infinitive
largīrī – *to give*

Future infinitive
largītūrum/-am/-um esse – *to be going to give*

Present participle
largiēns, largientis – *giving; one who gives*

Future participle
largītūrus/-a/-um – *one who will give*

Gerund and Gerundive
largīrī, largiendī, etc. – *giving,* etc.; largiendus/-a/-um – *one who is given/must be given*

Deponent Verbs of the i-Conjugation

Personal forms using the participial stem

Perfect indicative

largītus/-a/-um sum	*I gave, have given, etc.*
largītus/-a/-um es	*you gave*
largītus/-a/-um est	*he/she/it gave*
largītī/-ae/-a sumus	*we gave*
largītī/-ae/-a estis	*you gave*
largītī/-ae/-a sunt	*they gave*

Pluperfect indicative

largītus/-a/-um eram	*I had given*
largītus/-a/-um erās	*you had given*
largītus/-a/-um erat	*he/she/it had given*
largītī/-ae/-a erāmus	*we had given*
largītī/-ae/-a erātis	*you had given*
largītī/-ae/-a erant	*they had given*

Future II

largītus/-a/-um erō	*I will have given*
largītus/-a/-um eris	*you will have given*
largītus/-a/-um erit	*he/she/it will have given*
largītī/-ae/-a erimus	*we will have given*
largītī/-ae/-a eritis	*you will have given*
largītī/-ae/-a erunt	*they will have given*

Perfect subjunctive

(Note that there is no single general rendering for Latin subjunctives. Only one possibility is given here.)

largītus/-a/-um sim	*I may have given*
largītus/-a/-um sīs	*you may have given*
largītus/-a/-um sit	*he/she/it may have given*
largītī/-ae/-a sīmus	*we may have given*
largītī/-ae/-a sītis	*you may have given*
largītī/-ae/-a sint	*they may have given*

Pluperfect subjunctive

largītus/-a/-um essem	*I might have given*
largītus/-a/-um essēs	*you might have given*
largītus/-a/-um esset	*he/she/it might have given*
largītī/-ae/-a essēmus	*we might have given*
largītī/-ae/-a essētis	*you might have given*
largītī/-ae/-a essent	*they might have given*

Nominal forms of the participial stem

Perfect infinitive

largītum/-am/-um esse – *to have given*

Perfect participle

largītus/-a/-um – *one who has given*

Consonant Conjugation

Personal forms using the present stem

Present indicative

regō	*I direct*
regis	*you direct*
regit	*he/she/it directs*
regimus	*we direct*
regitis	*you direct*
regunt	*they direct*

Imperfect indicative

regēbam	*I directed, was directing, etc.*
regēbās	*you directed*
regēbat	*he/she/it directed*
regēbāmus	*we directed*
regēbātis	*you directed*
regēbant	*they directed*

Future I

regam	*I will direct*
regēs	*you will direct*
reget	*he/she/it will direct*
regēmus	*we will direct*
regētis	*you will direct*
regent	*they will direct*

Present subjunctive

(Note that there is no single general rendering for Latin subjunctives. Only one possibility is given here.)

regam	*I may direct*
regās	*you may direct*
regat	*he/she/it may direct*
regāmus	*we may direct*
regātis	*you may direct*
regant	*they may direct*

Imperfect subjunctive

regerem	*I might direct*
regerēs	*you might direct*
regeret	*he/she/it might direct*
regerēmus	*we might direct*
regerētis	*you might direct*
regerent	*they might direct*

Imperative

rege	*direct!*
regite	*direct!*

Future imperative

regitō	*you shall direct!*
regitō	*he/she/it shall direct!*
regitōte	*you shall direct!*
reguntō	*they shall direct!*

Nominal forms of the present and participial stems

Present infinitive

regere – *to direct*

Future infinitive

rectūrum/-am/-um esse – *to be going to direct*

Present participle

regēns, regentis – *directing; one who directs*

Future participle

rectūrus/-a/-um – *one who will direct*

Gerund

regere, regendī, -ndo, ad -ndum/regere, regendo – *(the) directing, of (the) directing, etc.*

Consonant Conjugation

Personal forms using the present stem

Present indicative

reg**or**	*I am directed*
reg**eris**	*you are directed*
reg**itur**	*he/she/it is directed*
reg**imur**	*we are directed*
reg**iminī**	*you are directed*
reg**untur**	*they are directed*

Imperfect indicative

reg**ēbar**	*I was directed, was being directed, etc.*
reg**ēbāris**	*you were directed*
reg**ēbātur**	*he/she/it was directed*
reg**ēbāmur**	*we were directed*
reg**ēbāminī**	*you were directed*
reg**ēbantur**	*they were directed*

Future I

reg**ar**	*I will be directed*
reg**ēris**	*you will be directed*
reg**ētur**	*he/she/it will be directed*
reg**ēmur**	*we will be directed*
reg**ēminī**	*you will be directed*
reg**entur**	*they will be directed*

Present subjunctive

(Note that there is no single general rendering for Latin subjunctives. Only one possibility is given here.)

reg**ar**	*I may be directed*
reg**āris**	*you may be directed*
reg**ātur**	*he/she/it may be directed*
reg**āmur**	*we may be directed*
reg**āminī**	*you may be directed*
reg**antur**	*they may be directed*

Imperfect subjunctive

reg**erer**	*I might be directed*
reg**erēris**	*you might be directed*
reg**erētur**	*he/she/it might be directed*
reg**erēmur**	*we might be directed*
reg**erēminī**	*you might be directed*
reg**erentur**	*they might be directed*

Imperative

–

Future imperative

–

Nominal forms of the present and participial stems

Present infinitive

reg**ī** – *to be directed*

Future infinitive

rect**um īrī** – *to be going to be directed*

Present participle

–

Future participle

–

Gerundive

reg**endus/-a/-um** – *one who is being directed/must be directed*

Consonant Conjugation

Personal forms using the perfect stem

Perfect indicative

rēxī	*I directed, have directed, etc.*
rēxistī	*you directed*
rēxit	*he/she/it directed*
rēximus	*we directed*
rēxistis	*you directed*
rēxērunt	*they directed*

Pluperfect indicative

rēxeram	*I had directed*
rēxerās	*you had directed*
rēxerat	*he/she/it had directed*
rēxerāmus	*we had directed*
rēxerātis	*you had directed*
rēxerant	*they had directed*

Future II

rēxerō	*I will have directed*
rēxeris	*you will have directed*
rēxerit	*he/she/it will have directed*
rēxerimus	*we will have directed*
rēxeritis	*you will have directed*
rēxerint	*they will have directed*

Perfect subjunctive

(Note that there is no single general rendering for Latin subjunctives. Only one possibility is given here.)

rēxerim	*I may have directed*
rēxeris	*you may have directed*
rēxerit	*he/she/it may have directed*
rēxerimus	*we may have directed*
rēxeritis	*you may have directed*
rēxerint	*they may have directed*

Pluperfect subjunctive

rēxissem	*I might have directed*
rēxissēs	*you might have directed*
rēxisset	*he/she/it might have directed*
rēxissēmus	*we might have directed*
rēxissētis	*you might have directed*
rēxissent	*they might have directed*

Nominal forms of the perfect stem

Perfect active infinitive
rēxisse – *to have directed*

Perfect active participle
–

Consonant Conjugation

Personal forms using the participial stem

Perfect indicative

rēctus/-a/-um sum	*I have been directed*
rēctus/-a/-um es	*you have been directed*
rēctus/-a/-um est	*he/she/it has been directed*
rēctī/-ae/-a sumus	*we have been directed*
rēctī/-ae/-a estis	*you have been directed*
rēctī/-ae/-a sunt	*they have been directed*

Pluperfect indicative

rēctus/-a/-um eram	*I had been directed*
rēctus/-a/-um erās	*you had been directed*
rēctus/-a/-um erat	*he/she/it had been directed*
rēctī/-ae/-a erāmus	*we had been directed*
rēctī/-ae/-a erātis	*you had been directed*
rēctī/-ae/-a erant	*they had been directed*

Future II

rēctus/-a/-um erō	*I will have been directed*
rēctus/-a/-um eris	*you will have been directed*
rēctus/-a/-um erit	*he/she/it will have been directed*
rēctī/-ae/-a erimus	*we will have been directed*
rēctī/-ae/-a eritis	*you will have been directed*
rēctī/-ae/-a erunt	*they will have been directed*

Perfect subjunctive

(Note that there is no single general rendering for Latin subjunctives. Only one possibility is given here.)

rēctus/-a/-um sim	*I may have been directed*
rēctus/-a/-um sīs	*you may have been directed*
rēctus/-a/-um sit	*he/she/it may have been directed*
rēctī/-ae/-a sīmus	*we may have been directed*
rēctī/-ae/-a sītis	*you may have been directed*
rēctī/-ae/-a sint	*they may have been directed*

Pluperfect subjunctive

rēctus/-a/-um essem	*I might have been directed*
rēctus/-a/-um essēs	*you might have been directed*
rēctus/-a/-um esset	*he/she/it might have been directed*
rēctī/-ae/-a essēmus	*we might have been directed*
rēctī/-ae/-a essētis	*you might have been directed*
rēctī/-ae/-a essent	*they might have been directed*

Nominal forms of the participial stem

Perfect passive infinitive

rēctum/-am/-um esse – *to have been directed*

Perfect passive participle

rēctus/-a/-um – *directed; one who has been directed*

Deponent Verbs of the Consonant Conjugation

Personal forms using the present stem

Present indicative
sequor	*I follow*
sequeris	*you follow*
sequitur	*he/she/it follows*
sequimur	*we follow*
sequiminī	*you follow*
sequuntur	*they follow*

Imperfect indicative
sequ**ēba**r	*I followed, was following,* etc.
sequ**ēbā**ris	*you followed*
sequ**ēbā**tur	*he/she/it followed*
sequ**ēbā**mur	*we followed*
sequ**ēbā**minī	*you followed*
sequ**ēba**ntur	*they followed*

Future I
sequ**ar**	*I will follow*
sequ**ēr**is	*you will follow*
sequ**ēt**ur	*he/she/it will follow*
sequ**ēm**ur	*we will follow*
sequ**ēm**inī	*you will follow*
sequ**e**ntur	*they will follow*

Present subjunctive
(Note that there is no single general rendering for Latin subjunctives. Only one possibility is given here.)

sequ**ar**	*I may follow*
sequ**ār**is	*you may follow*
sequ**āt**ur	*he/she/it may follow*
sequ**ām**ur	*we may follow*
sequ**ām**inī	*you may follow*
sequ**a**ntur	*they may follow*

Imperfect subjunctive
sequ**erer**	*I might follow*
sequ**erēr**is	*you might follow*
sequ**erēt**ur	*he/she/it might follow*
sequ**erēm**ur	*we might follow*
sequ**erēm**inī	*you might follow*
sequ**ere**ntur	*they might follow*

Imperative
sequ**ere**	*follow!*
sequ**imin**ī	*follow!*

Future imperative
sequ**itor**	*you shall follow!*
sequ**itor**	*he/she/it shall follow!*
–	
sequ**u**ntur	*they shall follow!*

Nominal forms of the present and participial stems

Present infinitive
sequ**ī** – *to follow*

Future infinitive
secūt**ūrum/-am/-um esse** – *to be going to follow*

Present participle
sequ**ēn**s, sequ**entis** – *following; one who follows*

Future participle
secūt**ūrus/-a/-um** – *one who will follow*

Gerund and Gerundive
sequ**ī**, sequ**endī**, etc. – *(the) following,* etc.; sequ**endus/-a/-um** – *one who is going to be followed/ must be followed*

Deponent Verbs of the Consonant Conjugation

Personal forms using the participial stem

Perfect indicative

secūtus/-a/-um sum	*I followed, have followed, etc.*
secūtus/-a/-um es	*you followed*
secūtus/-a/-um est	*he/she/it followed*
secūtī/-ae/-a sumus	*we followed*
secūtī/-ae/-a estis	*you followed*
secūtī/-ae/-a sunt	*they followed*

Pluperfect indicative

secūtus/-a/-um eram	*I had followed*
secūtus/-a/-um erās	*you had followed*
secūtus/-a/-um erat	*he/she/it had followed*
secūtī/-ae/-a erāmus	*we had followed*
secūtī/-ae/-a erātis	*you had followed*
secūtī/-ae/-a erant	*they had followed*

Future II

secūtus/-a/-um erō	*I will have followed*
secūtus/-a/-um eris	*you will have followed*
secūtus/-a/-um erit	*he/she/it will have followed*
secūtī/-ae/-a erimus	*we will have followed*
secūtī/-ae/-a eritis	*you will have followed*
secūtī/-ae/-a erunt	*they will have followed*

Perfect subjunctive

(Note that there is no single general rendering for Latin subjunctives. Only one possibility is given here.)

secūtus/-a/-um sim	*I may have followed*
secūtus/-a/-um sīs	*you may have followed*
secūtus/-a/-um sit	*he/she/it may have followed*
secūtī/-ae/-a sīmus	*we may have followed*
secūtī/-ae/-a sītis	*you may have followed*
secūtī/-ae/-a sint	*they may have followed*

Pluperfect subjunctive

secūtus/-a/-um essem	*I might have followed*
secūtus/-a/-um essēs	*you might have followed*
secūtus/-a/-um esset	*he/she/it might have followed*
secūtī/-ae/-a essēmus	*we might have followed*
secūtī/-ae/-a essētis	*you might have followed*
secūtī/-ae/-a essent	*they might have followed*

Nominal forms of the participial stem

Perfect infinitive

secūtum/-am/-um esse – *to have followed*

Perfect participle

secūtus/-a/-um – *one who has followed*

Mixed Conjugation

Personal forms using the present stem

Present indicative
capiō	*I catch*
capis	*you catch*
capit	*he/she/it catches*
capimus	*we catch*
capitis	*you catch*
capiunt	*they catch*

Imperfect indicative
capiēbam	*I caught, was catching, etc.*
capiēbās	*you caught*
capiēbat	*he/she/it caught*
capiēbāmus	*we caught*
capiēbātis	*you caught*
capiēbant	*they caught*

Future I
capiam	*I will catch*
capiēs	*you will catch*
capiet	*he/she/it will catch*
capiēmus	*we will catch*
capiētis	*you will catch*
capient	*they will catch*

Present subjunctive
(Note that there is no single general rendering for Latin subjunctives. Only one possibility is given here.)
capiam	*I may catch*
capiās	*you may catch*
capiat	*he/she/it may catch*
capiāmus	*we may catch*
capiātis	*you may catch*
capiant	*they may catch*

Imperfect subjunctive
caperem	*I might catch*
caperēs	*you might catch*
caperet	*he/she/it might catch*
caperēmus	*we might catch*
caperētis	*you might catch*
caperent	*they might catch*

Imperative
cape	*catch!*
capite	*catch!*

Future imperative
capitō	*you shall catch!*
capitō	*he/she/it shall catch!*
capitōte	*you shall catch!*
capiuntō	*they shall catch!*

Nominal forms of the present and participial stems

Present infinitive
capere – *to catch*

Future infinitive
captūrum/-am/-um esse – *to be going to catch*

Present participle
capiēns, capientis – *catching; one who catches*

Future participle
captūrus/-a/-um – *one who will catch*

Gerund
capere, capiendī, -ndo, ad -ndum/capere, capiendo – *(the) catching, of (the) catching*, etc.

Mixed Conjugation

Personal forms using the present stem

Present indicative

capior	*I am caught*
caperis	*you are caught*
capitur	*he/she/it is caught*
capimur	*we are caught*
capiminī	*you are caught*
capiuntur	*they are caught*

Imperfect indicative

capiēbar	*I was caught, was being caught, etc.*
capiēbāris	*you were caught*
capiēbātur	*he/she/it was caught*
capiēbāmur	*we were caught*
capiēbāminī	*you were caught*
capiēbantur	*they were caught*

Future I

capiar	*I will be caught*
capiēris	*you will be caught*
capiētur	*he/she/it will be caught*
capiēmur	*we will be caught*
capiēminī	*you will be caught*
capientur	*they will be caught*

Present subjunctive

(Note that there is no single general rendering for Latin subjunctives. Only one possibility is given here.)

capiar	*I may be caught*
capiāris	*you may be caught*
capiātur	*he/she/it may be caught*
capiāmur	*we may be caught*
capiāminī	*you may be caught*
capiantur	*they may be caught*

Imperfect subjunctive

caperer	*I might be caught*
caperēris	*you might be caught*
caperētur	*he/she/it might be caught*
caperēmur	*we might be caught*
caperēminī	*you might be caught*
caperentur	*they might be caught*

Imperative

–

Future imperative

–

Nominal forms of the present and participial stems

Present infinitive

capī – *to be caught*

Future infinitive

captum īrī – *to be going to be caught*

Present participle

–

Future participle

–

Gerundive

capiendus/-a/-um – *one who is being caught/must be caught*

Mixed Conjugation

Personal forms using the perfect stem

Perfect indicative

cēpī	*I caught, have caught*
cēpistī	*you caught*
cēpit	*he/she/it caught*
cēpimus	*we caught*
cēpistis	*you caught*
cēpērunt	*they caught*

Pluperfect indicative

cēperam	*I had caught*
cēperās	*you had caught*
cēperat	*he/she/it had caught*
cēperāmus	*we had caught*
cēperātis	*you had caught*
cēperant	*they had caught*

Future II

cēperō	*I will have caught*
cēperis	*you will have caught*
cēperit	*he/she/it will have caught*
cēperimus	*we will have caught*
cēperitis	*you will have caught*
cēperint	*they will have caught*

Perfect subjunctive

(Note that there is no single general rendering for Latin subjunctives. Only one possibility is given here.)

cēperim	*I may have caught*
cēperis	*you may have caught*
cēperit	*he/she/it may have caught*
cēperimus	*we may have caught*
cēperitis	*you may have caught*
cēperint	*they may have caught*

Pluperfect subjunctive

cēpissem	*I might have caught*
cēpissēs	*you might have caught*
cēpisset	*he/she/it might have caught*
cēpissēmus	*we might have caught*
cēpissētis	*you might have caught*
cēpissent	*they might have caught*

Nominal forms of the perfect stem

Perfect active infinitive

cēpisse – *to have caught*

Perfect active participle

–

Mixed Conjugation

Personal forms using the participial stem

Perfect indicative
captus/-a/-um sum   *I have been caught*
captus/-a/-um es   *you have been caught*
captus/-a/-um est   *he/she/it has been caught*
captī/-ae/-a sumus   *we have been caught*
captī/-ae/-a estis   *you have been caught*
captī/-ae/-a sunt   *they have been caught*

Pluperfect indicative
captus/-a/-um eram *I had been caught*
captus/-a/-um erās *you had been caught*
captus/-a/-um erat *he/she/it had been caught*
captī/-ae/-a erāmus *we had been caught*
captī/-ae/-a erātis *you had been caught*
captī/-ae/-a erant *they had been caught*

Future II
captus/-a/-um erō *I will have been caught*
captus/-a/-um eris *you will have been caught*
captus/-a/-um erit *he/she/it will have been caught*
captī/-ae/-a erimus *we will have been caught*
captī/-ae/-a eritis *you will have been caught*
captī/-ae/-a erunt *they will have been caught*

Perfect subjunctive
(Note that there is no single general rendering for Latin subjunctives. Only one possibility is given here.)
captus/-a/-um sim   *I may have been caught*
captus/-a/-um sīs   *you may have been caught*
captus/-a/-um sit   *he/she/it may have been caught*
captī/-ae/-a sīmus   *we may have been caught*
captī/-ae/-a sītis   *you may have been caught*
captī/-ae/-a sint   *they may have been caught*

Pluperfect subjunctive
captus/-a/-um essem *I might have been caught*
captus/-a/-um essēs *you might have been caught*
captus/-a/-um esset *he/she/it might have been caught*
captī/-ae/-a essēmus *we might have been caught*
captī/-ae/-a essētis *you might have been caught*
captī/-ae/-a essent *they might have been caught*

Nominal forms of the participial stem

Perfect passive infinitive
captum/-am/-um esse – *to have been caught*

Perfect passive participle
captus/-a/-um – *caught; one who has been caught*

Deponent Verbs of the Mixed Conjugation

Personal forms using the present stem

Present indicative
patior	*I suffer*
pateris	*you suffer*
patitur	*he/she/it suffers*
patimur	*we suffer*
patiminī	*you suffer*
patiuntur	*they suffer*

Imperfect indicative
patiēbar	*I suffered, was suffering, etc.*
patiēbāris	*you suffered*
patiēbātur	*he/she/it suffered*
patiēbāmur	*we suffered*
patiēbāminī	*you suffered*
patiēbantur	*they suffered*

Future I
patiar	*I will suffer*
patiēris	*you will suffer*
patiētur	*he/she/it will suffer*
patiēmur	*we will suffer*
patiēminī	*you will suffer*
patientur	*they will suffer*

Present subjunctive
(Note that there is no single general rendering for Latin subjunctives. Only one possibility is given here.)
patiar	*I may suffer*
patiāris	*you may suffer*
patiātur	*he/she/it may suffer*
patiāmur	*we may suffer*
patiāminī	*you may suffer*
patiantur	*they may suffer*

Imperfect subjunctive
paterer	*I might suffer*
paterēris	*you might suffer*
paterētur	*he/she/it might suffer*
paterēmur	*we might suffer*
paterēminī	*you might suffer*
paterentur	*they might suffer*

Imperative
patere	*suffer!*
patiminī	*suffer!*

Future imperative
patitor	*you shall suffer!*
patitor	*he/she/it shall suffer!*
–	
patiuntor	*they shall suffer!*

Nominal forms of the present and participial stems

Present infinitive
patī – *to suffer*

Future infinitive
passūrum/-am/-um esse – *to be going to suffer*

Present participle
patiēns, patientis – *suffering; one who suffers*

Future participle
passūrus/-a/-um – *one who will suffer*

Gerund and Gerundive
patī, patiendī, etc. – *(the) suffering, etc.;* patiendus/-a/-um – *one who is suffered/must be suffered*

Deponent Verbs of the Mixed Conjugation

Personal forms using the participial stem

Perfect indicative

passus/-a/-um sum	*I suffered, have suffered, etc.*
passus/-a/-um es	*you suffered*
passus/-a/-um est	*he/she/it suffered*
passī/-ae/-a sumus	*we suffered*
passī/-ae/-a estis	*you suffered*
passī/-ae/-a sunt	*they suffered*

Pluperfect indicative

passus/-a/-um eram	*I had suffered*
passus/-a/-um erās	*you had suffered*
passus/-a/-um erat	*he/she/it had suffered*
passī/-ae/-a erāmus	*we had suffered*
passī/-ae/-a erātis	*you had suffered*
passī/-ae/-a erant	*they had suffered*

Future II

passus/-a/-um erō	*I will have suffered*
passus/-a/-um eris	*you will have suffered*
passus/-a/-um erit	*he/she/it will have suffered*
passī/-ae/-a erimus	*we will have suffered*
passī/-ae/-a eritis	*you will have suffered*
passī/-ae/-a erunt	*they will have suffered*

Perfect subjunctive

(Note that there is no single general rendering for Latin subjunctives. Only one possibility is given here.)

passus/-a/-um sim	*I may have suffered*
passus/-a/-um sīs	*you may have suffered*
passus/-a/-um sit	*he/she/it may have suffered*
passī/-ae/-a sīmus	*we may have suffered*
passī/-ae/-a sītis	*you may have suffered*
passī/-ae/-a sint	*they may have suffered*

Pluperfect subjunctive

passus/-a/-um essem	*I might have suffered*
passus/-a/-um essēs	*you might have suffered*
passus/-a/-um esset	*he/she/it might have suffered*
passī/-ae/-a essēmus	*we might have suffered*
passī/-ae/-a essētis	*you might have suffered*
passī/-ae/-a essent	*they might have suffered*

Nominal forms of the participial stem

Perfect infinitive

passum/-am/-um esse – *to have suffered*

Perfect participle

passus/-a/-um – *one who has suffered*

Irregular Verbs

Personal forms using the present stem

Present indicative

ferō	*I carry*
fers	*you carry*
fert	*he/she/it carries*
ferimus	*we carry*
fertis	*you carry*
ferunt	*they carry*

Imperfect indicative

ferēbam	*I carried, was carrying, etc.*
ferēbās	*you carried*
ferēbat	*he/she/it carried*
ferēbāmus	*we carried*
ferēbātis	*you carried*
ferēbant	*they carried*

Future I

feram	*I will carry*
ferēs	*you will carry*
feret	*he/she/it will carry*
ferēmus	*we will carry*
ferētis	*you will carry*
ferent	*they will carry*

Present subjunctive

(Note that there is no single general rendering for Latin subjunctives. Only one possibility is given here.)

feram	*I may carry*
ferās	*you may carry*
ferat	*he/she/it may carry*
ferāmus	*we may carry*
ferātis	*you may carry*
ferant	*they may carry*

Imperfect subjunctive

ferrem	*I might carry*
ferrēs	*you might carry*
ferret	*he/she/it might carry*
ferrēmus	*we might carry*
ferrētis	*you might carry*
ferrent	*they might carry*

Imperative

fer	*carry!*
ferte	*carry!*

Future imperative

fertō	*you shall carry!*
fertō	*he/she/it shall carry!*
fertōte	*you shall carry!*
feruntō	*they shall carry!*

Nominal forms of the present and participial stems

Present infinitive
ferre – *to carry*

Future infinitive
lātūrum/-am/-um esse – *to be going to carry*

Present participle
ferēns, ferentis – *carrying; one who carries*

Future participle
lātūrus/-a/-um – *one who will carry*

Gerund
ferre, ferendī, -ndo, ad -ndum/ferre, ferrendo – *(the) carrying, of (the) carrying, etc.*

Irregular Verbs

Personal forms using the present stem

Present indicative

feror	_I am carried_
ferris	_you are carried_
fertur	_he/she/it is carried_
ferimur	_we are carried_
feriminī	_you are carried_
feruntur	_they are carried_

Imperfect indicative

ferēbar	_I was carried, was being carried, etc._
ferēbāris	_you were carried_
ferēbātur	_he/she/it was carried_
ferēbāmur	_we were carried_
ferēbāminī	_you were carried_
ferēbantur	_they were carried_

Future I

ferar	_I will be carried_
ferēris	_you will be carried_
ferētur	_he/she/it will be carried_
ferēmur	_we will be carried_
ferēminī	_you will be carried_
ferentur	_they will be carried_

Present subjunctive

(Note that there is no single general rendering for Latin subjunctives. Only one possibility is given here.)

ferar	_I may be carried_
ferāris	_you may be carried_
ferātur	_he/she/it may be carried_
ferāmur	_we may be carried_
ferāminī	_you may be carried_
ferantur	_they may be carried_

Pluperfect subjunctive

ferrer	_I might be carred_
ferrēris	_you might be carried_
ferrētur	_he/she/it might be carried_
ferrēmur	_we might be carried_
ferrēminī	_you might be carried_
ferrentur	_they might be carried_

Imperative

–

Future imperative

–

Nominal forms of the present and participial stems

Present infinitive

ferrī – _to be carried_

Future infinitive

lātum īrī – _to be going to be carried_

Present participle

–

Future participle

–

Gerundive

ferendus/-a/-um – _one who is being carried/must be carried_

Irregular Verbs

Personal forms using the perfect stem

Perfect indicative

tulī	*I carried, have carried, etc.*
tulistī	*you carried*
tulit	*he/she/it carried*
tulimus	*we carried*
tulistis	*you carried*
tulērunt	*they carried*

Pluperfect indicative

tuleram	*I had carried*
tulerās	*you had carried*
tulerat	*he/she/it had carried*
tulerāmus	*we had carried*
tulerātis	*you had carried*
tulerant	*they had carried*

Future II

tulerō	*I will have carried*
tuleris	*you will have carried*
tulerit	*he/she/it will have carried*
tulerimus	*we will have carried*
tuleritis	*you will have carried*
tulerint	*they will have carried*

Perfect subjunctive (Note that there is no single general rendering for Latin subjunctives. Only one possibility is given here.)

tulerim	*I may have carried*
tuleris	*you may have carried*
tulerit	*he/she/it may have carried*
tulerimus	*we may have carried*
tuleritis	*you may have carried*
tulerint	*they may have carried*

Pluperfect subjunctive

tulissem	*I might have carried*
tulissēs	*you might have carried*
tulisset	*he/she/it might have carried*
tulissēmus	*we might have carried*
tulissētis	*you might have carried*
tulissent	*they might have carried*

Nominal forms of the perfect stem

Perfect active infinitive
tulisse – *to have carried*

Perfect active participle
–

Irregular Verbs

Personal forms using the participial stem

Perfect indicative

lātus/-a/-um sum	*I was carried, have been carried, etc.*
lātus/-a/-um es	*you were carried*
lātus/-a/-um est	*he/she/it was carried*
lātī/-ae/-a sumus	*we were carried*
lātī/-ae/-a estis	*you were carried*
lātī/-ae/-a sunt	*they were carried*

Pluperfect indicative

lātus/-a/-um eram	*I had been carried*
lātus/-a/-um erās	*you had been carried*
lātus/-a/-um erat	*he/she/it had been carried*
lātī/-ae/-a erāmus	*we had been carried*
lātī/-ae/-a erātis	*you had been carried*
lātī/-ae/-a erant	*they had been carried*

Future II

lātus/-a/-um erō	*I will have been carried*
lātus/-a/-um eris	*you will have been carried*
lātus/-a/-um erit	*he/she/it will have been carried*
lātī/-ae/-a erimus	*we will have been carried*
lātī/-ae/-a eritis	*you will have been carried*
lātī/-ae/-a erunt	*they will have been carried*

Perfect subjunctive (Note that there is no single general rendering for Latin subjunctives. Only one possibility is given here.)

lātus/-a/-um sim	*I may have been carried*
lātus/-a/-um sīs	*you may have been carried*
lātus/-a/-um sit	*he/she/it may have been carried*
lātī/-ae/-a sīmus	*we may have been carried*
lātī/-ae/-a sītis	*you may have been carried*
lātī/-ae/-a sint	*they may have been carried*

Pluperfect subjunctive

lātus/-a/-um essem	*I might have been carried*
lātus/-a/-um essēs	*you might have been carried*
lātus/-a/-um esset	*he/she/it might have been carried*
lātī/-ae/-a essēmus	*we might have been carried*
lātī/-ae/-a essētis	*you might have been carried*
lātī/-ae/-a essent	*they might have been carried*

Nominal forms of the participial stem

Perfect passive infinitive
lātum/-am/-um esse – *to have been carried*

Perfect passive participle
lātus/-a/-um – *carried; one who has been carried*

Irregular Verbs

Personal forms using the present stem

Present indicative

sum	*I am*
es	*you are*
est	*he/she/it is*
sumus	*we are*
estis	*you are*
sunt	*they are*

Imperfect indicative

eram	*I was, was being,* etc.
erās	*you were*
erat	*he/she/it was*
erāmus	*we were*
erātis	*you were*
erant	*they were*

Future I

erō	*I will be*
eris	*you will be*
erit	*he/she/it will be*
erimus	*we will be*
eritis	*you will be*
erunt	*they will be*

Present subjunctive
(Note that there is no single general rendering for Latin subjunctives. Only one possibility is given here.)

sim	*I may be*
sīs	*you may be*
sit	*he/she/it may be*
sīmus	*we may be*
sītis	*you may be*
sint	*they may be*

Imperfect subjunctive

essem	*I might be*
essēs	*you might be*
esset	*he/she/it might be*
essēmus	*we might be*
essētis	*you might be*
essent	*they might be*

Imperative

es	*be!*
este	*be!*

Future imperative

estō	*you shall be!*
estō	*he/she/it shall be!*
estōte	*you shall be!*
suntō	*they shall be!*

Nominal forms of the present and participial stems

Present infinitive
esse – *to be*

Future infinitive
futūrum/-am/-um esse; fore – *to be going to be*

Present participle
–

Future participle
futūrus/-a/-um – *future; one who will be*

Gerund
–

Irregular Verbs

Personal forms using the perfect stem

Perfect indicative

fuī	*I was, have been, etc.*
fuistī	*you were*
fuit	*he/she/it was*
fuimus	*we were*
fuistis	*you were*
fuērunt	*they were*

Pluperfect indicative

fueram	*I had been*
fuerās	*you had been*
fuerat	*he/she/it had been*
fuerāmus	*we had been*
fuerātis	*you had been*
fuerant	*they had been*

Future II

fuerō	*I will have been*
fueris	*you will have been*
fuerit	*he/she/it will have been*
fuerimus	*we will have been*
fueritis	*you will have been*
fuerint	*they will have been*

Perfect subjunctive
(Note that there is no single general rendering for Latin subjunctives. Only one possibility is given here.)

fuerim	*I may have been*
fueris	*you may have been*
fuerit	*he/she/it may have been*
fuerimus	*we may have been*
fueritis	*you may have been*
fuerint	*they may have been*

Pluperfect subjunctive

fuissem	*I might have been*
fuissēs	*you might have been*
fuisset	*he/she/it might have been*
fuissēmus	*we might have been*
fuissētis	*you might have been*
fuissent	*they might have been*

Nominal forms of the perfect stem

Perfect active infinitive
fuisse – *to have been*

Perfect active participle
–

Irregular Verbs

Personal forms using the present stem

Present indicative

possum	*I am able, can, etc.*
potes	*you are able*
potest	*he/she/it is able*
possumus	*we are able*
potestis	*you are able*
possunt	*they are able*

Imperfect indicative

poteram	*I was able, used to be able, etc.*
poterās	*you were able*
poterat	*he/she/it was able*
poterāmus	*we were able*
poterātis	*you were able*
poterant	*they were able*

Future I

poterō	*I will be able*
poteris	*you will be able*
poterit	*he/she/it will be able*
poterimus	*we will be able*
poteritis	*you will be able*
poterunt	*they will be able*

Present subjunctive
(Note that there is no single general rendering for Latin subjunctives. Only one possibility is given here.)

possim	*I may be able*
possīs	*you may be able*
possit	*he/she/it may be able*
possīmus	*we may be able*
possītis	*you may be able*
possint	*they may be able*

Imperfect subjunctive

possem	*I might be able*
possēs	*you might be able*
posset	*he/she/it might be able*
possēmus	*we might be able*
possētis	*you might be able*
possent	*they might be able*

Imperative

–

Future imperative

–

Nominal forms of the present stem

Present infinitive
posse – *to be able, can*

Future infinitive
–

Present participle
–

Future participle
–

Gerund
–

Irregular Verbs

Personal forms using the perfect stem

Perfect indicative

potuī	*I was able, have been able, could, etc.*
potuistī	*you were able*
potuit	*he/she/it was able*
potuimus	*we were able*
potuistis	*you were able*
potuērunt	*they were able*

Pluperfect indicative

potueram	*I had been able*
potuerās	*you had been able*
potuerat	*he/she/it had been able*
potuerāmus	*we had been able*
potuerātis	*you had been able*
potuerant	*they had been able*

Future II

potuerō	*I will have been able*
potueris	*you will have been able*
potuerit	*he/she/it will have been able*
potuerimus	*we will have been able*
potueritis	*you will have been able*
potuerint	*they will have been able*

Perfect subjunctive

(Note that there is no single general rendering for Latin subjunctives. Only one possibility is given here.)

potuerim	*I may have been able*
potueris	*you may have been able*
potuerit	*he/she/it may have been able*
potuerimus	*we may have been able*
potueritis	*you may have been able*
potuerint	*they may have been able*

Pluperfect subjunctive

potuissem	*I might have been able*
potuissēs	*you might have been able*
potuisset	*he/she/it might have been able*
potuissēmus	*we might have been able*
potuissētis	*you might have been able*
potuissent	*they might have been able*

Nominal forms of the perfect stem

Perfect active infinitive

potuisse – *to have been able*

Perfect active participle

–

Irregular Verbs

Personal forms using the present stem

Present indicative

prōsum	*I am useful*
prōdes	*you are useful*
prōdest	*he/she/it is useful*
prōsumus	*we are useful*
prōdestis	*you are useful*
prōsunt	*they are useful*

Imperfect indicative

prōderam	*I was useful, was being useful, etc.*
prōderās	*you were useful*
prōderat	*he/she/it was useful*
prōderāmus	*we were useful*
prōderātis	*you were useful*
prōderant	*they were useful*

Future I

prōderō	*I will be useful*
prōderis	*you will be useful*
prōderit	*he/she/it will be useful*
prōderimus	*we will be useful*
prōderitis	*you will be useful*
prōderunt	*they will be useful*

Present subjunctive

(Note that there is no single general rendering for Latin subjunctives. Only one possibility is given here.)

prōsim	*I may be useful*
prōsīs	*you may be useful*
prōsit	*he/she/it may be useful*
prōsīmus	*we may be useful*
prōsītis	*you may be useful*
prōsint	*they may be useful*

Imperfect subjunctive

prōdessem	*I might be useful*
prōdessēs	*you might be useful*
prōdesset	*he/she/it might be useful*
prōdessēmus	*we might be useful*
prōdessētis	*you might be useful*
prōdessent	*they might be useful*

Imperative

prōdes	*be useful!*
prōdeste	*be useful!*

Future imperative

–

Nominal forms of the present and perfect stems

Present infinitive

prōdesse – *to be useful*

Future infinitive

–

Present participle

–

Future participle

prōfutūrus/-a/-um – *one who will be useful*

Gerund

–

Irregular Verbs

Personal forms using the perfect stem

Perfect indicative

prōfuī	*I was useful, have been useful, etc.*
prōfuistī	*you were useful*
prōfuit	*he/she/it was useful*
prōfuimus	*we were useful*
prōfuistis	*you were useful*
prōfuērunt	*they were useful*

Pluperfect indicative

prōfueram	*I had been useful*
prōfuerās	*you had been useful*
prōfuerat	*he/she/it had been useful*
prōfuerāmus	*we had been useful*
prōfuerātis	*you had been useful*
prōfuerant	*they had been useful*

Future II

prōfuerō	*I will have been useful*
prōfueris	*you will have been useful*
prōfuerit	*he/she/it will have been useful*
prōfuerimus	*we will have been useful*
prōfueritis	*you will have been useful*
prōfuerint	*they will have been useful*

Perfect subjunctive

(Note that there is no single general rendering for Latin subjunctives. Only one possibility is given here.)

prōfuerim	*I may have been useful*
prōfueris	*you may have been useful*
prōfuerit	*he/she/it may have been useful*
prōfuerimus	*we may have been useful*
prōfueritis	*you may have been useful*
prōfuerint	*they may have been useful*

Pluperfect subjunctive

prōfuissem	*I might have been useful*
prōfuissēs	*you might have been useful*
prōfuisset	*he/she/it might have been useful*
prōfuissēmus	*we might have been useful*
prōfuissētis	*you might have been useful*
prōfuissent	*they might have been useful*

Nominal forms of the perfect stem

Perfect active infinitive

prōfuisse – *to have been useful*

Perfect active participle

–

Irregular Verbs

Personal forms using the present stem

Present indicative
volō	*I wish*
vīs	*you wish*
vult	*he/she/it wishes*
volumus	*we wish*
vultis	*you wish*
volunt	*they wish*

Imperfect indicative
volēbam	*I wished, was wishing, etc.*
volēbās	*you wished*
volēbat	*he/she/it wished*
volēbāmus	*we wished*
volēbātis	*you wished*
volēbant	*they wished*

Future I
volam	*I will wish*
volēs	*you will wish*
volet	*he/she/it will wish*
volēmus	*we will wish*
volētis	*you will wish*
volent	*they will wish*

Present subjunctive
(Note that there is no single general rendering for Latin subjunctives. Only one possibility is given here.)

velim	*I may wish*
velīs	*you may wish*
velit	*he/she/it may wish*
velīmus	*we may wish*
velītis	*you may wish*
velint	*they may wish*

Imperfect subjunctive
vellem	*I might wish*
vellēs	*you might wish*
vellet	*he/she/it might wish*
vellēmus	*we might wish*
vellētis	*you might wish*
vellent	*they might wish*

Imperative
–

Future imperative
–

Nominal forms of the present stem

Present infinitive
velle – *to wish*

Future infinitive
–

Present participle
volēns, volentis – *wishing; one who wishes*

Future participle
–

Gerund
–

Irregular Verbs

Personal forms using the perfect stem

Perfect indicative
voluī	*I wished, have wished, etc.*
voluistī	*you wished*
voluit	*he/she/it wished*
voluimus	*we wished*
voluistis	*you wished*
voluērunt	*they wished*

Pluperfect indicative
volueram	*I had wished*
voluerās	*you had wished*
voluerat	*he/she/it had wished*
voluerāmus	*we had wished*
voluerātis	*you had wished*
voluerant	*they had wished*

Future II
voluerō	*I will have wished*
volueris	*you will have wished*
voluerit	*he/she/it will have wished*
voluerimus	*we will have wished*
volueritis	*you will have wished*
voluerint	*they will have wished*

Perfect subjunctive
(Note that there is no single general rendering for Latin subjunctives. Only one possibility is given here.)
voluerim	*I may have wished*
volueris	*you may have wished*
voluerit	*he/she/it may have wished*
voluerimus	*we may have wished*
volueritis	*you may have wished*
voluerint	*they may have wished*

Pluperfect subjunctive
voluissem	*I might have wished*
voluissēs	*you might have wished*
voluisset	*he/she/it might have wished*
voluissēmus	*we might have wished*
voluissētis	*you might have wished*
voluissent	*they might have wished*

Nominal forms of the perfect stem

Perfect active infinitive
voluisse – *to have wished*

Perfect active participle
–

Irregular Verbs

Personal forms using the present stem

Present indicative

nōlō	*I am unwilling*
nōn vīs	*you are unwilling*
nōn vult	*he/she/it is unwilling*
nōlumus	*we are unwilling*
nōn vultis	*you are unwilling*
nōlunt	*they are unwilling*

Imperfect indicative

nōlēbam	*I was unwilling, used to be unwilling, etc.*
nōlēbās	*you were unwilling*
nōlēbat	*he/she/it was unwilling*
nōlēbāmus	*we were unwilling*
nōlēbātis	*you were unwilling*
nōlēbant	*they were unwilling*

Future I

nōlam	*I will be unwilling*
nōlēs	*you will be unwilling*
nōlet	*he/she/it will be unwilling*
nōlēmus	*we will be unwilling*
nōlētis	*you will be unwilling*
nōlent	*they will be unwilling*

Present subjunctive

(Note that there is no single general rendering for Latin subjunctives. Only one possibility is given here.)

nōlim	*I may be unwilling*
nōlīs	*you may be unwilling*
nōlit	*he/she/it may be unwilling*
nōlīmus	*we may be unwilling*
nōlītis	*you may be unwilling*
nōlint	*they may be unwilling*

Imperfect subjunctive

nōllem	*I might be unwilling*
nōllēs	*you might be unwilling*
nōllet	*he/she/it might be unwilling*
nōllēmus	*we might be unwilling*
nōllētis	*you might be unwilling*
nōllent	*they might be unwilling*

Imperative

nōlī [turbāre]	*don't [disturb]!*
nōlīte [turbāre]	*don't [disturb]!*

Future imperative

nōlītō [turbāre]	*you shall not [disturb]!*
nōlītō [turbāre]	*he/she/it shall not [disturb]!*
nōlītōte [turbāre]	*you shall not [disturb]!*
nōluntō [turbāre]	*they shall not [disturb]!*

Nominal forms of the present stem

Present infinitive

nōlle – *to be unwilling*

Future infinitive

–

Present participle

nōlēns, nōlentis – *being unwilling*

Future participle

–

Gerund

–

Irregular Verbs

Personal forms using the perfect stem

Perfect indicative

nōluī	_I was unwilling, have been unwilling, etc._
nōluistī	_you were unwilling_
nōluit	_he/she/it was unwilling_
nōluimus	_we were unwilling_
nōluistis	_you were unwilling_
nōluērunt	_they were unwilling_

Pluperfect indicative

nōlueram	_I had been unwilling_
nōluerās	_you had been unwilling_
nōluerat	_he/she/it had been unwilling_
nōluerāmus	_we had been unwilling_
nōluerātis	_you had been unwilling_
nōluerant	_they had been unwilling_

Future II

nōluerō	_I will have been unwilling_
nōlueris	_you will have been unwilling_
nōluerit	_he/she/it will have been unwilling_
nōluerimus	_we have been unwilling_
nōlueritis	_you will have been unwilling_
nōluerint	_they have been unwilling_

Perfect subjunctive

(Note that there is no single general rendering for Latin subjunctives. Only one possibility is given here.)

nōluerim	_I may have been unwilling_
nōlueris	_you may have been unwilling_
nōluerit	_he/she/it may have been unwilling_
nōluerimus	_we may have been unwilling_
nōlueritis	_you may have been unwilling_
nōluerint	_they may have been unwilling_

Pluperfect subjunctive

nōluissem	_I might have been unwilling_
nōluissēs	_you might have been unwilling_
nōluisset	_he/she/it might have been unwilling_
nōluissēmus	_we might have been unwilling_
nōluissētis	_you might have been unwilling_
nōluissent	_they might have been unwilling_

Nominal forms of the perfect stem

Perfect active infinitive

nōluisse – _to have been unwilling_

Perfect active participle

–

Irregular Verbs

Personal forms using the present stem

Present indicative

mālō	*I prefer*
māvīs	*you prefer*
māvult	*he/she/it prefers*
mālumus	*we prefer*
māvultis	*you prefer*
mālunt	*they prefer*

Imperfect indicative

mālēbam	*I preferred, used to prefer, etc.*
mālēbās	*you preferred*
mālēbat	*he/she/it preferred*
mālēbāmus	*we preferred*
mālēbātis	*you preferred*
mālēbant	*they preferred*

Future I

mālam	*I will prefer*
mālēs	*you will prefer*
mālet	*he/she/it will prefer*
mālēmus	*we will prefer*
mālētis	*you will prefer*
mālent	*they will prefer*

Present subjunctive

(Note that there is no single general rendering for Latin subjunctives. Only one possibility is given here.)

mālim	*I may prefer*
mālīs	*you may prefer*
mālit	*he/she/it may prefer*
mālīmus	*we may prefer*
mālītis	*you may prefer*
mālint	*they may prefer*

Imperfect subjunctive

māllem	*I might prefer*
māllēs	*you might prefer*
māllet	*he/she/it might prefer*
māllēmus	*we might prefer*
māllētis	*you might prefer*
māllent	*they might prefer*

Imperative

–

Future imperative

–

Nominal forms of the present stem

Present infinitive

mālle – *to prefer*

Future infinitive

–

Present participle

–

Future participle

–

Gerund

–

Irregular Verbs

Personal forms using the perfect stem

Perfect indicative

māluī	*I preferred, have preferred, etc.*
māluistī	*you preferred*
māluit	*he/she/it preferred*
māluimus	*we preferred*
māluistis	*you preferred*
māluērunt	*they preferred*

Pluperfect indicative

mālueram	*I had preferred*
māluerās	*you had preferred*
māluerat	*he/she/it had preferred*
māluerāmus	*we had preferred*
māluerātis	*you had preferred*
māluerant	*they had preferred*

Future II

māluerō	*I will have preferred*
mālueris	*you will have preferred*
māluerit	*he/she/it will have preferred*
māluerimus	*we will have preferred*
mālueritis	*you will have preferred*
māluerint	*they will have preferred*

Perfect subjunctive

(Note that there is no single general rendering for Latin subjunctives. Only one possibility is given here.)

māluerim	*I may have preferred*
mālueris	*you may have preferred*
māluerit	*he/she/it may have preferred*
māluerimus	*we may have preferred*
mālueritis	*you may have preferred*
māluerint	*they may have preferred*

Pluperfect subjunctive

māluissem	*I might have preferred*
māluissēs	*you might have preferred*
māluisset	*he/she/it might have preferred*
māluissēmus	*we might have preferred*
māluissētis	*you might have preferred*
māluissent	*they might have preferred*

Nominal forms of the perfect stem

Perfect active infinitive

māluisse – *to have preferred*

Perfect active participle

–

Irregular Verbs

Personal forms using the present stem

Present indicative

eō	*I go*
īs	*you go*
it	*he/she/it goes*
īmus	*we go*
ītis	*you go*
eunt	*they go*

Imperfect indicative

ībam	*I went, was going,* etc.
ībās	*you went*
ībat	*he/she/it went*
ībāmus	*we went*
ībātis	*you went*
ībant	*they went*

Future I

ībō	*I will go*
ībis	*you will go*
ībit	*he/she/it will go*
ībimus	*we will go*
ībitis	*you will go*
ībunt	*they will go*

Present subjunctive
(Note that there is no single general rendering for Latin subjunctives. Only one possibility is given here.)

eam	*I may go*
eās	*you may go*
eat	*he/she/it may go*
eāmus	*we may go*
eātis	*you may go*
eant	*they may go*

Imperfect subjunctive

īrem	*I might go*
īrēs	*you might go*
īret	*he/she/it might go*
īrēmus	*we might go*
īrētis	*you might go*
īrent	*they might go*

Imperative

ī	*go!*
īte	*go!*

Future imperative

ītō	*you shall go!*
ītō	*he/she/it shall go!*
ītōte	*you shall go!*
euntō	*they shall go!*

Nominal forms of the present and participial stems

Present infinitive
īre – *to go*

Present participle
iēns, euntis – *going; one who goes*

Future infinitive
itūrum/-am/-um esse – *to be going to go*

Future participle
itūrus/-a/-um – *one who will go*

Gerund
īre, eundī, -ndo, ad -ndum/īre, eundo – *(the) going, of (the going),* etc.

Irregular Verbs

Personal forms using the perfect stem

Perfect indicative

iī	*I went, have gone, etc.*
īstī	*you went*
iit	*he/she/it went*
iimus	*we went*
īstis	*you went*
iērunt	*they went*

Pluperfect indicative

ieram	*I had gone*
ierās	*you had gone*
ierat	*he/she/it had gone*
ierāmus	*we had gone*
ierātis	*you had gone*
ierant	*they had gone*

Future II

ierō	*I will have gone*
ieris	*you will have gone*
ierit	*he/she/it will have gone*
ierimus	*we will have gone*
ieritis	*you will have gone*
ierint	*they will have gone*

Perfect subjunctive

(Note that there is no single general rendering for Latin subjunctives. Only one possibility is given here.)

ierim	*I may have gone*
ieris	*you may have gone*
ierit	*he/she/it may have gone*
ierimus	*we may have gone*
ieritis	*you may have gone*
ierint	*they may have gone*

Pluperfect subjunctive

īssem	*I might have gone*
īssēs	*you might have gone*
īsset	*he/she/it might have gone*
īssēmus	*we might have gone*
īssētis	*you might have gone*
īssent	*they might have gone*

Nominal forms of the perfect stem

Perfect active infinitive

īsse – *to have gone*

Perfect active participle

–

Irregular Verbs

Personal forms using the present stem

Present indicative

fīō	*I become*
fīs	*you become*
fit	*he/she/it becomes*
fīmus	*we become*
fītis	*you become*
fīunt	*they become*

Imperfect indicative

fīēbam	*I became, was becoming, etc.*
fīēbās	*you became*
fīēbat	*he/she/it became*
fīēbāmus	*we became*
fīēbātis	*you became*
fīēbant	*they became*

Future I

fīam	*I will become*
fīēs	*you will become*
fīet	*he/she/it will become*
fīēmus	*we will become*
fīētis	*you will become*
fīent	*they will become*

Present subjunctive

(Note that there is no single general rendering for Latin subjunctives. Only one possibility is given here.)

fīam	*I may become*
fīās	*you may become*
fīat	*he/she/it may become*
fīāmus	*we may become*
fīātis	*you may become*
fīant	*they may become*

Imperfect subjunctive

fierem	*I might become*
fierēs	*you might become*
fieret	*he/she/it might become*
fierēmus	*we might become*
fierētis	*you might become*
fierent	*they might become*

Imperative

fī	*become!*
fīte	*become!*

Future imperative

–

Nominal forms of the present stem

Present infinitive

fierī – *to become, to be made, to happen*

Future infinitive

factum īrī – *to be going to become/be made*
fore *or* futūrum/-am/-um esse – *to be going to happen*

Present participle

–

Future participle

(futūrus/-a/-um) – *one who will; become/ be made*

Gerundive

faciendus/-a/-um – *one who is becoming/being made; must become/be made*

Irregular Verbs

Personal forms using the participial stem

Perfect indicative

factus/-a/-um sum	*I became, have become, etc.*
factus/-a/-um es	*you became*
factus/-a/-um est	*he/she/it became*
factī/-ae/-a sumus	*we became*
factī/-ae/-a estis	*you became*
factī/-ae/-a sunt	*they became*

Pluperfect indicative

factus/-a/-um eram	*I had become*
factus/-a/-um erās	*you had become*
factus/-a/-um erat	*he/she/it had become*
factī/-ae/-a erāmus	*we had become*
factī/-ae/-a erātis	*you had become*
factī/-ae/-a erant	*they had become*

Future II

factus/-a/-um erō	*I will have become*
factus/-a/-um eris	*you will have become*
factus/-a/-um erit	*he/she/it will have become*
factī/-ae/-a erimus	*we will have become*
factī/-ae/-a eritis	*you will have become*
factī/-ae/-a erunt	*they will have become*

Perfect subjunctive

(Note that there is no single general rendering for Latin subjunctives. Only one possibility is given here.)

factus/-a/-um sim	*I may have become*
factus/-a/-um sīs	*you may have become*
factus/-a/-um sit	*he/she/it may have become*
factī/-ae/-a sīmus	*we may have become*
factī/-ae/-a sītis	*you may have become*
factī/-ae/-a sint	*they may have become*

Pluperfect subjunctive

factus/-a/-um essem	*I might have become*
factus/-a/-um essēs	*you might have become*
factus/-a/-um esset	*he/she/it might have become*
factī/-ae/-a essēmus	*we might have become*
factī/-ae/-a essētis	*you might have become*
factī/-ae/-a essent	*they might have become*

Nominal forms of the participial stem

Perfect infinitive

factum/-am/-um esse – *to have become, to have been made*

Perfect participle

factus/-a/-um – *made; one who has become/been made*

Defective Verb

Personal forms using the perfect stem

Perfect indicative
(Note that this verb is perfect in form, but present in meaning.)

memini	*I remember*
meministi	*you remember*
meminit	*he/she/it remembers*
meminimus	*we remember*
meministis	*you remember*
meminērunt	*they remember*

Pluperfect indicative

memineram	*I remembered*
meminerās	*you remembered*
meminerat	*he/she/it remembered*
meminerāmus	*we remembered*
meminerātis	*you remembered*
meminerant	*they remembered*

Future II

meminerō	*I will remember*
memineris	*you will remember*
meminerit	*he/she/it will remember*
meminerimus	*we will remember*
memineritis	*you will remember*
meminerint	*they will remember*

Perfect subjunctive
(Note that there is no single general rendering for Latin subjunctives. Only one possibility is given here.)

meminerim	*I may remember*
memineris	*you may remember*
meminerit	*he/she/it may remember*
meminerimus	*we may remember*
memineritis	*you may remember*
meminerint	*they may remember*

Pluperfect subjunctive

meminissem	*I might remember*
meminissēs	*you might remember*
meminisset	*he/she/it might remember*
meminissēmus	*we might remember*
meminissētis	*you might remember*
meminissent	*they might remember*

Imperative

mementō	*remember!*
mementōte	*remember!*

Future imperative

–

Nominal forms of the perfect stem

Perfect infinitive
meminisse – *to remember*

Perfect participle
–

Defective Verb

Personal forms using the perfect stem

Perfect indicative
(Note that this verb is perfect in form, but present in meaning.)

ōdī	*I hate*
ōdistī	*you hate*
ōdit	*he/she/it hates*
ōdimus	*we hate*
ōdistis	*you hate*
ōdērunt	*they hate*

Pluperfect indicative

ōderam	*I hated*
ōderās	*you hated*
ōderat	*he/she/it hated*
ōderāmus	*we hated*
ōderātis	*you hated*
ōderant	*they hated*

Future II

ōderō	*I will hate*
ōderis	*you will hate*
ōderit	*he/she/it will hate*
ōderimus	*we will hate*
ōderitis	*you will hate*
ōderint	*they will hate*

Perfect subjunctive
(Note that there is no single general rendering for Latin subjunctives. Only one possibility is given here.)

ōderim	*I may hate*
ōderis	*you may hate*
ōderit	*he/she/it may hate*
ōderimus	*we may hate*
ōderitis	*you may hate*
ōderint	*they may hate*

Pluperfect subjunctive

ōdissem	*I might hate*
ōdissēs	*you might hate*
ōdisset	*he/she/it might hate*
ōdissēmus	*we might hate*
ōdissētis	*you might hate*
ōdissent	*they might hate*

Nominal forms of the perfect and participial stems

Perfect infinitive
ōdisse – *to hate*

Future participle
ōsūrus/-a/-um – *one who will hate*

Principal Parts of Important Verbs

Verbs of the a-Conjugation

Perfect using v

1	amāre	amō	amāvī	amātum	to love
2	laudāre	laudō	laudāvī	laudātum	to praise

Perfect using u

3	domāre	domō	domuī	domitum	to tame
4	secāre	secō	secuī	sectum	to cut, sever
5	vetāre	vetō	vetuī	vetitum	to forbid

Perfect using reduplication

6	dare	dō	dedī	datum	to give
7	circumdare	circumdō	circumdedī	circumdatum	to surround, envelop
8	stāre	stō	stetī	stātūrus	to stand
9	circumstāre	circumstō	circumstetī	–	to stand around, surround
10	cōnstāre	cōnstō	cōnstitī	cōnstātūrus	to consist, to be correct
		cōnstat	cōnstitit		it is correct/was correct
11	instāre	instō	institī	–	to approach, to threaten
12	obstāre	obstō	obstitī	–	to oppose, hinder
13	praestāre	praestō	praestitī	praestātūrus	(dat.) to excel
					(acc.) to provide, supply
	praestat	praestitit			it is/was better
14	restāre	restō	restitī	–	to be left over, remain

Perfect using lengthening

15	(ad)iuvāre	(ād)iuvō	(ad)iūvī	(ad)iūtum	to support, help
		iuvat	iūvit		it pleases/pleased
16	lavāre	lavō	lāvī	–	to wash
				lautus	clean, washed

Deponent verbs

17	lavārī	lavor	lautus sum	to wash
18	aemulārī	aemulor	aemulātus sum	to emulate
19	arbitrārī	arbitror	arbitrātus sum	to believe, think
20	auxiliārī	auxilior	auxiliātus sum	to help
21	comitārī	comitor	comitātus sum	to accompany
22	cōnārī	cōnor	cōnātus sum	to attempt, try
23	percontārī	percontor	percontātus sum	to inquire
24	cōntiōnārī	cōntiōnor	cōntiōnātus sum	to give a speech
25	recordārī	recordor	recordātus sum	to remember
26	cūnctārī	cūnctor	cūnctātus sum	to hesitate

27	indīgnārī	indīgnor	indīgnātus sum	to scorn, deem unworthy
28	dominārī	dominor	dominātus sum	to dominate, rule
29	glōriārī	glōrior	glōriātus sum	to boast, brag
30	grātulārī	grātulor	grātulātus sum	to congratulate
31	(ad/co)hortārī	(ad/co)hortor	(ad/co)hortātus sum	to urge, to exhort
32	imitārī	imitor	imitātus sum	to imitate
33	interpretārī	interpretor	interpretātus sum	to decide, to construe, to interpret
34	laetārī	laetor	laetātus sum	to be glad, rejoice
35	minārī	minor	minātus sum	to threaten
36	minitārī	minitor	minitātus sum	to threaten
37	(ad)mirārī	(ad)miror	(ad)mirātus sum	to admire, to be surprised
38	miserārī	miseror	miserātus sum	to regret
39	morārī	moror	morātus sum	to devote attention to
40	opīnārī	opīnor	opīnātus sum	to opine, to think
41	perīclitārī	perīclitor	perīclitātus sum	to try, to endanger
42	populārī	populor	populātus sum	to ravage, devastate
43	praedārī	praedor	praedātus sum	to acquire loot; to obtain food by hunting/preying
44	precārī	precor	precātus sum	to beg, entreat
45	proeliārī	proelior	proeliātus sum	to fight
46	(cōn)sectārī	(cōn)sector	(cōn)sectātus sum	to hunt down
47	(cōn)sōlārī	(cōn)sōlor	(cōn)sōlātus sum	to console, comfort
48	speculārī	speculor	speculātus sum	to observe, to spy out
49	(per)scrūtārī	(per)scrūtor	(per)scrūtātus sum	to search through, to investigate carefully
50	āspernārī	āspernor	āspernātus sum	to despise, disdain
51	cōnspicārī	cōnspicor	cōnspicātus sum	to catch sight of
52	suspicārī	suspicor	suspicātus sum	to mistrust, to suppose
53	testārī	testor	testātus sum	to testify
54	obtestārī	obtestor	obtestātus sum	to call to witness, to implore
55	tūtārī	tūtor	tūtātus sum	to protest
56	vagārī	vagor	vagātus sum	to wander, roam
57	vēnārī	vēnor	vēnātus sum	to hunt
58	venerārī	veneror	venerātus sum	to venerate
59	versārī	versor	versātus sum	to dwell

Verbs of the e-Conjugation

Perfect using v

60	complēre	compleō	complēvī	complētum	to finish, complete
61	implēre	impleō	implēvī	implētum	to fill, complete
62	dēlēre	dēleō	dēlēvī	dēlētum	to destroy
63	flēre	fleō	flēvī	flētum	to weep, cry

Perfect using u

64	arcēre	arceō	arcuī	–	to ward off, keep away
65	coercēre	coerceō	coercuī	coercitum	to enclose, to restrain, to limit
66	exercēre	exerceō	exercuī	–	to exercise, practice
				exercitātus	trained, skilled
				exercitus	plagued, troubled
67	habēre	habeō	habuī	habitum	to have, hold
68	adhibēre	adhibeō	adhibuī	adhibitum	to use, employ, to invite, bring in
69	prohibēre	prohibeō	prohibuī	prohibitum	to prohibit
70	dēbēre	dēbeō	dēbuī	dēbitum	to owe, to have to (must), to thank
71	praebēre	praebeō	praebuī	praebitum	to make available, provide
72	merēre	mereō	meruī	meritum	to earn, deserve
73	monēre	moneō	monuī	monitum	to warn
74	admonēre	admoneō	admonuī	admonitum	to admonish, to caution
75	nocēre	noceō	nocuī	nocitūrus	to harm
76	placēre	placeō	placuī	–	to please
		placet	placuit	placitum	it pleases/pleased
77	tacēre	taceō	tacuī	–	to be silent
				tacitus	discreet, secretive
78	terrēre	terreō	terruī	territum	to frighten
79	perterrēre	perterreō	perterruī	perterritum	to terrify, frighten greatly
80	docēre	doceō	docuī	doctum	to teach
81	miscēre	misceō	miscuī	mixtum	to mix
82	tenēre	teneō	tenuī	–	to hold, to possess
83	abstinēre	abstineō	abstinuī	–	to keep away, to abstain
84	continēre	contineō	continuī	–	to hold in position, to retain
				contentus	content(ed)
85	obtinēre	obtineō	obtinuī	obtentum	to obtain, to prevail, to occupy
86	pertinēre	pertineō	pertinuī	–	to extend, to relate to
87	retinēre	retineō	retinuī	retentum	to restrain, to retain
88	sustinēre	sustineō	sustinuī	(sustentātum)	to hold back, to support
89	cēnsēre	cēnseō	cēnsuī	cēnsum	to think, suppose, to assess
90	carēre	careō	caruī	–	to be without, to lack
91	egēre	egeō	eguī	–	to need, to be without
92	dolēre	doleō	doluī	–	to suffer, feel pain
93	horrēre	horreō	horruī	–	to dread, shudder at
94	iacēre	iaceō	iacuī	–	to lie, be situated
95	latēre	lateō	latuī	–	to lie hidden
96	ēminēre	ēmineō	ēminuī	–	to excel, be prominent
97	imminēre	immineō	–	–	to overhang, to threaten
98	pārēre	pāreō	pāruī	–	to obey
99	appārēre	appāreō	appāruī	–	to appear
		appāret	appāruit		it is/was apparent

100	patēre	pateō	patuī	–	to extend, to lie open
101	studēre	studeō	studuī	–	to strive, to busy oneself with
102	timēre	timeō	timuī	–	to fear, be afraid
103	valēre	valeō	valuī	–	to be healthy, to be influential, to prevail
104	vigēre	vigeō	vīguī	–	to be strong or vigorous

Perfect using s

105	augēre	augeō	auxī	auctum	to increase, to promote
106	torquēre	torqueō	torsī	tortum	to turn, twist, to torture
107	ārdēre	ārdeō	ārsī	ārsūrus	to burn, to glow
108	haerēre	haereō	haesī	haesūrus	to stick, cling to
109	iubēre	iubeō	iussī	iussum	to order
110	manēre	maneō	mānsī	mānsūrus	to stay, to wait for
111	permanēre	permaneō	permānsī	permānsūrus	to remain, to endure
112	rīdēre	rīdeō	rīsī	rīsum	to laugh, to laugh at
113	suādēre	suādeō	suāsī	suāsum	to recommend, to urge
114	persuādēre	persuādeō	persuāsī	persuāsum	to persuade (ut), to convince (AcI)
115	fulgēre	fulgeō	fulsī	–	to shine, to glow
116	lūcēre	lūceō	lūxī	–	to shine, to be apparent
117	urgēre	urgeō	ursī	–	to urge, spur on

Perfect using reduplication
No reduplication in the compound.

118	pendēre	pendeō	pependī	–	to hang, hang down
119	impendēre	impendeō	–	–	to be imminent, impend
120	spondēre	spondeō	spopondī	spōnsum	to promise, give a pledge
121	respondēre	respondeō	respondī*	respōnsum	to answer, respond

Perfect using lengthening

122	cavēre	caveō	cāvī	cautum	to beware of (acc.), to avoid
123	favēre	faveō	fāvī	fautum	to favor, support
124	movēre	moveō	mōvī	mōtum	to move
125	commovēre	commoveō	commōvī	commōtum	to move, to provoke
126	permovēre	permoveō	permōvī	permōtum	to move deeply, to influence
127	removēre	removeō	remōvī	remōtum	to remove
128	sedēre	sedeō	sēdī	sessum	to sit
129	obsidēre	obsideō	obsēdī	obsessum	to besiege
130	possidēre	possideō	possēdī	possessum	to possess
131	vidēre	videō	vīdī	vīsum	to see
132	invidēre	invideō	invīdī	invīsum	to envy
133	prōvidēre	prōvideō	prōvīdī	prōvīsum	to foresee (acc.), to provide for (dat.)

Deponent verbs

134	pollicērī	polliceor	pollicitus sum	to promise
135	merērī	mereor	meritus sum	to earn, to deserve, merit
136	miserērī	misereor	miseritus sum	to pity, to have mercy
137	verērī	vereor	veritus sum	to revere, to fear, to dread
138	rērī	reor	ratus sum	to suppose, to reckon
139	tuērī	tueor	–	to protect
			tutus	safe, protected
140	intuērī	intueor	–	to consider, regard
141	fatērī	fateor	fassus sum	to admit, confess
142	cōnfitērī	cōnfiteor	cōnfessus sum	to confess
143	profitērī	profiteor	professus sum	to declare, to profess
144	medērī	medeor	–	to heal

Semideponent verbs

145	solēre	soleō	solitus sum	to be accustomed to
146	audēre	audeō	ausus sum	to dare
147	gaudēre	gaudeō	gāvīsus sum	to be glad, rejoice

Verbs of the i-Conjugation

Perfect using v

148	audīre	audiō	audīvī	audītum	to hear
149	sepelīre	sepeliō	sepelīvī	sepultum	to bury, inter

Perfect using u

150	aperīre	aperiō	aperuī	apertum	to open
151	operīre	operiō	operuī	opertum	to cover, to conceal
152	dēsilīre	dēsiliō	dēsiluī	–	to leap down

Perfect using s

153	haurīre	hauriō	hausī	haustum	to drink, swallow
154	exhaurīre	exhauriō	exhausī	exhaustum	to exhaust
155	saepīre	saepiō	saepsī	saeptum	to surround
156	sancīre	sanciō	sānxī	sānctum	to ordain, to ratify
157	vincīre	vinciō	vīnxī	vīnctum	to bind, fetter
158	sentīre	sentiō	sēnsī	sēnsum	to feel, think
159	cōnsentīre	cōnsentiō	cōnsēnsī	cōnsēnsum	to be in agreement
160	dissentīre	dissentiō	dissēnsī	dissēnsum	to dissent

Perfect using reduplication

161	reperīre	reperiō	repperī	repertum	to find out, discover
162	comperīre	comperiō	comperī	compertum	to learn, to verify

Perfect using lengthening

163	venīre	veniō	vēnī	ventum	to come
164	circumvenīre	circumveniō	circumvēnī	circumventum	to encircle, surround
165	convenīre	conveniō	convēnī	conventum	to convene, to suit, fit
166	invenīre	inveniō	invēnī	inventum	to invent
167	pervenīre	perveniō	pervēnī	perventum	to come to, to arrive
168	subvenīre	subveniō	subvēnī	subventum	to come to help, assist

Deponent verbs

169	blandīrī	blandior	blandītus sum	to flatter
170	largīrī	largior	largītus sum	to give generously
171	mentīrī	mentior	mentītus sum	to lie, deceive
172	mōlīrī	mōlior	mōlītus sum	to set in motion, undertake
173	partīrī	partior	partītus sum	to divide
174	potīrī	potior	potītus sum	to get possession of (abl.)
175	sortīrī	sortior	sortītus sum	to cast or draw lots
176	assentīrī	assentior	assēnsus sum	to assent
177	adorīrī	adorior	adortus sum	to come to grips, to begin work
178	experīrī	experior	expertus sum	to test, put to the test
179	opperīrī	opperior	oppertus sum	to wait (for), to await
180	mētīrī	mētior	mēnsus sum	to measure
181	ōrdīrī	ōrdior	ōrsus sum	to begin

Verbs of the Consonant Conjugation

Perfect using v

182	cernere	cernō	(crēvī)	(crētum)	to see, sight
183	dēcernere	dēcernō	dēcrēvī	dēcrētum	to decide, determine
184	discernere	discernō	discrēvī	discrētum	to discern, to distinguish
185	sēcernere	sēcernō	sēcrēvī	sēcrētum	to separate
186	serere	serō	sēvī	satum	to sow, plant
187	spernere	spernō	sprēvī	sprētum	to spurn
188	sternere	sternō	strāvī	strātum	to spread, strew
189	sinere	sinō	sīvī	situm	to allow, permit
190	dēsinere	dēsinō	dēsiī	dēsitum	to cease, desist
191	terere	terō	trīvī	trītum	to rub, wear away

192	quaerere	quaerō	quaesīvī	quaesītum	to see, inquire (ex, ab)
193	exquīrere	exquīrō	exquīsīvī	exquīsītum	to seek out, to examine
194	petere	petō	petīvī	petītum	to ask (for), to aim at
195	appetere	appetō	appetīvī	appetītum	to desire
196	expetere	expetō	expetīvī	expetītum	to aspire to
197	repetere	repetō	repetīvī	repetītum	to repeat, to demand back
198	suppetere	suppetō	suppetīvī	–	to be on hand, to be sufficient (for)
199	arcessere	arcessō	arcessīvī	arcessītum	to send for, summon
200	capessere	capessō	capessīvī	capessītum	to grasp, take
201	lacessere	lacessō	lacessīvī	lacessītum	to provoke, challenge
202	crēscere	crēscō	crēvī	–	to grow, increase
203	pāscere	pāscō	pāvī	pāstum	to feed, to pasture
204	quiēscere	quiēscō	quiēvī	–	to rest
205	assuēscere	assuēscō	assuēvī	– / assuētus	to get used to / accustomed
206	cōnsuēscere	cōnsuēscō	cōnsuēvī	–	to get used to
207	nōscere	nōscō	nōvī	– / nōtus	to examine, to recognize / known, acquainted
208	cōgnōscere	cōgnōscō	cōgnōvī	cōgnitum	to examine, learn
209	īgnōscere	īgnōscō	īgnōvī	īgnōtum	to pardon, forgive
210	adolēscere	adolēscō	adolēvī	– / adultus	to grow up, mature / mature, adult
211	ascīscere	ascīscō	ascīvī	ascītum	to admit, approve of
212	concupīscere	concupīscō	concupīvī	concupītum	to desire

Perfect using u

213	gemere	gemō	gemuī	–	to sigh, groan
214	gignere	gignō	genuī	genitum	to give birth to, to beget
215	pōnere	pōnō	posuī	positum	to set, place, lay
216	compōnere	compōnō	composuī	compositum	to compose, to put together
217	dēpōnere	dēpōnō	dēposuī	dēpositum	to take off, to deposit
218	dispōnere	dispōnō	disposuī	dispositum	to distribute, to order, manage
219	expōnere	expōnō	exposuī	expositum	to set out, to publish
220	impōnere	impōnō	imposuī	impositum	to impose, put upon
221	prōpōnere	prōpōnō	prōposuī	prōpositum	to propose
222	alere	alō	aluī	al(i)tum	to nourish, feed
223	colere	colō	coluī	cultum	to cultivate, to honor, to inhabit
224	incolere	incolō	incoluī	–	to live (in), to inhabit
225	cōnsulere	cōnsulō	cōnsuluī	cōnsultum	to consult (acc.), to take care of (dat.)
226	serere	serō	seruī	sertum	to sow, plant, to put in a row
227	dēserere	dēserō	dēseruī	dēsertum	to desert

228	disserere	disserō	disseruī	(disputātum)	to discuss, to explain
229	cōnsenēscere	cōnsenēscō	cōnsenuī	–	to grow old
230	conticēscere	conticēscō	conticuī	–	to fall silent
231	convalēscere	convalēscō	convaluī	–	to become healthy or strong
232	ērubēscere	ērubēscō	ērubuī	–	to blush
233	ingemīscere	ingemīscō	ingemuī	–	to sigh
234	ingravēscere	ingravēscō	–	–	to grow heavy
235	pertimēscere	pertimēscō	pertimuī	–	to become very scared (of)

Perfect using s

236	scrībere	scrībō	scrīpsī	scrīptum	to write
237	prōscrībere	prōscrībō	prōscrīpsī	prōscrīptum	to make public, to proscribe
238	dīcere	dīcō	dīxī	dictum	to say, speak
239	indīcere	indīcō	indīxī	indictum	to announce
240	praedīcere	praedīcō	praedīxī	praedictum	to predict
241	dūcere	dūcō	dūxī	ductum	to lead, to consider, regard
242	abdūcere	abdūcō	abdūxī	abductum	to lead away, to detach
243	addūcere	addūcō	addūxī	adductum	to lead to, to induce
244	condūcere	condūcō	condūxī	conductum	to bring together, to unite, join
		condūcit	condūxit		it is/was profitable
245	dēdūcere	dēdūcō	dēdūxī	dēductum	to divert
246	indūcere	indūcō	indūxī	inductum	to lead in, to induce, influence
247	perdūcere	perdūcō	perdūxī	perductum	to conduct, bring through
248	prōdūcere	prōdūcō	prōdūxī	prōductum	to lead forward, to reveal
249	redūcere	redūcō	redūxī	reductum	to lead back, to reduce
250	subdūcere	subdūcō	subdūxī	subductum	to lead up, to transfer
251	trādūcere	trādūcō	trādūxī	trāductum	to lead across
252	trahere	trahō	trāxī	tractum	to draw, drag
253	contrahere	contrahō	contrāxī	contractum	to tighten, contract
254	dētrahere	dētrahō	dētrāxī	dētractum	to take away, to drag down
255	vehere	vehō	vēxī	vectum	to convey, to pass, ride
256	cōnflīgere	cōnflīgō	cōnflīxī	cōnflictum	to flee
257	regere	regō	rēxī	rēctum	to rule, guide, to manage, direct
258	corrigere	corrigō	corrēxī	corrēctum	to correct
259	ērigere	ērigō	ērēxī	ērēctum	to raise, to rouse
260	porrigere	porrigō	porrēxī	porrēctum	to extend, stretch out
261	pergere	pergō	perrēxī	–	to proceed
262	surgere	surgō	surrēxī	–	to rise, lift
263	tegere	tegō	tēxī	tēctum	to cover
264	prōtegere	prōtegō	prōtēxī	prōtēctum	to protect
265	cingere	cingō	cīnxī	cīnctum	to encircle, surround

Conjugation

266	fingere	fingō	finxī	fictum	to make up a story
267	pingere	pingō	pīnxī	pictum	to paint
268	stringere	stringō	strīnxī	strictum	to draw tight, to draw, to strip off
269	exstinguere	exstinguō	exstinxī	exstinctum	to extinguish
270	distinguere	distinguō	distinxī	distinctum	to distinguish
271	fluere	fluō	flūxī	–	to flow
272	exstruere	exstruō	exstrūxī	exstrūctum	to pile up, to build
273	instruere	instruō	instrūxī	instrūctum	to prepare, to fit out, to instruct
274	vīvere	vīvō	vīxī	vīctūrus	to live
275	contemnere	contemnō	contempsī	contemptum	to look down on, to disregard
276	gerere	gerō	gessī	gestum	to carry, to carry on
277	ūrere	ūrō	ussī	ustum	to burn
278	mittere	mittō	mīsī	missum	to send
279	admittere	admittō	admīsī	admissum	to admit, to permit
280	āmittere	āmittō	āmīsī	āmissum	to lose
281	committere	committō	commīsī	commissum	to bring together, to entrust
282	dēmittere	dēmittō	dēmīsī	dēmissum	to let fall, to sink
283	dīmittere	dīmittō	dīmīsī	dīmissum	to send away, to abandon
284	omittere	omittō	omīsī	omissum	to lay aside, to omit
285	permittere	permittō	permīsī	permissum	to permit
286	prōmittere	prōmittō	prōmīsī	prōmissum	to promise
287	remittere	remittō	remīsī	remissum	to send back, remit
288	cēdere	cēdō	cessī	cessūrus	to give way, yield
289	accēdere	accēdō	accessī	accessūrus	to approach, to be added to
290	concēdere	concēdō	concessī	concessum	to concede, to submit
291	dēcēdere	dēcēdō	dēcessī	–	to disappear, to die
292	discēdere	discēdō	discessī	–	to depart, to abandon
293	excēdere	excēdō	excessī	–	to go out, go away
294	incēdere	incēdō	incessī	–	to advance, to march along
295	prōcēdere	prōcēdō	prōcessī	–	to proceed
296	sēcēdere	sēcēdō	sēcessī	–	to withdraw, to secede
297	succēdere	succēdō	successī	–	to advance, to follow
298	claudere	claudō	clausī	clausum	to close, shut
299	inclūdere	inclūdō	inclūsī	inclūsum	to shut up, enclose
300	interclūdere	interclūdō	interclūsī	interclūsum	to blockade
301	dīvidere	dīvidō	dīvīsī	dīvīsum	to divide
302	laedere	laedō	laesī	laesum	to strike, to injure
303	lūdere	lūdō	lūsī	lūsum	to play, to jest
304	plaudere	plaudō	plausī	plausum	to applaud
305	vādere	vādō	–	–	to go, to walk
306	ēvādere	ēvādō	ēvāsī	ēvāsūrus	to evade, to avoid
307	invādere	invādō	invāsī	invāsūrus	to invade
308	figere	figō	fīxī	fīxum	to fasten, fix

309	trānsfīgere	trānsfīgō	trānsfīxī	trānsfīxum	to pierce
310	flectere	flectō	flexī	flexum	to bend
311	spargere	spargō	sparsī	sparsum	to scatter, sprinkle
312	premere	premō	pressī	pressum	to press
313	opprimere	opprimō	oppressī	oppressum	to oppress
314	exārdēscere	exārdēscō	exārsī	–	to flare up

Perfect using reduplication
*Reduplication usually is not present in the compounds

315	sistere	sistō	stetī (stitī)	statum	to stop, to cause to stand
316	cōnsistere	cōnsistō	cōnstitī	–	to exist, to be established
317	dēsistere	dēsistō	dēstitī	–	to stop, desist
318	ex(s)istere	ex(s)istō	exstitī	–	to appear; to be
319	resistere	resistō	restitī	–	to resist
320	canere	canō	cecinī	(cantātum)	to sing, to play an instrument
321	tangere	tangō	tetigī	tāctum	to touch
322	contingere	contingō	contigī*	contāctum	to touch, to attain (to)
		contingit	contigit*		it comes/came to pass
323	tendere	tendō	tetendī	tentum	to stretch, tighten
324	contendere	contendō	contendī*	contentum	to hasten, to struggle
325	intendere	intendō	intendī*	intentum	to aim
326	ostendere	ostendō	ostendī*	–	to show, exhibit
327	cadere	cadō	cecidī	cāsūrus	to fall
328	accidere	accidō	accidī*	–	to happen, occur
		accidit	accidit*		it happens/happened
329	concidere	concidō	concidī*	–	to fall down
330	incidere	incidō	incidī*	–	to fall in with, to happen
331	occidere	occidō	occidī*	–	to fall, fall down
332	caedere	caedō	cecīdī	caesum	to fell, to kill
333	occīdere	occīdō	occīdī*	occīsum	to strike down, kill
334	pendere	pendō	pependī	pēnsum	to weight, to pay
335	impendere	impendō	impendī*	impēnsum	to expend, to devote (to)
336	currere	currō	cucurrī	cursum	to run
337	concurrere	concurrō	concurrī*	concursum	to concur, to coincide
338	occurrere	occurrō	occurrī*	–	to run to meet
339	fallere	fallō	fefellī	–	to deceive, to slip by
		fallit	fefellit	falsus	it escapes/escaped the notice/false
340	dēdere	dēdō	dēdidī	dēditum	to surrender, hand over
341	ēdere	ēdō	ēdidī	ēditum	to put forth, give out
342	prōdere	prōdō	prōdidī	prōditum	to hand down, to reveal
343	reddere	reddō	reddidī	redditum	to pay back
344	trādere	trādō	trādidī	trāditum	to hand over, to bequeath

345	abdere	abdō	abdidī	abditum	to conceal
346	addere	addō	addidī	additum	to add to
347	crēdere	crēdō	crēdidī	crēditum	to believe
348	perdere	perdō	perdidī	perditum	to ruin, destroy, to lose
349	vendere	vendō	vendidī	venditum	to sell
350	condere	condō	condidī	conditum	to put out of sight
351	parcere	parcō	pepercī	parsūrus	to spare
352	pellere	pellō	pepulī	pulsum	to beat, to drive out
353	dēpellere	dēpellō	dēpulī*	dēpulsum	to push out, to repel
354	expellere	expellō	expulī*	expulsum	to expel
355	impellere	impellō	impulī*	impulsum	to drive, impel
356	repellere	repellō	reppulī	repulsum	to repel, push back
357	bibere	bibō	bibī	–	to drink
358	pangere	pangō	pepigī	pāctum	to agree upon
359	findere	findō	fidī	fissum	to split
360	percellere	percellō	perculī	perculsum	to dismay, upset
361	pungere	pungō	pupugī	pūnctum	to puncture
362	scindere	scindō	scidī	scissum	to tear, split
363	rescindere	rescindō	rescidī	rescissum	to rescind
364	tollere	tollō	sustulī	sublātum	to lift, raise; to remove
365	tundere	tundō	tutudī	tūsum	to beat
366	poscere	poscō	poposcī	(postulātum)	to demand
367	dēposcere	dēposcō	dēposcī	–	to demand
368	discere	discō	didicī	–	to learn

Perfect using lengthening
*Some compounds form the perfect by using s

369	agere	agō	ēgī	āctum	to conduct
370	exigere	exigō	exēgī	exāctum	to expel, to finish
371	peragere	peragō	perēgī	perāctum	to complete
372	redigere	redigō	redēgī	redāctum	to render, to reduce
373	subigere	subigō	subēgī	subāctum	to subjugate
374	cōgere	cōgō	coēgī	coāctum	to collect, to compel
375	frangere	frangō	frēgī	frāctum	to break something
376	emere	emō	ēmī	ēmptum	to buy
377	adimere	adimō	adēmī	adēmptum	to take away
378	dirimere	dirimō	dirēmī	dirēmptum	to separate
379	dēmere	dēmō	dēmpsī*	dēmptum	to take away
380	prōmere	prōmō	prōmpsī*	prōmptum	to bring forth
381	sūmere	sūmō	sūmpsī*	sūmptum	to take
382	cōnsūmere	cōnsūmō	cōnsūmpsī*	cōnsūmptum	to consume, use
383	legere	legō	lēgī	lēctum	to read
384	colligere	colligō	collēgī	collēctum	to collect

385	dēligere	dēligō	dēlēgī	dēlēctum	to pick out, choose
386	ēligere	ēligō	ēlēgī	ēlēctum	to choose
387	dīligere	dīligō	dīlēxī*	dīlēctum	to esteem, love
388	intellegere	intellegō	intellēxī*	intellēctum	to understand
389	neglegere	neglegō	neglēxī*	neglēctum	to neglect
390	relinquere	relinquō	relīquī	relictum	to abandon, leave behind
391	vincere	vincō	vīcī	victum	to conquer
392	dēvincere	dēvincō	dēvīcī	dēvictum	to conquer utterly
393	convincere	convincō	convīcī	convictum	to convince, to demonstrate
394	rumpere	rumpō	rūpī	ruptum	to break, destroy
395	corrumpere	corrumpō	corrūpī	corruptum	to corrupt
396	irrumpere	irrumpō	irrūpī	irruptum	to break in
397	edere	edō	ēdī	ēsum	to eat
398	fundere	fundō	fūdī	fūsum	to pour (metal), to rout
399	diffundere	diffundō	diffūdī	diffūsum	to spread out, to cheer up
400	effundere	effundō	effūdī	effūsum	to pour out
401	cōnsīdere	cōnsīdō	cōnsēdī	cōnsessum	to settle, to take up a position
402	obsīdere	obsīdō	obsēdī	obsessum	to occupy

Perfect with no change in the present stem

403	accendere	accendō	accendī	accēnsum	to kindle
404	incendere	incendō	incendī	incēnsum	to set fire to
405	dēfendere	dēfendō	dēfendī	dēfēnsum	to defend
406	offendere	offendō	offendī	offēnsum	to offend
407	comprehendere	comprehendō	comprehendī	comprehēnsum	to embrace, to include
408	reprehendere	reprehendō	reprehendī	reprehēnsum	to blame
409	scandere	scandō	scandī	–	to climb
410	ascendere	ascendō	ascendī	ascēnsum	to ascend, climb up
411	dēscendere	dēscendō	dēscendī	dēscēnsum	to descend, climb down
412	trānscendere	trānscendō	trānscendī	trānscēnsum	to go across or over
413	vertere	vertō	vertī	versum	to turn
414	āvertere	āvertō	āvertī	āversum	to turn aside, avert
415	convertere	convertō	convertī	conversum	to change
416	ēvertere	ēvertō	ēvertī	ēversum	to overthrow, ruin
417	animadvertere	animadvertō	animadvertī	animadversum	to take notice of
418	āvellere	āvellō	āvellī	āvulsum	to tear away
419	excellere	excellō	–	–	to excel, to be eminent
420	furere	furō	–	–	to rage
421	vergere	vergō	–	–	to incline, slope
422	verrere	verrō	–	–	to sweep
423	vīsere	vīsō	–	–	to look at
424	minuere	minuō	minuī	minūtum	to decrease

Conjugation

425	statuere	statuō	statuī	statūtum	to set up, to decide
426	cōnstituere	cōnstituō	cōnstituī	cōnstitūtum	to set up, to place
427	īnstituere	īnstituō	īnstituī	īnstitūtum	to establish, institute
428	restituere	restituō	restituī	restitūtum	to restore
429	metuere	metuō	metuī	–	to fear
430	tribuere	tribuō	tribuī	tribūtum	to divide, to allot
431	distribuere	distribuō	distribuī	distribūtum	to distribute
432	induere	induō	induī	indūtum	to put on, clothe
433	exuere	exuō	exuī	exūtum	to undress, to deprive of
434	ruere	ruō	ruī	ruitūrus	to fall, to rush on, to destroy
435	obruere	obruō	obruī	obrutum	to overwhelm
436	arguere	arguō	arguī	(accusātum)	to allege, to accuse
437	congruere	congruō	congruī	–	to agree, coincide
438	luere	luō	luī	luitūrus	to pay, to atone
439	solvere	solvō	solvī	solūtum	to loosen, to pay back
440	absolvere	absolvō	absolvī	absolūtum	to acquit, to sum up
441	dissolvere	dissolvō	dissolvī	dissolūtum	to dissolve
442	volvere	volvō	volvī	volūtum	to roll, to revolve

Deponent verbs

443	fungī	fungor	fūnctus sum	to be engaged in (abl.)
444	dēfungī	dēfungor	dēfūnctus sum	to pass away
445	querī	queror	questus sum	to complain
446	loquī	loquor	locūtus sum	to speak
447	alloquī	alloquor	allocūtus sum	to speak to
448	colloquī	colloquor	collocūtus sum	to speak together
449	sequī	sequor	secūtus sum	to follow (acc.)
450	assequī	assequor	assecūtus sum	to gain, achieve
451	cōnsequī	cōnsequor	cōnsecūtus sum	to catch up with
452	exsequī	exsequor	exsecūtus sum	to accomplish, to pursue
453	persequī	persequor	persecūtus sum	to persecute
454	fruī	fruor	fruitūrus	to enjoy (abl.)
455	lābī	lābor	lāpsus sum	to glide, to slip and fall
456	ēlābī	ēlābor	ēlāpsus sum	to slip away
457	ūtī	ūtor	ūsus sum	to use (abl.)
458	nītī	nītor	nīsus/nīxus sum	to lean upon, to strive
459	amplectī	amplector	amplexus sum	to embrace, encircle
460	complectī	complector	complexus sum	to grasp, to include
461	nāscī	nāscor	nātus sum	to be born
462	nancīscī	nancīscor	na(n)ctus sum	to stumble on, find
463	ulcīscī	ulcīscor	ultus sum	to avenge
464	īrāscī	īrāscor	–	to get angry
			īrātus	irate, angry

465	adipīscī	adipīscor	adeptus sum	to obtain, to inherit
466	proficīscī	proficīscor	profectus sum	to depart, set out
467	comminīscī	comminīscor	commentus sum	to devise, think up
468	reminīscī	reminīscor	(recordātus sum)	to remember
469	oblīvīscī	oblīvīscor	oblītus sum	to forget
470	vēscī	vēscor	(vīxī)	to feed on
471	expergīscī	expergīscor	experrēctus sum	to awake
472	pacīscī	pacīscor	pactus sum	to make a bargain or agreement

Semideponent verbs

473	fīdere	fīdō	fīsus sum	to trust
474	cōnfīdere	cōnfīdō	cōnfīsus sum	to trust, rely (on)
475	diffīdere	diffīdō	diffīsus sum	to mistrust
476	revertī	revertor	revertī	to return
			reversus	returned
477	dēvertī	dēvertor	dēvertī	to resort to, to lodge

Verbs of the Mixed Conjugation

Perfect using v

478	cupere	cupiō	cupīvī	cupītum	to desire

Perfect using u

479	rapere	rapiō	rapuī	raptum	to seize, to pillage
480	dīripere	dīripiō	dīripuī	dīreptum	to plunder
481	ēripere	ēripiō	ēripuī	ēreptum	snatch away

Perfect using s

482	āspicere	āspiciō	āspexī	āspectum	to look at, observe
483	cōnspicere	cōnspiciō	cōnspexī	cōnspectum	to attract attention
484	dēspicere	dēspiciō	dēspexī	dēspectum	to look down on, to despise
485	prōspicere	prōspiciō	prōspexī	prōspectum	to foresee, to look out for
486	respicere	respiciō	respexī	respectum	to respect, to consider
488	concutere	concutiō	concussī	concussum	to shake
487	quatere	quatiō	–	–	to shake
489	excutere	excutiō	excussī	excussum	to shake out or off
490	percutere	percutiō	percussī	percussum	to strike, to pierce

Perfect using reduplication

491	parere	pariō	peperī	partum (paritūrus)	to produce, to give birth to, to acquire

Perfect using lengthening

492	capere	capiō	cēpī	captum	to seize, take
493	accipere	accipiō	accēpī	acceptum	to receive, accept, to learn
494	concipere	concipiō	concēpī	conceptum	to receive, to contain
495	dēcipere	dēcipiō	dēcēpī	dēceptum	to deceive, mislead
496	excipere	excipiō	excēpī	exceptum	to take out, to receive
497	percipere	percipiō	percēpī	perceptum	to perceive
498	praecipere	praecipiō	praecēpī	praeceptum	to anticipate
499	recipere	recipiō	recēpī	receptum	to keep back, to accept
500	suscipere	suscipiō	suscēpī	susceptum	to undertake
501	incipere	incipiō	coepī	inceptum (coeptum)	to begin, start
502	facere	faciō	fēcī	factum	to do, to make
503	patefacere	patefaciō	patefēcī	patefactum	to open
504	satisfacere	satisfaciō	satisfēcī	satisfactum	to satisfy (dat.)
505	afficere	afficiō	affēcī	affectum	to affect
506	cōnficere	cōnficiō	cōnfēcī	cōnfectum	to complete, prepare
507	dēficere	dēficiō	dēfēcī	dēfectum	to lack, be left without, be wanting
508	efficere	efficiō	effēcī	effectum	to bring about, to effect
509	interficere	interficiō	interfēcī	interfectum	to kill, to destroy
510	perficere	perficiō	perfēcī	perfectum	to complete, to accomplish
511	praeficere	praeficiō	praefēcī	praefectum	to put in charge
512	prōficere	prōficiō	prōfēcī	prōfectum	to make, accomplish
513	reficere	reficiō	refēcī	refectum	to rebuild, repair
514	iacere	iaciō	iēcī	iactum	to throw, hurl
515	adicere	adiciō	adiēcī	adiectum	to add (to)
516	conicere	coniciō	coniēcī	coniectum	to throw into
517	dēicere	dēiciō	dēiēcī	dēiectum	to throw down
518	ēicere	ēiciō	ēiēcī	ēiectum	to throw out, eject
519	inicere	iniciō	iniēcī	iniectum	to throw into, to instill feeling
520	obicere	obiciō	obiēcī	obiectum	to throw before; to object
521	subicere	subiciō	subiēcī	subiectum	to subject
522	trāicere	trāiciō	trāiēcī	trāiectum	to transfer, to transport
523	fodere	fodiō	fōdī	fossum	to dig, to stab
524	fugere	fugiō	fūgī	fugitūrus	to flee, to avoid
		fugit	fūgit		it escapes/escaped
525	cōnfugere	cōnfugiō	cōnfūgī	–	to flee
526	effugere	effugiō	effūgī	–	to escape
527	profugere	profugiō	profūgī	–	to run away from

Irregular Verbs

Deponent verbs

528	orīrī	orior	ortus sum	to emerge, arise
529	exorīrī	exorior	exortus sum	to emerge, arise
530	morī	morior	mortuus sum	to die
			moritūrus	one who is going to die
531	patī	patior	passus sum	to suffer, to permit
532	perpetī	perpetior	perpessus sum	to endure to the full
533	gradī	gradior	gressus sum	to walk, step
534	aggredī	aggredior	aggressus sum	to advance, to attack
535	ēgredī	ēgredior	ēgressus sum	to go out
536	ingredī	ingredior	ingressus sum	to enter into
537	prōgredī	prōgredior	prōgressus sum	to go forward, make progress

Irregular Verbs

esse and its compounds

538	esse	sum	fui	–	to be
539	abesse	absum	āfui	–	to be absent
540	adesse	adsum	affuī/adfuī	–	to be present, to help
541	dēesse	dēsum	dēfuī	–	to be lacking/missing
542	inesse	insum	(fuī)	–	to be in, to be involved in
543	interesse	intersum	interfuī	–	to take part in
		interest	interfuit	–	it is/was important
544	praeesse	praesum	praefuī	–	to be in charge of
545	superesse	supersum	superfuī	–	to be left over, to survive
546	posse	possum	potuī	–	to be able (can)
547	prōdesse	prōsum	prōfuī	–	to be useful

ferre and its compounds

548	ferre	ferō	tulī	lātum	to carry, bring
549	afferre	afferō	attulī	allātum	to bring to
550	auferre	auferō	abstulī	ablātum	to take away
551	cōnferre	cōnferō	cōntulī	collātum	to bring together, to compare
552	dēferre	dēferō	dētulī	dēlātum	to offer, to submit
553	differre	differō	distulī	dīlātum	to delay, to differ
554	efferre	efferō	extulī	ēlātum	to bring out, to carry out for burial
555	īnferre	īnferō	īntulī	illātum	to bring in, to inflict
556	offerre	offerō	obtulī	oblātum	to offer

557	perferre	perferō	pertulī	perlātum	to bear, endure to the end
558	referre	referō	rettulī	relātum	to refer, to bring back (news)
		rēfert	rētulit		what makes/made the difference
559	trānsferre	trānsferō	trānstulī	trānslātum	to transfer, to bring across
560	(tollere)	(tollō)	sustulī	sublātum	to lift, to take away

īre and its compounds

561	īre	eō	iī	itum	to go
562	abīre	abeō	abiī	abitum	to go away
563	adīre	adeō	adiī	aditum	to go to
564	coīre	coeō	coiī	coitum	to gather, meet
565	exīre	exeō	exiī	exitum	to go out
566	obīre	obeō	obiī	obitum	to go to meet, to attend to, to die
567	perīre	pereō	periī	peritum	to perish
568	praeterīre	praetereō	praeteriī	praeteritum	to pass, go by
		praeterit	praeteriit		it escapes/escaped
569	subīre	subeō	subiī	subitum	to undergo
570	trānsīre	trānseō	trānsiī	trānsitum	to go over, cross
571	vēnīre	vēneō	vēniī	–	to be sold
572	velle	volō	voluī	–	to be willing, will, want
573	nōlle	nōlō	nōluī	–	to be unwilling, wish not to
574	mālle	mālō	māluī	–	to prefer

Important Impersonal Verbs

575	accidere	accidit	accidit	it happens
576	appārēre	appāret	appāruit	it is apparent
577	condūcere	condūcit	condūxit	it is useful
578	cōnstāre	cōnstat	cōnstitit	it is well known
579	contingere	contingit	contigit	it turns out
580	decēre	decet	decuit	it is fitting
581	dēdecēre	dēdecet	dēdecuit	it is not fitting
582	ēvenīre	ēvenit	ēvēnit	it happens
583	expedīre	expedit	–	it is useful
584	fallere	fallit	fefellit	it escapes (me), is unknown
585	fugere	fugit	fūgit	it escapes (me), is unknown
586	interesse	interest	interfuit	it concerns
587	iuvāre	iuvat	iūvit	it is a pleasure
588	libēre	libet	libuit	it pleases

589	licēre	licet	licuit	it is permitted
590	liquēre	liquet	–	it is proven
591	miserēre	miseret	–	it grieves
592	oportēre	oportet	oportuit	it is desirable/proper
593	paenitēre	paenitet	paenituit	it causes regret
594	pigēre	piget	piguit	it displeases
595	placēre	placet	placuit	it pleases
596	praestāre	praestat	praestitit	it is better
597	praeterīre	praeterit	praeteriit	it escapes (me), is unknown
598	pudere	pudet	puduit	it causes shame
599	rēferre	rēfert	rētulit	it is important, it concerns
600	taedēre	taedet	taesum est	it wearies, bores

Alphabetical List of Verbs

The number following the verb is the number under which it is listed in the section "Principal Parts of Important Verbs."

The letters indicate the appropriate conjugation tables. The following abbreviations are used:

aC = a-conjugation (amāre)
aD = deponent verb of the a-conjugation (hortārī)
cC = consonant conjugation (regere)
cD = deponent verb of the consonant conjugation (sequī)
dV = defective verb
eC = e-conjugation (monēre)
eD = deponent verb of the e-conjugation (verērī)
iC = i-conjugation (audīre)
iD = deponent verb of the i-conjugation (largīrī)
iV = irregular verb
mC = mixed conjugation (capere)
mD = deponent verb of the mixed conjugation (patī)
SD = semideponent verb of the corresponding conjugation

For conjugating the compounds of irregular verbs, the simple verb is used as an example.
The verbs used as examples are highlighted in blue in the alphabetical list.
A number with no indication of conjugation represents an impersonal verb.

A

abdere .... 345 cC
abdūcere............... 242 cC
abesse .... 539 iV esse
abīre .... 562 iV īre
absolvere .... 440 cC
abstinēre............... 83 eC
accēdere .... 289 cC
accendere.............. 403 cC
accidere...........328 cC, 575
accipere............... 493 mC
addere .... 346 cC
addūcere............... 243 cC
adesse .... 540 iV esse
adhibēre .... 68 eC
adhortārī................ 31 aD
adicere................. 515 mC
adimere................ 377 cC
adipīscī ....465 cD
adīre .... 563 iV īre
adiuvāre .... 15 aC

admirārī.................. 37 aD
admittere .... 279 cC
admonēre............... 74 eC
adolēscere .... 210 cC
adorīrī.................. 177 iD
aemulārī .... 18 aD
afferre............ 549 iV ferre
afficere................ 505 mC
agere................... 369 cC
aggredī................ 534 mD
alere .... 222 cC
alloquī ....447 cD
amāre .... 1 aC
āmittere................ 280 cC
amplectī ....459 cD
animadvertere .... 417 cC
aperīre.................. 150 iC
appārēre .... 99 eC, 576
appetere .... 195 cC
arbitrārī................. 19 aD
arcēre.................... 64 eC
arcessere............... 199 cC

ārdēre.................. 107 eC
arguere .... 436 cC
ascendere.............. 410 cC
ascīscere .... 211 cC
āspernārī................. 50 aD
āspicere............... 482 mC
assentīrī .... 176 iD
assequī.................450 cD
assuēscere .... 205 cC
audēre .... 146 eSD
audīre.................. 148 iC
auferre............. 550 iV ferre
augēre.................. 105 eC
auxiliārī.................. 20 aD
āvellere .... 418 cC
āvertere................ 414 cC

B

bibere.................. 357 cC
blandīrī .... 169 iD

C

cadere.................. 327 cC
caedere .... 332 cC
canere .... 320 cC
capere.................. 492 mC
capessere .... 200 cC
carēre .... 90 eC
cavēre.................. 122 eC
cēdere.................. 288 cC
cēnsēre .... 89 eC
cernere.................182 cC
cingere..................265 cC
circumdare.............. 7 aC
circumstāre .... 9 aC
circumvenīre........... 164 iC
claudere.................298 cC
coepī (see incipere)....501 mC
coercēre.................. 65 eC
cōgere ....374 cC
cōgnōscere..............208 cC
cohortārī.................31 aD
coīre ....564 iV īre
colere ....223 cC
colligere ....384 cC
colloquī.................448 cD
comitārī.................21 aD
comminīscī...............467 cD
committere ....281 cC
commovēre ....125 eC
comperīre.............. 162 iC
complectī ....460 cD
complēre................. 60 eC
compōnere..............216 cC
comprehendere.........407 cC
cōnārī...................22 aD
concēdere...............290 cC
concidere ....329 cC
concipere ....494 mC
concupīscere...........212 cC
concurrere ....337 cC
concutere ....488 mC
condere ....350 cC
condūcere ....244 cC, 577
cōnferre...........551 iV ferre
cōnficere...............506 mC

cōnfīdere.............. 474 cSD
cōnfitērī.................142 eD
cōnflīgere..............256 cC
cōnfugere ....525 mC
congruere...............437 cC
conicere................516 mC
cōnsectārī...............46 aD
cōnsenēscere ....229 cC
cōnsentīre .... 159 iC
cōnsequī ....451 cD
cōnsīdere...............401 cC
cōnsistere...............316 cC
cōnsōlārī................47 aD
cōnspicārī...............51 aD
cōnspicere ....483 mC
cōnstāre ....10 aC, 578
cōnstituere............426 cC
cōnsuēscere...........206 cC
cōnsulere ....225 cC
cōnsūmere ....382 cC
contemnere ....275 cC
contendere.............324 cC
conticēscere ....230 cC
continēre .... 84 eC
contingere ....322 cC, 579
cōntiōnārī................24 aD
contrahere ....253 cC
convalēscere...........231 cC
convenīre .... 165 iC
convertere ....415 cC
convincere ....393 cC
corrigere ....258 cC
corrumpere ....395 cC
crēdere.................347 cC
crēscere................202 cC
cūnctārī..................26 aD
cupere .... 478 mC
currere..................336 cC

D

dare....................... 6 aC
dēbēre .... 70 eC
dēcēdere ....291 cC
decēre....................580

dēcernere .... 183 cC
dēcipere............... 495 mC
dēdecēre...................581
dēdere ....340 cC
dēdūcere...............245 cC
dēesse .... 541 iV esse
dēfendere..............405 cC
dēferre............552 iV ferre
dēficere .... 507 mC
dēfungī ....444 cD
dēicere .... 517 mC
dēlēre.................... 62 eC
dēligere.................385 cC
dēmere ....379 cC
dēmittere ....282 cC
dēpellere................353 cC
dēpōnere...............217 cC
dēposcere..............367 cC
dēscendere.............411 cC
dēserere ....227 cC
dēsilīre.................. 152 iC
dēsinere.................190 cC
dēsistere................317 cC
dēspicere .... 484 mC
dētrahere ....254 cC
dēvertī .... 477 cSD
dēvincere ....392 cC
dīcere ....238 cC
differre...........553 iV ferre
diffīdere .... 475 cSD
diffundere...............399 cC
dīligere ....387 cC
dīmittere...............283 cC
dirimere.................378 cC
dīripere .... 480 mC
discēdere ....292 cC
discere ....368 cC
discernere...............184 cC
dispōnere...............218 cC
dissentīre .... 160 iC
disserere................228 cC
dissolvere...............441 cC
distinguere..............270 cC
distribuere..............431 cC
dīvidere.................301 cC

īrāscī.....................464 cD
īre........................ 561 iV
irrumpere ....396 cC
iubēre.................109 eC
iuvāre.............15 aC, 587

L

lābī.......................455 cD
lacessere...............201 cC
laedere.................302 cC
laetārī..................34 aD
largīrī ....170 iD
latēre ....95 eC
laudāre...................2 aC
lavāre ....16 aC
lavārī.......................17 aD
legere ....383 cC
libēre 588
licēre......................589
liquēre 590
loquī ....446 cD
lūcēre ....116 eC
lūdere ....303 cC
luere ....438 cC

M

mālle.....................574 iV
manēre...................110 eC
medērī ....144 eD
meminisse ....dV
mentīrī..................171 iD
merēre ....72 eC
merērī...................135 eD
mētīrī ....180 iD
metuere ....429 cC
minārī....................35 aD
minitārī..................36 aD
minuere ....424 cC
mirārī....................37 aD
miscēre ....81 eC
miserārī..................38 aD
miserēre 591
miserērī..................136 eD

mittere..................278 cC
mōlīrī ....172 iD
monēre....................73 eC
morārī......................39 aD
morī.....................530 mD
movēre...................124 eC

N

nancīscī..................462 cD
nāscī ....461 cD
neglegere ....389 cC
nītī.......................458 cD
nocēre ....75 eC
nōlle ....573 iV
nōscere ....207 cC

O

obicere...................520 mC
obīre ....566 īre
oblīvīscī..................469 cD
obruere ....435 cC
obsidēre ....129 eC
obsīdere ....402 cC
obstāre.....................12 aC
obtestārī..................54 aD
obtinēre...................85 eC
occidere...................331 cC
occīdere...................333 cC
occurrere.................338 cC
ōdisse ....dV
offendere ....406 cC
offerre ....556 iV ferre
omittere ....284 cC
operīre ....151 iC
opīnārī.....................40 aD
oportēre....................592
opperīrī ....179 iD
opprimere.................313 cC
ōrdīrī......................181 iD
orīrī ....528 mD
ostendere ....326 cC

P

pacīscī ....472 cD
paenitēre 593
pangere..................358 cC
parcere...................351 cC
parere ....491 mC
pārēre....................98 eC
partīrī...................173 iD
pāscere..................203 cC
patefacere ....503 mC
patēre...................100 eC
patī ....531 mD
pellere ....352 cC
pendēre..................118 eC
pendere ....334 cC
peragere ....371 cC
percellere ....360 cC
percipere................497 mC
percontārī.................23 aD
percutere ....490 mC
perdere ....348 cC
perdūcere ....247 cC
perferre ....557 iV ferre
perficere ....510 mC
pergere ....261 cC
perīclitārī.................41 aD
perīre ....567 iV īre
permanēre ....111 eC
permittere ....285 cC
permovēre ....126 eC
perpetī...................532 mD
perscrūtārī.................49 aD
persequī ....453 cD
persuādēre ....114 eC
perterrēre................79 eC
pertimēscere ....235 cC
pertinēre...................86 eC
pervenīre..................167 iC
petere....................194 cC
pigēre.....................594
pingere ....267 cC
placēre.............76 eC, 595
plaudere ....304 cC
pollicērī..................134 eD
pōnere ....215 cC

Alphabetical List of Verbs Principal Parts

tenēre.................... 82 eC
terere................... 191 cC
terrēre.................. 78 eC
testārī...................53 aD
timēre..................102 eC
tollere..................364 cC
tollere.............560 iV ferre
torquēre...............106 eC
trādere..................344 cC
trādūcere..............251 cC
trahere..................252 cC
trāicere.............. 522 mC
trānscendere...........412 cC
trānsferre.........559 iV ferre
trānsfigere.............309 cC
trānsīre.............570 iV īre
tribuere................430 cC
tuērī....................139 eD

tundere.................365 cC
tūtārī....................55 aD

U

ulcīscī...................463 cD
ūrere....................277 cC
urgēre..................117 eC
ūtī.......................457 cD

V

vādere..................305 cC
vagārī....................56 aD
valēre...................103 eC
vehere..................255 cC
velle....................572 iV
vēnārī...................57 aD

vendere.................349 cC
venerārī.................58 aD
venīre...................163 iC
vēnīre...............571 iV īre
verērī...................137 eD
vergere.................421 cC
verrere.................422 cC
versārī...................59 aD
vertere..................413 cC
vēscī....................470 cD
vetāre.................... 5 aC
vidēre...................131 eC
vigēre...................104 eC
vincere..................391 cC
vincīre.................. 157 iC
vīsere...................423 cC
vīvere...................274 cC
volvere.................442 cC

Index

Index

Index

Index

Index